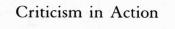
Criticism in Action

Criticism in Action

ENLIGHTENMENT EXPERIMENTS
IN POLITICAL WRITING

Dena Goodman

Cornell University Press

ITHACA AND LONDON

First published 1989 by Cornell University Press.

Library of Congress Cataloging-in-Publication Data

Goodman, Dena, 1952–
  Criticism in action.

  Bibliography: p.
  Includes index.
    1. Political science—France—History—18th century. 2. Enlightenment.
3. France—Intellectual life—18th century. 4. Montesquieu, Charles de Secondat, baron de, 1689–1755. Lettres persanes. 5. Rousseau, Jean-Jacques. Discours sur l'origine et les fondements de l'inégalité parmi les hommes. 6. Diderot, Denis, 1713–1784. Supplément au voyage de Bougainville. I. Title.
JA84.F8G57 1989   320'.0944   88-47915
ISBN 0-8014-2201-9 (alk. paper)

Printed in the United States of America

The paper in this book is acid-free and meets the guidelines for permanence and durability of the Committee on Production Guidelines for Book Longevity of the Council on Library Resources.

For my parents

Contents

Acknowledgments

I t is hard to know where to begin this note of thanks, but perhaps the best place is the University of Chicago, where I was introduced to the Enlightenment. There Keith Baker became both a guide and a source of unfailing support. I thank him and my other teachers as well: Leonard Krieger and Françoise Meltzer. And I thank my graduate-school friends, especially Susan Kadlec Mahoney, Gary Kates, and Anthea Waleson.

During my three years at Stanford University I found a whole new set of colleagues in the Berkeley French History Group. In the best atmosphere one can imagine, they too helped me to sharpen my ideas and shape the thinking that eventually produced this book. I thank them all, but especially Lynn Hunt, Susanna Barrows, Herrick Chapman, Suzanne Desan, and Lloyd Kramer.

Two old friends, Isaac Kramnick and Constance Louise Thorpe, helped me to clarify my thinking at two crucial points that I'm sure they have completely forgotten. I haven't, and I thank them too.

A Susan B. Anthony Fellowship from the American Association of University Women and a supplementary travel grant from the University of Chicago enabled me to begin the work that developed into this book.

I also thank the anonymous readers who supported this book and made suggestions that have helped me to strengthen it. Renée Palmer generously helped with copy reading. And I thank John Ackerman of Cornell University Press, who had faith in this book from the start.

Finally, I offer this book as a gift to my parents, without whom . . .

D. G.

Criticism in Action

Philosophers have only interpreted the world in various ways. The point, however, is to change it.

KARL MARX

Introduction

Historians of the Enlightenment, like other intellectual historians, tend to focus on the ideas expressed by the great writers of the age they study, often taking for granted the structures by which these ideas are formed and upon which they are framed. Criticism of this traditional approach has come primarily from social historians, who remind the intellectual historian that the idea must be viewed also as a material object, as black marks on a printed page, bound between covers and sold in the marketplace. Between the book and the idea, however, is the text: that somewhat less than material object which is at the same time more than simply a collection of ideas. Both the traditional and the social historian of ideas see through the text to the object, real or ideal, of their own concern. I, however, would like to posit the text as the proper object for the study of what may be called the history of intellectual activity. For the text is not just the major product of such activity; it embodies that action. The text is an act.[1] It is the common ground on which human beings as writers and readers meet to engage with one another and the world they wish to represent, to criticize, and even to change. If we are to understand how intellectual activity can change the world, we must look not simply at ideas or at books but at texts. To look at texts, furthermore, is to analyze the ways they are and can be read, and to examine the implications of those readings. In the end, it is not authors but texts that act upon readers; and it is only readers who can act upon the world.

[1] I am here reversing Paul Ricoeur's argument in "The Model of the Text: Meaningful Action Considered as a Text," in *Interpretive Social Science: A Reader*, ed. Paul Rabinow and William M. Sullivan (Berkeley, 1979), pp. 73–101.

This book is intended as a foray into the history of Enlightenment intellectual activity. I take as my objects of study three major texts of the French Enlightenment: Montesquieu's *Lettres persanes*, Rousseau's *Discours sur l'inégalité* (the *Second Discours*), and Diderot's *Supplément au Voyage de Bougainville*. My focus on texts of social and political criticism leads me to ask what form each act of criticism takes, what purpose it aims to serve, and what possibilities it holds out. I tend not to consider very closely the substance of the criticism or its relationship to the world beyond the text. I take it as an open question whether these critical texts aim to change the world, but I do assume that criticism implies the need for change. Ultimately, I would like to know how writers might change the world through the writing of texts. While the question is mine, it is original neither to me nor even to the person who gave it its most famous formulation: Karl Marx. It is the quintessential question of the Enlightenment, central to the project of Enlightenment itself, the direct corollary of Diderot's description of a "good dictionary" as one that will "change the common way of thinking."

Thus, while texts are acts, they are not isolated acts. If we are to make sense of eighteenth-century texts, they must be situated within the larger historical context of the Old Regime and in relation to one another as moments in the larger set of actions that are known collectively as the Enlightenment. The point of such contextualizing is not to determine in retrospect the validity of particular critical acts but to understand them: how they work, what their purpose is, and how successful they are in achieving their goals. To understand texts as acts is to understand them historically, to situate them in the particular time and place in which they are meaningful as actions.

The disillusionment with the absolute monarchy that set in during the final years of Louis xiv's reign opened up new questions about how to do social and political criticism. With the Regency came Montesquieu's *Lettres persanes*: the first attempt to write political criticism for a public without writing for a prince; the first attempt at political writing for the modern age. With the *Lettres persanes*, Montesquieu turned his back on the king as the basis of political reform and set a new direction for practical political criticism in the eighteenth century.

The traditional assumption that social reform must begin with the recognized holder of political power, that criticism must reflect the hierarchical nature of society by directing itself to the highest authority in that hierarchy, had made the king both the subject of criticism and the implied reader of critical texts. With the *Lettres persanes*, Montesquieu rejected the king as both the subject of criticism and the reader to whom that criticism should be directed. In so doing he made necessary the search for a means of reform that did not simply follow from the reform of the prince and for a new readership that could effect the reform of society. As the eighteenth century progressed, the need for such reform seemed increasingly urgent and the experiments in political writing multiplied. With the focus off the king, the way was opened for a whole range of criticism that was to penetrate and explore the very structure and bases of state and society. The depth of Rousseau's truly fundamental critique of modern society and the breadth of Diderot's efforts to shape a critical and active readership extended the range of criticism opened up by the *Lettres persanes*.

The three texts that I have chosen to analyze are by no means ordinary, but they are typical of the Enlightenment. All three are literary masterpieces that represent the best of Enlightenment critical writing. I have turned my attention to them, however, not because they are "great" but because the literary and the political are equally important in them. In fact, their richness lies in the high level of self-consciousness they reflect as works of literature and political criticism.

Though extraordinary, these texts are not anomalous. To the contrary, a defining feature of the Enlightenment lies in the way it brought together the literary and critical dimensions of the writer's task. The citizens of the eighteenth-century Republic of Letters were the first to see themselves in both the literary and the political terms that the name of their community implies. They not only took seriously but articulated for the first time the public responsibility of the writer as critic. Indeed, it is as moments in the articulation of this responsibility that I see the crucial relationship among the three texts under study here: each was a conscious act carried out by a leading figure in the Enlightenment's civic project to change the common way of thinking.

It is in this way that these texts can be understood as active forces in the world, forces that shape the thinking and acting of particular individuals who are engaged with them in the act of reading and who form a community of discourse within the greater social, political, and intellectual contexts by which history is defined. And while a full social history of Enlightenment intellectual activity remains to be written, this book is at least a foray into the historical analysis of Enlightenment texts as critical activity. But how is such an analysis to be undertaken? What approach should the intellectual historian use to analyze properly these textual acts? Historians, for the most part, have looked at texts either as the repositories of ideas or as documents of some greater historical phenomenon. But Dominick LaCapra cautions us that "the historian who reads texts either as mere documents or as formal entities . . . does not read them historically precisely because he or she does not read them as texts."[2]

To read Enlightenment texts as texts is above all to attend to the literary forms that shape them. The eighteenth century was an age of experimentation—in literature as in politics and science. From the literary historian's point of view, the eighteenth century was an age of generic anarchy: the rigid classicism of the previous century gave way to a profusion of forms drawn from life itself—the letter, the correspondence, the memoir, the dialogue, the history. Out of these forms was shaped the narrative novel that has come to dominate modern literary production since the nineteenth century. Montesquieu, Rousseau, and Diderot were all experimenters in the forms of writing, and each text to be examined here employs one of these experimental literary forms. The *Lettres persanes*, the *Second Discours*, and the *Supplément* were experiments not only in political writing, but in writing itself.

All of these texts impose upon the reader the question of the relationship between the form of criticism and its aims. They demand of us a critical approach not only to the object of criticism but also to the critical text. The literary forms that eighteenth-century critics devised do not, as is so often claimed, serve merely as candy coatings on philosophical pills, hiding dangerous messages. Rather, they reveal the structures of the critical methods their authors employed. But what critical approach are we to use that will be adequate to three such different texts? Is there a single type of analysis that is sensitive to the very different kinds of activity taking place in them? In our own age of criticism, have we invented the one analytical tool that can reveal the workings of all texts? I don't think so. What the present state of literary criticism provides is an array of critical approaches whose very variety opens up texts in new ways, a pluralism that makes possible a critical discourse that can be sensitive and responsive to the variety of individual texts.

In this book I have employed certain methods of analysis because they are responsive to the particular texts I want to analyze. Thus, while all three analyses that I will engage in here are formal, each is determined by the form of the text being analyzed. Montesquieu's epistolary text calls for an analysis that can account for the static relationships implied in the arrangement of discrete letters; Rousseau's hypothetical history, by contrast, demands a narrative analysis; and an adequate treatment of Diderot's dialogue must focus on dialogic relationships. My analysis of the *Lettres persanes* is thus primarily semiotic and grammatical, while

---

[2]Dominick LaCapra, "Rethinking Intellectual History and Reading Texts," in *Modern European Intellectual History: Reappraisals and New Perspectives*, ed. LaCapra and Steven L. Kaplan (Ithaca, 1982), p. 81.

that of the *Second discours* is narrative, and that of the *Supplément* is rhetorical. This is not to say that sign, narrative, and rhetoric are the exclusive and discrete concerns of one or another of these three texts. Rather, as each text has its own critical project, so the analysis of each text must reveal the uniqueness of that project by being sensitive to the particular form used to carry it out. Equally important is the way in which the author has shaped that form to the ends of his project. Forms are not, in the hands of great writers, simply convenient and prefabricated frames on which to hang ideas; rather, literary form becomes the very basis of creative experimentation that in the end cannot be distinguished from, because it is at the very heart of, the critical project itself.[3]

Because the texts I am concerned with here are experiments not simply in writing but in political writing, textual analysis must open out to the contextual worlds they are trying to criticize and shape. The bridge between these worlds—the world in which the text is created, the world created by the text, and the world the text is attempting to shape—is the reader. All texts, LaCapra reminds us, "are events in the history of language. To understand these multivalent events as complex uses of language, one must learn to pose anew the question of 'what really happens' in them and in the reader who actually reads them."[4] To understand "what happens" in a text—what the text is doing—is to understand what the reader is being asked to do both in reading and as a result of reading it.

What a reader is asked to do in reading (or in order to read) a text is a result of what LaCapra calls the "worklike," or formal, aspect of the text, which "engages the reader in recreative dialogue with the text and the problem it raises."[5] For both reader and writer, the worklike implies what J. L. Austin calls a "performative" use of language—language that does not merely say something, does not merely refer to something else, but that itself constitutes a form of action meant to have an effect on its world.[6]

What a reader is asked to do *as a result of* reading a text arises directly out of what he is asked to do *in* reading it. The way in which the reading shapes the reader as a reader shapes him as well as a potential agent in the world. It is thus in the relationship between what the reader is asked to do in reading and as a result of reading texts that an answer might be

---

[3]For a refreshing discussion of the importance of form in literary history and the history of ideas see Jean Ehrard, "Histoire des idées et histoire littéraire," in *Problèmes et méthodes de l'histoire littéraire* (Paris, 1974), p. 74–79.

[4]LaCapra, "Rethinking Intellectual History," p. 81.

[5]Ibid., p. 53.

[6]J. L. Austin, *How to Do Things with Words*, 2d ed. (Cambridge, Mass., 1975), pp. 5–7.

found to the question of how philosophers are to change the world. For while the text stands as mediator between ideas and their contextual world, representing and interpreting it, it is the reader who must mediate between the text and the world. As the text acts upon the reader, demanding a particular kind of activity in reading, so it may call the reader to act upon the world in a particular fashion.

Whereas Marx asked how philosophers are to change the world, I now ask how readers are to do so. This question becomes relevant only at that point in history when the reading public becomes the reader of social and political criticism and when the public itself begins to be constituted as a political agent. That transformation occurred in France during the eighteenth century.[7] The general methodological questions about how to analyze texts, about how to do intellectual history, thus bring us back to the particularity of the historical moment.

A Mirror for Princes

From the sixteenth to the eighteenth century, the field of practical political criticism was dominated by works in the genre of the *speculum principis* (mirror for princes). This genre can be distinguished from other forms of political writing because it is necessarily practical, critical, and particular, arising as it does out of the relationship between a reigning prince and his adviser. Although the history of the mirror for princes has been traced from a treatise given to Nicocles of Cyprus by Isocrates in the fourth century B.C., the height of its popularity and importance came in the early modern period when monarchies were on the rise all over Europe. Between 1513 and 1519, the modern genre was launched as the premier form of political criticism in Machiavelli's *Prince*, More's *Utopia*, Erasmus' *Education of a Christian Prince*, Castiglione's *Book of the Courtier*, and, in France, Seyssel's *Monarchie de France* and Budé's *De l'institution du prince*. Throughout Europe, writers emerged who were eager to advise their ever more powerful princes.[8]

Only exceptionally, as in the case of Machiavelli's *Prince*, did political

---

[7]Jürgen Habermas, *L'Espace public: Archéologie de la publicité comme dimension constitutive de la société bourgeoise*, trans. Marc B. de Launay (Paris, 1986); Keith Michael Baker, "Politics and Public Opinion under the Old Regime: Some Reflections," in *Press and Politics in Pre-Revolutionary France*, ed. Jack R. Censer and Jeremy D. Popkin (Berkeley, 1987), pp. 204–46.

[8]For a history of the *speculum principis* from Isocrates to Erasmus, see Lester K. Born, Introduction to *The Education of a Christian Prince*, by Desiderius Erasmus (New York, 1936).

writing of this kind redefine basic political principles so fundamentally that it was in time elevated to the canon of works in the history of political thought. Yet unoriginal as most of these texts may be, out of this practical strain in political thought developed the political texts of the Enlightenment. The men of the Enlightenment were nothing if they were not practical, critical, and enmeshed in the particularities of eighteenth-century politics. The author of *L'Esprit des lois* was first the author of the *Lettres persanes*; the author of the *Contrat social* was already the author of two critical discourses.

But while Enlightenment political criticism was practical and rooted in historical particularity, it also broke with the mirror for princes tradition in a fundamental way. That break was made first and most consciously by Montesquieu with the *Lettres persanes*, a story about an adviser who flees his prince's court when it becomes clear that his advice will not be taken. Usbek, and with him Montesquieu, turns his back on his prince and is left with the enormous challenge of finding a new subject and a new object of political criticism. We can best understand the revolution in criticism effected by Montesquieu by looking at the *Lettres persanes* in relation to the last great exemplar of the *speculum principis* in France: Fénelon's *Aventures de Télémaque*.

What follows is thus a brief analysis of *Télémaque*. This analysis proceeds from a discussion first of genre, then of the particular form of the text, and finally of the political argument structured by and presented in it. After suggesting what the mirror-for-princes tradition implies generically, how texts written in that tradition operate, and the state of the art in France toward the end of Louis xiv's reign, I will turn to the way in which the *Lettres persanes* rejects both Fénelon's text and the tradition that it represents. I can then turn to the question of how Montesquieu deals with the problem of criticism and reform once the king has been removed from the center of the political picture. I will then deal with each subsequent text—Rousseau's *Second Discours* and Diderot's *Supplément*—in the same way and according to this new problematic: how to do political criticism and achieve political reform when the king is no longer at the center of political hopes. But before we can understand that new world, let us go back to the seventeenth century, when the monarchy and the monarch were supreme in France and a writer emerged to play the role of mirror.

As early modern princes became stronger, taking upon themselves more and more of the available power in society to the advantage of the state, the critical voices may have become louder, but they certainly did not change their style. In France, the monarchy simply attracted attention to itself, even if that attention became increasingly critical. By the second half of the seventeenth century, Louis xiv's policy of strengthening the relationship between king and subject at the expense of local and personal ties of allegiance, as well as the various institutional means established to centralize power and authority in the monarchy, could not but reaffirm the prince as the key to political change.[9] Not surprisingly, then, it was toward the end of the reign of Louis xiv that the mirror-for-princes tradition reached its highest literary expression in France. At the close of the seventeenth century, after Louis's supreme attempt to impose his will on the nation through the revocation of the Edict of Nantes, and after the exhaustion of years of costly wars, luxury, and the taxes constantly levied to pay for them, the man chosen by this king to be preceptor to the royal children wrote perhaps the finest piece of literature in the mirror-for-princes tradition.

In August 1689, François de Salignac de La Mothe-Fénelon was named preceptor of the duke of Burgundy, the presumed heir to the throne of France. Ten years later, only a few months after he was definitively deprived of this office, he published *Les Aventures de Télémaque*, which was written for the young prince but which Louis xiv rightly saw as highly critical of himself. *Télémaque* shows the reader how to be a good prince and a good courtier, both giving the prince advice and providing models of good advisers. Fénelon's ideal adviser is a mentor to his prince, for the guise taken by Minerva, the goddess under whose protection the young Telemachus learns the ways of kingship, is that of the wise preceptor Mentor. And while Mentor, like Castiglione's "perfect courtier," constantly exhorts his prince to be virtuous, the classical model for *Télémaque* is quite different from that of the *Book of the Courtier*.

Whereas Castiglione had taken for his literary model Plato's *Symposium*, a conversation among friends that leads to a game whose object is to define an ideal, Fénelon's starting point is Homer's *Odyssey*. The book opens on the island of Calypso where Telemachus, who has undertaken his own travels in search of his father, has been shipwrecked. At Calypso's request he recounts the story of his adventures to that point, featuring encounters with people, places, and gods familiar to the classically educated seventeenth-century reader. After Telemachus makes a narrow escape from the sensual trap of Calypso's island, the adventures continue. A narrator now takes over where Telemachus had left off.

Throughout his travels, the young prince is accompanied by Mentor, who, as the spirit of wisdom, helps him in different ways. Mentor is most

[9]Roland Mousnier, *The Institutions of France under the Absolute Monarchy, 1598–1789: Society and the State*, trans. Brian Pearce (Chicago, 1974), pp. 107–8.

immediately useful in getting Telemachus out of scrapes into which his passions, impetuosity, and naive ignorance constantly lead him. Each of these crises, moreover, provides a lesson for the young prince that contributes to his growing maturity. Mentor thus helps Telemachus in this second way of making a man out of him. Finally, Mentor instructs the prince directly and indirectly in the particular art of statecraft that his royal birth requires him to master. Although the three aspects of Telemachus' education reinforce one another, it is this third, political formation that sets Fénelon's work squarely in the tradition of political criticism, and Mentor in the tradition of princely courtiers. To complicate, and thus to enrich, matters, Fénelon presents both Telemachus and the reader with numerous examples of other kings and other courtiers. The encounters and experiences of Telemachus in his voyages thereby constitute examples for the reader of good and bad kingship, good and bad advice. These examples, moreover, are always subject to the interpretation of Mentor, who never fails to draw from them the appropriate lessons.

The classical voyage provides the primary model for *Télémaque*, although the modern voyage and the utopian literature it spawned inform the work as well. Fénelon's version of Utopia is the island of Bétique. Like More's Utopia and its seventeenth-century successors, Fénelon's Bétique is a society in which nature is rational and utility leads to happiness. Bétique, according to Telemachus, was a nation that, "following the law of nature, was at the same time [very] wise and [very] happy."[10]

In *Télémaque*, however, the voyage itself, rather than a single ideal society, is the focus of the story. As in the Homeric epic, the voyage is more than simply a device to reinforce a sense of realism which will lend credibility to the account of the discovered land.[11] Like Ulysses before him, Telemachus seeks not to discover new lands but to regain what had been lost. Only in overcoming obstacles to their desires do these two travelers achieve the kind of wisdom that is their true, if unanticipated, discovery. "The wisest lessons of Ulysses will not be as useful to you,"

[10]François de Salignac de La Mothe-Fénelon, *Les Aventures de Télémaque* (Paris, 1968), p. 212. All subsequent references to this work will be given in the text. All translations, here and throughout this book, are my own unless I have noted otherwise. It is also possible to view Bétique in the tradition of Atlantis, since its location (near the straits of Gibraltar) and the almost mythical fame by which Telemachus knows of it are reminiscent of the ancient ideal. As an ideal, however, Bétique goes far beyond the antimaterialistic simplicity of Atlantis.

[11]Geoffrey Atkinson, *The Extraordinary Voyage in French Literature before 1700* (New York, 1920), pp. 162–63.

Mentor tells Telemachus, "as his long absence and the troubles you are suffering in seeking him" (*Télémaque*, p. 502).

By taking as his model the ancient voyage, with its many ports of call, rather than the modern utopian voyage, which centers on a single discovered land, Fénelon is able to introduce into his narrative an imperfect but reformable country in contrast to the ideal. The utopian Bétique, which is never actually visited (which need not be visited since, as a rational ideal, it is accessible through the mind), is overshadowed by Salente, a country that suffers from many of the excesses of contemporary France and that is reformed under the guidance of Mentor. The Salentine episode, in which a chastened ruler straightens his bent will to the path of political virtue, is both the culmination of Telemachus' voyage and the illusion that Montesquieu's Usbek will unveil in the opening pages of the *Lettres persanes*.

Unlike voyagers to utopian lands, Telemachus and Mentor bring more to the lands they visit than they are able to take away. In Crete, Telemachus, infused with the wisdom of Mentor/Minerva, is chosen king because of his understanding of the ancient laws of Minos, but he declines the offer. Later he is offered another kingship and again refuses. Each time he declares his desire to return to his own poor land, Ithaca, to rule there as is his duty (*Télémaque*, books 5 and 16).

Thus Bétique stands only as an ideal that Telemachus cannot obtain. More important, the description of Bétique is followed directly by the sojourn at Salente, where Telemachus learns that in Mentor he already has all the wisdom he needs to be a good king. For even though Telemachus has many adventures and meets many people in his travels, his wisdom is derived not so much from those experiences as from the mentor he has brought with him: his own reason whose guidance he must learn to appreciate and accept.

Telemachus' voyage, like that of Ulysses before him, is ultimately a voyage of self-discovery. It is because Telemachus' wisdom is his own that the text focuses on Salente, in need of wise reform, rather than on the ideal Bétique. It is significant that Bétique is described during an evening of recreation after a sublime musical performance. The whole episode occurs at night and at sea, giving it a dreamlike quality (*Télémaque*, book 7). Like music, the contemplation of the ideal is no more than a pastime, bringing with it the true pleasure that is based not on sensuality but on wisdom: "There is nothing either austere or affected about wisdom," says Mentor: "she alone gives true pleasure. . . . She knows how to mix games and laughter with grave and serious business; she prepares for pleasure with toil, and she provides relaxation from toil with pleasure" (*Télémaque*, p. 203). After this evening of wise pleasures

Telemachus and Mentor find themselves in Salente, where they are immediately caught up in the real-life problems of kingship.

While the question of the relationship between princes and their advisers is a recurrent theme in *Télémaque*, the importance of good advisers is nowhere so central as in the section on Salente. Upon their arrival the two strangers are heralded by the priest of Jupiter as the saviors of Salente, "a young hero whom Wisdom leads by the hand" (*Télémaque*, p. 227). While the "young hero" goes off to prove himself on the battlefield of a just war, Mentor undertakes the domestic reforms necessary to restore the health of the Salentine state. While youthful courage goes to war (under the aegis of Minerva, of course), wisdom stays home, seeing to the prosperity of the realm. But before any reforms are proposed, Fénelon makes clear that the possibility of such reforms depends upon the king's willingness to listen to a sincere disinterested counselor, just as the sorry state of affairs is the result of his weakness in following the advice of treacherous flatterers. Before he gives any advice at all, Mentor tells the king that he aims to speak freely and thereby to get him used to "hearing things called by their names." No one else, he says, has dared speak this way to the king, and therefore, "you see only half the truth, and that wrapped in pretty packages." The king agrees, admitting that he has never found anyone "who loved me enough to court my displeasure in speaking the whole truth" (*Télémaque*, pp. 264–65). Indeed, as he now confesses, the story of his life is the story of a king who chose the voice of flattery over that of sincere counsel. This is the story we learn in book 11 of *Télémaque*, the story, he says, of "all the misfortunes into which I was led by a false friend who flattered my passions in the hope that in turn I would flatter his" (*Télémaque*, p. 268).

Book 11 tells the story of these three men: the king, Idomeneus; the flatterer and favorite, Protesilas; and the wise and virtuous courtier, Philocles. Although at first Philocles' sincerity had pleased Idomeneus, the then king of Crete was unable to uphold his commitment to keep listening to him and thus to protect himself from the flattery of Protesilas (*Télémaque*, pp. 294–95). Protesilas then managed to have Philocles disgraced and exiled, leaving himself in full command at home. "From that moment," Idomeneus recalls, "no one spoke freely in my council meetings; the truth withdrew from me; error, which makes ready the fall of kings, punished me for having sacrificed Philocles to the cruel ambition of Protesilas. . . . I feared that the truth would break through the clouds and that it would reach me despite the flatterers; for, since I no longer had the strength to follow it, the light of truth was simply a nuisance to me" (*Télémaque*, pp. 302–3). With Protesilas in full control of the country, Idomeneus then left to fight in the Trojan War. On his return, the people, who had reached the limits of a life of oppression, rebelled, and Idomeneus was forced to flee with his now indispensable adviser. Together they founded Salente on the coast of Italy. Once there, they picked up where they had left off in Crete for, as Idomeneus later admits, "all experience is useless to soft and lazy princes who live without thinking" (*Télémaque*, p. 304).

Had it not been for the timely arrival of Mentor, Salente would surely have gone the way of Crete. "But you have finally opened my eyes," Idomeneus tells Mentor, "and you have inspired in me the courage I was lacking to free myself from servitude" (*Télémaque*, p. 304). Mentor then convinces Idomeneus to send Protesilas into exile and to recall the virtuous Philocles. Although Mentor realizes that the path of virtue may not be as pleasant as the easy ways of vice and understands that to kings "all free and generous speech seems haughty, critical, and seditious," he is firm in telling Idomeneus what as a king he really needs: "You need a man who loves only the truth and you, who loves you more than you know how to love yourself, who tells you the truth in spite of you, who forces a way through all your defenses. And that necessary man is Philocles" (*Télémaque*, pp. 308, 309).

Just as Telemachus has the wisdom he needs, Idomeneus has the wise and virtuous adviser he needs: all they have to do is to learn from adverse experiences to recognize what they have and then to develop the will to use it. The problem is not to find wisdom but to choose to follow it after one's eyes have been opened to its beneficent rays. Like Beatrice in Dante's *Divine Comedy*, Mentor as Minerva in human form represents a divine wisdom that can help man to overcome the weakness of his will to do good and thus allow him to follow the path of reason and virtue. In Philocles, Idomeneus had had an adviser who gave him exactly the same advice that Mentor brings him, but only Mentor can give him the strength and courage to follow it. With Mentor at his side, Idomeneus banishes the evil flatterer and recalls Philocles to his court. At this point, however, he runs into an unanticipated snag.

Idomeneus' agent finds Philocles living a life of contentment and self-sufficiency in a cave on a mountainside. Revered by the people, he spends his time sculpting images of the gods and reading a handful of inspirational books. His involuntary exile from the corrupt world of court politics has turned out to be the best thing that ever happened to him. "Protesilas has betrayed himself in wishing to betray the king and to destroy me," Philocles explains; "but he has not harmed me. To the contrary, he has given me the greatest of gifts: he has delivered me from the tumult and the servitude of worldly affairs; I owe him my precious solitude and all the innocent pleasures it allows me" (*Télémaque*, p. 314).

Philocles, who has found tranquillity on Samos, has no desire to return to what he considers the servitude of worldly affairs.

Idomeneus' messenger does all he can to convince the virtuous man that he ought to return to court. Doesn't he want to see his friends and family again? Think of how the king will interpret this rebuff. Most significant, however, is the following argument: "But you, who fear the gods and love duty, doesn't serving your king, helping him in doing all the good he wants to do and making so many people happy, mean anything to you? Is it legitimate to abandon yourself to a primitive philosophy [philosophie sauvage], to prefer yourself over the rest of the human race, and to love your own rest better than the happiness of your fellow citizens?" (Télémaque, p. 315). The contemplative ideal and personal happiness are here challenged by the duty of a subject to aid his prince and serve the people, his fellow citizens. Like that of Bétique, this ideal brings pleasure, but it must be thought of as a dream or a moment of recreation, of relaxation in preparation for the necessary labor of public service. Just as the prince must remember always that his first responsibility is to serve his people, so too is it the courtier's responsibility to serve his prince and, through him, his fellow citizens. Philocles, after consulting his gods, returns to Salente.

Salente, which at the arrival of Telemachus and Mentor had been on the verge of self-destruction, has now been fully restored through reform, but also through the restoration of a true order at court based on reason and virtue. The vicious, tyrannical court of Protesilas has been overturned, and the virtuous, beneficent one of Philocles put in its place. The process by which this feat was accomplished began with the king's willingness to change his ways, to listen to the truth uttered by a sincere adviser over the insidious lies of the flatterer. Once the will was in place, it was only a matter of following wise counsel and, from time to time, shoring up that will by listening to the voice of divine wisdom. And to make sure that the new ways would be lasting, a whole new court system had to be put in place, in addition to the laws and institutions by which the nation was to be governed. This new court is the meeting ground of private virtue and public service, personal happiness and national prosperity. Once this new style of princely court, with its own system of courtiership based on sincerity and virtue is installed, Mentor's task is over, and he waits only for Telemachus' return to finish the journey back to Ithaca. Book 11 ends affirming the true pedagogical aim of the reform of Salente: "Minerva, in the guise of Mentor, thus established in Salente all the best laws and the most useful precepts of government, less in order to make the realm of Idomeneus flourish than to show Telemachus, on his return, a concrete example of what a wise government can

do to make its people happy and to give lasting glory to a good king"
(*Télémaque*, p. 322).

The lesson of the Salente episode is reinforced by every other adventure recounted in the book. The story of Idomeneus, Philocles, and
Protesilas, with its lesson about the proper relationship between kings
and courtiers, as well as between private virtue and public service, is
simply the most elaborate expression of the major theme that runs
through Fénelon's text. Each adventure approaches the problem of kingship and courtiership from a different angle, but from each the same
lesson is drawn.

The very structure of *Télémaque*, based as it is on the ancient imaginary voyage with its many adventures, is at the bottom of this process of
reinforcement. Although the text is narrative, it is only minimally linear.
That is, the episodes do not build upon one another in such a way as to
generate the question "What happens next?" in the reader's mind. Indeed, the end, the regaining of Ithaca and Ulysses, has been assured from
the beginning both by explicit divine prediction and by the reader's
knowledge of Homer. The process of reinforcement and intensification
is based not on a narrative building to a climax but on the reiteration of
the same lesson as it is drawn from different narrative examples, each
presenting the problem in a slightly different way. The text should thus
be read primarily as a series of exemplary tales, each of which delivers
the same message, rather than as a single narrative whose end gives
meaning teleologically to the beginning and middle.[12] Underlying Fénelon's use of this epic narrative structure are epistemological and rhetorical assumptions with significant implications for political criticism, assumptions that Montesquieu rejects in the *Lettres persanes*, where the epic
voyage is replaced by the epistolary voyage.

From the beginning of *Télémaque* it is obvious that both Fénelon and
Mentor know all that they and their audience need to know. Their job is
to convey the knowledge they possess to Telemachus and to the reader.
And since Telemachus has Mentor as guide, and both Louis xiv and the
young duke of Burgundy already have Fénelon in their service as adviser
and tutor, these princes can be said already to "possess" the wisdom and
knowledge they need to rule well. As already noted, the voyagers in this
book bring wisdom and knowledge to the strange lands they visit, instead of discovering a new learning, as do the utopian voyagers modeled

---

[12]Aristotle recognized the essential difference between epic and tragic narrative in the
Poetics. Erich Auerbach elaborates on the definition of the epic as episodic in *Mimesis:
The Representation of Reality in Western Literature*, trans. Willard Trask (New York,
1957), p. 3.

on More's Hythloday. Epistemologically, therefore, Fénelon begins from a position of certainty. The basis of this certainty lies in religious faith, for it is through the goddess Minerva in the guise of Mentor that Telemachus (as well as Idomeneus and other kings encountered) learns his lessons.

Even when guaranteed by divine wisdom, however, epistemological certainty does not eliminate the need for rhetorical argument. Knowledge having been arrived at already, rhetoric must now move the will to accept its guidance. The rhetorical proof is thus a means not of arriving at a solution but simply of persuading the reader to follow a course of action that has already been deemed correct by other means. Each of Telemachus' adventures, each story related in the text, functions as this kind of rhetorical proof, a proof always of the same argument: that a healthy state depends upon a virtuous prince, and that virtuous princes depend upon virtuous advisers dedicated to public service. All specific recommendations for economic, social, and political reforms elaborated in the text depend in turn upon this premise. Thus, while Fénelon does suggest some major reforms, they never break through the structure of monarchical rule. As Nannerl Keohane remarks of the whole group of reformers who gathered around the young duke of Burgundy, their schemes depended upon the "sincere good will of the monarch," on a reforming king who would listen to good advisers.[13]

Montesquieu's *Lettres persanes* begins precisely where Fénelon's *Aventures de Télémaque* leaves off, for it is the sincere adviser's failure to be heard at court that causes him to start out upon his own journey. The story of Idomeneus and Philocles is here retold, but this time from the point of view of Philocles, the virtuous adviser. With Montesquieu's Persian, Usbek, however, we embark on a very different kind of voyage, one constructed not of exemplary tales that reinforce a single theme but of letters that break down the absolutist unity underlying Fénelon's work. The theme of princely virtue, directed by divine wisdom with the aid of good advisers, becomes for Montesquieu a premise to be called into question and eventually rejected. The unquestioned assumption that only through the reform of the king could reform of the nation and the state be effected is finally shattered. The door is open for new experiments in criticism which will take full advantage of literary forms to structure novel ways of examining the constitution of society and the activity of politics.

---

[13]Nannerl O. Keohane, *Philosophy and the State in France: The Renaissance to the Enlightenment* (Princeton, 1980), p. 346.

PART I

MONTESQUIEU

The Epistolary Form of Criticism

CHAPTER ONE

The Comparative
Critical Method

In 1721, six years after the death of Louis xiv, Charles-Louis de Secondat, baron de Montesquieu, a young man of thirty-two, published his *Lettres persanes*. The letters, each one carefully dated, begin in 1711 and end in 1720. They thus chronicle the waning years of the Sun King's reign and the first heady years of the regency of the duc d'Orléans. The chroniclers are two Persians who have left the court of their own king, both for political reasons and to seek the wisdom of the West.

As in Fénelon's *Télémaque*, we are embarked on a voyage with two travelers, one young and naive, the other older and wiser. But here the resemblance ends. The older man, Usbek, may think himself wise, but his travels shatter his self-confidence as he is repeatedly confronted with conflicting truths. Usbek's companion, Rica, is young and naive, but his openness makes him more able to learn from his experiences and adapt to the new society in which he finds himself. Even more telling is that Usbek, while on a voyage of self-discovery as important for his future ability to take up his political responsibilities as Telemachus' was for his, does not return from his travels ready to take up the reins of government. There is no Ithaca waiting patiently for Usbek's return, but a harem that, in his absence and because of it, falls apart. The story of a wise ruler putting his kingdom in order under the guidance of his own reason and virtue, strengthened by divine wisdom, is displaced by a new story: one about a polity that falls into disorder and a ruler who, though his sole concern is to know truth and to act virtuously, is helpless to restore an order he had maintained through false principles.

This is the story that Montesquieu chose to tell. The telling of such a complex tale demanded a complex form. Whereas *Télémaque* was a constructive exercise, with each adventure compounding its simple mes-

19

sage, the *Lettres persanes* charts both the negative paths of the breakdown
of the harem, of the French monarchy, and of Usbek's wisdom and the
positive trajectory of Usbek's attempt to construct a new theoretical basis
for social and political order. No narrative form, no matter how complex, could carry these two opposing thrusts in such a way as to maintain
the tension between them. No narrative form could contain the conflicting voices and conflicting truths, the multiple plots and themes that
intersect in the complexity of Usbek's many faces as human being, citizen, minister, master, and husband. And no narrative form could leave
the contradictions and conflicts raised by the story of Usbek's life and
travels so hopelessly unresolved and so squarely in the lap of the reader.

In the epistolary form, invented but only minimally exploited before,
Montesquieu found a form that could serve his needs. Although there
were a number of models for the *Lettres persanes*, the most obvious is a
popular seventeenth-century work, *L'Espion turc*, by Jean-Paul Marana.
Marana's foreign hero recorded his observations of the French capital in
letters sent home between the years 1637 and 1682.[1] But what had been
in the work of Marana simply a clever, if transparent, vehicle for social
and political satire became in Montesquieu's hands a form of writing that
fused literary and critical ends. In the *Lettres persanes*, Montesquieu does
not simply use a literary form, he reinvents it. The greatness of the
Lettres persanes as criticism depends upon its complexity and sophistica-
tion as literature, its exploitation of the epistolary form that Marana had
merely used.

As the *Lettres persanes* demonstrates, the epistolary form was potentially highly complex.[2] Since there was no narrator, it could match the
synthetic, constructive tendency of the narrative with the analytic aims of
the critic. Without a narrator, the reader would have to figure out both
what to think and what to do. There is thus a structural irony embedded
in this text. The active force, that which moves the reader forward, is not
a plot but the reader himself, who is forced to construct the various
narrative and thematic lines from the discrete letters handed to him. As
the reader, seated passively in his chair, is forced into the role of actor in
order to understand (and thus to enjoy) the book, the narrative surface of
the fiction is seen through to the unchanging principles that underlie it,
defining as they do the particular societies in which the characters move.
The narrative momentum of the fiction that carries the passive reader
along is counteracted and overwhelmed by the structural relationships

---

[1]Charles E. Kany, *The Beginnings of the Epistolary Novel in France, Italy, and Spain*
(Berkeley, 1937), pp. 99–100.

[2]An excellent general study of the epistolary form is Janet Gurkin Altman, *Epistolarity:
Approaches to a Form* (Columbus, O., 1982).

that define society and call for critical activity for their comprehension.[3] It is this critical activity that later writers such as Diderot will try to harness and direct toward the goals of social and political reform.

The epistolary form of the *Lettres persanes* makes this transfer of textual dynamism possible by requiring the reader to make connections between the letters as discrete textual units. Unlike previous historians who tried to comprehend social reality, Montesquieu provides neither the temporal and causal links associated with the secular historiographical tradition nor the figural and divinely absolute ones of St. Augustine and later Christian historians.[4] Rather, by giving the reader the letters alone, without any overpowering narrative coherence, he sets the terms for a secular but ahistorical—that is, a *critical*—reading of the text whose end is precisely to determine the principles of social relations without recourse either to God or to history. In the epistolary form can be located the first stage of the sociological revolution that Roger Caillois attributes to Montesquieu and the *Lettres persanes*.[5]

In the *Lettres persanes*, Montesquieu develops a polyphonic epistolary form to create a structure of references and cross-references that, like the cross-references in Diderot's *Encyclopédie* thirty years later, "clarify the object, indicate its close connections with those that touch it immediately, and its more distant connections with others with which one would think it unrelated; recall common ideas and analogous principles; fortify the consequences; interweave the branch to the trunk, and give to the whole that unity so favorable to the establishment of the truth and to persuasion." Like the *Encyclopédie*'s cross-references, the lexical references that force the reader to make connections between discrete letters have a more radical, critical function as well. "They will oppose ideas to each other," explains Diderot; "they will show how principles contrast with each other; they will attack, shake, secretly overturn ridiculous opinions that one would not dare insult openly. If the author is impartial, they will always have the double function of confirming and refuting; of troubling and reconciling."[6] The result is synthesis, but a critical synthesis, one that is dependent upon the activity of the reader for the connections that hold it together and, at the same time, call it into question.

[3]See Dena Goodman, "Towards a Critical Vocabulary for Interpretive Fictions of the Eighteenth Century," *Kentucky Romance Quarterly* 31 (Fall 1984): 259–68.

[4]I depend here upon Auerbach's distinction between hypotaxic and parataxic structures of historical interpretation in *Mimesis*, pp. 61–66, 86–106.

[5]Preface to *Oeuvres complètes*, by Montesquieu, 2 vols. (Paris, 1949–51), 1:v–vi.

[6]*Encyclopédie, ou Dictionnaire raisonné des sciences, des arts et des métiers*, ed. [Denis] Diderot and [Jean le Rond] d'Alembert, 35 vols. (Paris, 1751–80; rpt. Stuttgart–Bad Cannstatt, 1966), 5:642A.

Woven together in this critical fashion are two societies defined principally by their political systems: despotism and absolute monarchy. While changes occur on the surface of the two societies, their constitutions remain untouched, and it is the constitution of society that Montesquieu seeks to define in the *Lettres persanes*. While the definition of France's social constitution is not fully worked out in the course of the *Lettres persanes*, a critical method for achieving such a definition is clearly demonstrated.

The method elaborated by Montesquieu in the *Lettres persanes*, which I call the "comparative critical method," operates on three distinct but complementary levels of the text. The narrative surface of the *Lettres persanes* displays the comparative critical method most obviously. The Persians all use it in their observations on the West and their native Persia. This surface, moreover, is overlaid upon two other fundamental and structural levels of the text that show this method to be that of its author as well. These two deeper levels of the text reveal not what the characters think but what the author is doing.

The Epistolary Form

"The world is a tissue of relationships that change and intermingle," writes Jean Rousset of the *Lettres persanes*; "this is what the reader understands in the play alone of these innumerable letters that, before his eyes, are exchanged and intersect, that depart from and arrive at endlessly different points."[7] Through the creation of a complex network of epistolary exchanges, Montesquieu represents the world as constituted by human relations. More precisely, he represents not the world in general but the particular Persian world of Usbek, Rica, and their correspondents. By analogy, that other social whole, contemporary France, is created out of its own human and relational fabric. Again, Montesquieu's sociological approach is evident here in this representation of the social whole as what Norbert Elias calls a "figuration": "a formation consisting of many individual people" that can both survive and change as an entity independently of the individuals of which it is made up at any particular time.[8] But whereas Elias's focus on system over individual derives from his rejection of common sense and traditional historiographical notions of independent action as the determinant force in history, Montesquieu's

---

[7]Jean Rousset, *Forme et signification: Essais sur les structures littéraires de Corneille à Claudel* (Paris, 1962), p. 85.

[8]Norbert Elias, *The Court Society*, trans. Edmund Jephcott (New York, 1984), pp. 140–42.

leads him to this sad conclusion as if against his will. While Montesquieu clearly shares Elias's fascination with systems of human relations, that fascination never supplants the frustration and the pathos of the individual who struggles to break out of the entanglements of the social web, which keep the individual at the center of Montesquieu's representation of a social world that cannot be mastered.

As the representation of society in the *Lettres persanes* is fundamentally humane and relational, so the critical method that emerges from it is based upon the common sense of human beings. Common sense, rather than divine revelation, allows people to make comparisons and connections among social and individual particulars to arrive at a critical understanding of themselves and their societies. Unlike divine revelation, common sense is distinctly human, the reasoning faculty common to all human beings.[9]

If in the end the *Lettres persanes* is a representation of a social whole, a totality of interconnected human relations, this whole is arrived at only through the partial visions of the many correspondents. On another level, the parts of the social whole can be seen as the particular relationships—between husband and wives, between master and slaves, and between friends—that each correspondence marks. The reader is made aware of the partiality and particularity of both individuals and individual relationships throughout the *Lettres persanes*. "This intersecting of voices permits equally, on occasion, the initiation of a real discussion, where pros and cons are opposed," writes Pierre Testud. "In general, this is Montesquieu's intellectual attitude: to look at a question in various ways, thanks to the philosophical dialogue that the epistolary form naturally institutes, just as it permitted one to see a given society—the harem—from different angles. And in this case as in that one, the result is the same: nothing is simply imposed upon us."[10]

This determination not to impose answers upon the reader, but rather to present opposing views (even if they are not always presented fairly), pushes critical activity beyond the spheres of characters and implied author to that of the implied reader.[11] The reader, being implied by the

[9]On common sense in the eighteenth century, see Louise Marcil-Lacoste, "Le 'Dogmatisme' des philosophes: L'Origine d'une distorsion," *Studies on Voltaire and the Eighteenth Century* 190 (1980): 210.

[10]"Les *Lettres persanes*, roman épistolaire," *Revue d'Histoire Littéraire de la France* 66 (October–December 1966): 645.

[11]On the implied author—that author constructed by the reader through his reading of the text, as distinguished from the biographical author—see Wayne C. Booth, *The Rhetoric of Fiction* (Chicago, 1961). On the implied reader, see Wolfgang Iser, *The Implied Reader: Patterns of Communication in Prose Fiction from Bunyan to Beckett* (Baltimore, 1974). The concept of the implied reader depends upon the understanding that a text is

dropping of moral and social issues in his lap, is implicated as well, as the problems unresolved in the text become his to worry over and solve. But the text gives him more than just the topics of critical discourse; it gives him a method for approaching them as well, as he is forced to make cultural comparisons and through them to analyze the various social, political, and religious components of his own society. Such comparative and analytical activity is based on the exercise of a common sense that, being universal, can attend to all particular points of view.[12] To the extent that the partial visions of Montesquieu's characters, embodied in the discrete letters they write, imply an external reader who will make comparisons and connections between them, that implied reader is necessarily endowed with a common sense.[13]

Each Persian letter presents not only a partial but an immediate vision of the world. Although Montesquieu does not go to the lengths of novelistic immediacy attained later by Rousseau, in the famous letter written by St. Preux in Julie's closet, or by Laclos, in Valmont's letter written with his mistress's back serving as writing desk, the *Lettres persanes* does indeed capitalize on this formal property of the letter. The first-person style of the epistolary genre not only reveals the limitations of particular points of view but also creates what Bertil Romberg calls "a vibrant uncertainty" out of the simultaneity of experience and narration.[14] The partiality and uncertainty that arise from the immediacy of first-person narration depend, furthermore, on the constantly recreated distinction between the limited visions and voices of the characters and the greater world that the reader is attempting to put together to make sense of what he reads. And that world is constantly compared with, measured against, the world in which the reader lives.

---

only virtual until it is read and that the realizing of that potential requires certain attitudes, activities, and other characteristic features that are then attributed to the implied reader. Depending on the analysis, the implied reader can be specific to a text or a genre, or it can refer to the generalized nature of texts or narrative. I use the term in its most specific sense, referring here to the reader implied in the *Lettres persanes*.

[12]See Henri Coulet, "La Distanciation dans le roman et le conte philosophique," in *Roman et lumières au XVIIIe siècle*, ed. W. Kraus et al. (Paris, 1970), p. 444; and Wayne C. Booth, *A Rhetoric of Irony* (Chicago, 1974).

[13]"Usually the letter does not call forth a response and is condemned to insignificance. Except for the implied reader who will discover in the order of the letters a meaning and in their juxtaposition a language. He will be able to perceive certain temporal concordances (two letters written the same day), spatial ones (written the same day and coming from the same place), or textual ones (letters that are consecutive in the text and offer an obvious connection between them). These concordances are always significant." Réal Ouellet and Hélène Vachon, *"Lettres persanes" de Montesquieu* (Paris, 1976), p. 79.

[14]Bertil Romberg, *Studies in the Narrative Technique of the First-Person Novel* (Stockholm, 1962), p. 53.

Montesquieu's use of the immediacy of the letter thus emphasizes the distinction between what Paul Ricoeur calls "situation" and "world." Spoken discourse, Ricoeur argues, refers to the limited world of the situation of speaker and interlocutor. Written discourse, on the other hand, frees its reference from that immediate situation, opening out into a world beyond.

> Thus we speak about the "world" of Greece, not to designate any more what were the situations for those who lived them, but to designate the non-situational references which outlive the effacement of the first and which henceforth are offered as possible modes of being, as symbolic dimensions of our being-in-the-world. . . . Only writing, in freeing itself, not only from its author, but from the narrowness of the dialogic situation, reveals the destination of discourse as projecting a world.[15]

In the interior of the *Lettres persanes*, the dialogic situations are those of the senders and receivers of the letters, while the world is that of Montesquieu and his reader. Being a text, however, the *Lettres persanes* must also escape the situational references of Montesquieu's intentions to create a world in Ricoeur's full sense of the word. The reader's activity of determining the network of references that make of the partial situations of the characters a textual whole can be extended in the realization that the text as a text must project yet another world. As a result of this process, which the reader himself conducts, his own situation becomes a world, freed from the immediacy of his participation in it and thus made a potential object of his criticism.

In one sense what Montesquieu asks his reader to do in the *Lettres persanes* is to analyze a series of documents much as a historian or judge would, or even as a diplomat or general might, in determining a course of action on the basis of conflicting reports. In Montesquieu's day, almost all novels were published in documentary form: as memoirs, as histories, and as letters. "With the novel of experience replacing the novel of imagination," writes François Jost, "it is no less fictive. What disappears is the omniscience of the author."[16] Dorothy Thelander makes this same point in her study of *Les Liaisons dangereuses*:

> If the author of an epistolary novel has been successful in his creation of illusion, the reader, at least for the moment, accepts the letters as documents. From the multiple views, he must correct it as he goes along with

---

[15]Ricoeur, "Model of the Text," pp. 78–79.
[16]François Jost, "Le Roman épistolaire et la technique narrative au xviiie siècle," *Comparative Literature Studies* 3 (1966): 399.

the new information he receives. While in a sense the reader may be said to recreate any novel for himself, he does so with minimal guidance from the author in this *genre*, much as he is forced in daily life to probe not only what is said or written or done by several people, but what is omitted.[17]

The epistolary documents of which the *Lettres persanes* is composed are similarly presented to the reader for critical analysis, an analysis that is possible only when they are viewed in relation to each other and to the reader's own world.

If the critical activity of Usbek and Rica interests and amuses the reader, the epistolary form in which it is presented forces him to contribute to that activity if he is even to understand the book he reads. As Réal Ouellet points out, the epistolary is an open form, one that "demands of the reader to make himself, in his turn, the creator, to give birth, in his turn, to the work."[18] Just as Usbek and Rica compare the two societies of Persia and Paris, so too does the reader learn to make his own comparative analyses. Through the fiction of the novel he is able to criticize France with Rica and Usbek; through the epistolarity of the text he steps back from the characters and analyzes further the limitations of their particular visions of that world and their own.

As the reader analyzes his world critically, at a distance from the characters, he is also creating it as an object of criticism through a distancing from himself and his own partial and particular vision. The reader learns not simply to universalize his experience but to see beyond it to the problem of constructing universals by which his society might be governed. As he gains an understanding of the particularity of the constitution of absolutist France, he begins to think also of the validity of that constitution in the greater context of humanity. The comparative critical method in which the *Lettres persanes* initiates the reader is thus based upon an attention to cultural particularity and an assumption both of a common sense and of the possibility of other human universals.

As the epistolary form of the *Lettres persanes* makes evident, any society is composed of a closed network of human relations. Since the letters published by Montesquieu are wholly Persian, written to and from Persians (aside from a few letters inserted in others), the societies of East and West are kept apart as mutually distinct relational networks.

[17]Dorothy R. Thelander, *Laclos and the Epistolary Novel* (Geneva, 1963), p. 15.
[18]Ouellet, "Deux Théories romanesques au xviiie siècle: Le Roman 'bourgeois' et le roman épistolaire," *Études Littéraires* 1 (August 1968): 249. See also Jean Ehrard, "Tradition et innovation dans la littérature du xviiie siècle: Les Idées et les formes," in *La Littérature des Lumières en France et en Pologne: Ésthétique. Terminologie. Échanges* (Warsaw, 1976), pp. 22–23. Ehrard finds openness to be typical of the eighteenth century and most apparent in Diderot's dialogues.

And the process of critical definition that ensues within the epistolary framework reinforces the image of stasis and closure of a particular society, even as the dynamic openness of the reader's critical activity is demanded. In fact, the critical activity of the reader is what allows him to distance himself from the society in which he participates actively so as to see that society as an object of analysis and capable of definition. It is to this process of analysis and definition that I will now turn.

Despotism Defined in Discourse

The story told in the *Lettres persanes* is of a voyage to the West. The Persian nobleman Usbek and his young friend Rica are perhaps the first of their countrymen to make such a journey for the purpose of seeking wisdom—or so we are told in Usbek's first letter.[19] The love of knowledge, however, is not the only, or even the more important, reason for the journey, as Usbek reveals to his friend Rustan in letter VIII. The voyage is primarily a flight: having, like Philocles in Crete, run afoul of the despotic regime in Ispahan through the sincerity of his counsel, Usbek is forced to flee first the court and then the country. In contrast to the Cretan case, however, this flight marks a complete rupture between the king and his counselor, for sincere counsel is shown to be impossible within the despotic political system. In fact, Usbek's naive belief in the Fénelonian ideal of sincere counsel, shattered even before the first letter is written, is what led to his flight. Thus sincere counsel, deprived of its role, deprived of the ear of the prince, is set free of the courtly context, to establish itself as independent criticism. Usbek leaves the political sphere of the Persian despotism as a seeker of wisdom, and through that search he becomes a critic of the despotic system he had fled.

Usbek's story thus begins by defining narratively an opposition between the political despotism of Persia and an independent sphere of criticism. Once the counselor has been set free of the despotic state, he is able to be truly critical. But what does it mean to be critical? What is this critical activity that is opposed here to the political activity of the despotic court?

In the course of the *Lettres persanes* the reader learns the characteristics of criticism through cross-cultural comparisons of East and West. Not simply sincerity or truth telling, as Usbek initially believes, critical activity emerges as a way of thinking that is not possible within a despo-

---

[19]All references to the *Lettres persanes* are to the critical edition by Paul Vernière (Paris, 1975) and to J. Robert Loy's translation of *The Persian Letters* by Montesquieu. English translation copyright © 1961 by Harper & Row, Publishers, Inc. Reprinted by permission of the publisher. All letters will be referred to in the text by number.

tism or any system based on absolutist thinking. Criticism is the episte-mological adversary of absolutist thinking, based upon the human reason known as common sense rather than on dogmas, divine or otherwise. Unlike Telemachus and Idomeneus, who had all the wisdom they needed to be wise rulers, Usbek not only learns from his voyage but learns too how to be critical of what he had previously been taught. Indeed, reversing completely the pedagogical itinerary of the Fénelo-nian/Homeric voyage, the one thing that Usbek does not know, in the end, is himself. He does, however, learn a great deal about social, politi-cal, and ethical systems. Usbek's initial political polarization of virtuous truth telling, on the one hand, and despotism, on the other, is trans-formed into an epistemological opposition between criticism and absolut-ism, two fundamentally different forms of understanding. The journey to the West that places the counselor outside the polity also places him in a new social environment that spawns the critical process of analysis through comparison. The analytical, critical method, however, defines once again the extreme tension between criticism and absolutist politics. With his rejection of absolutism on epistemological grounds, the critic places himself in opposition to the despot. This opposition is finally revealed clearly in Usbek himself, as the gulf widens between his ideas as a social critic and his actions as a domestic despot in the harem. With the final exchange of letters between Usbek and his wives and eunuchs, the polarization of criticism and absolutist politics is complete.

In the course of the *Lettres persanes*, the reader may not learn how to change the political system, but he does learn how to analyze and crit-icize it on a radically fundamental level. And the focus of this analysis and criticism is not Persian despotism but French absolutism. The def-inition of oriental despotism established in the first few letters of the text, before Usbek arrives in Paris, is itself a crucial critical tool in the sub-sequent analysis of French society, for the analytic and critical represen-tation of French society is built out of cross-cultural comparisons and contrasts.

Usbek's letter VIII to Rustan introduces the major terms by which oriental despotism is defined in the *Lettres persanes*. It does so within the narrative context of Usbek's revelation of his motives for leaving Persia and traveling to the West. In the short narrative of his troubles within the political system of Persia, Usbek sets up a naive opposition between sincere and despotic discourse that is transformed later into the opposi-tion between criticism and absolutism.

A lexical, semiotic, and rhetorical analysis of letter VIII will thus expose the starting point for the development of a critical method, while defining the absolute and ideal poles of despotism and sincerity between which both politics and criticism must operate. By lexical I mean an analysis of the key terms of this letter and the despotism that they define. By semiotic analysis I mean simply the elucidation of a theory of verbal signs that is implicit in this letter and that has implications for the text as a whole. This semiotic axis of language, which defines the relationship between the word as referent and its external reference, as well as that between the word and the idea, is complemented by a rhetorical axis that defines the relationship between speaker and hearer in their use of language. Here I follow Ricoeur's reading of Aristotle's *Rhetoric*: "In short, rhetoric is a phenomenon of the intersubjective and dialogical dimension of the public use of speech."[20] This admittedly schematic and intentionally unambiguous way of dividing up the functions of language between the symbolic and the human or political is meant to disclose difficulties in the text created by Usbek's own naive opposition of these two axes in his understanding of himself in opposition to the despotic court that he flees.

In letter viii Usbek explains to Rustan the circumstances that led to his departure from Persia. Although Usbek had written in his first letter that he and Rica were off in search of Western wisdom, a deeper, political motivation for the journey is now revealed. The political explanation of letter viii, however, does not simply replace but is added to the intellectual one of letter i, thus modifying the simple significance of the search for knowledge. The intellectual and the political form the dual bases of Usbek's action here and throughout the *Lettres persanes*.

Usbek chooses the politically defined and defining moment of his entry into the royal court at Ispahan as the starting point of his narrative explanation in letter viii. Upon his entering the court, thus taking up his role as member of the polity, the story that constitutes the explanation of his present action begins. In so beginning his tale, Usbek has marked the bounds of his explanation for leaving Persia—and thus the bounds of the text as the story of his journey to the West—as political.[21]

Like Philocles before him, Usbek entered the political arena with a highly apolitical goal: to unmask vice by speaking always the truth. As he explains: "I carried truth to the very steps of the throne. I spoke there

---

[20]Paul Ricoeur, *The Rule of Metaphor: Interdisciplinary Studies in the Creation of Meaning in Language*, trans. Robert Czerny (Toronto, 1977), p. 29.

[21]Usbek's autobiography is echoed in that of his First Eunuch in the letter that directly follows this one. The eunuch also picks the moment of his entry into the political structure of which he is a member as a starting point, the moment of his castration (letter ix).

a hitherto unknown language; I brought flattery to confusion, and astonished at once both the worshippers and their idol" (letter VIII).[22] Usbek's
purpose was apolitical in two senses: first, because it disregarded totally
the actual political system in which Usbek was operating, as he soon
found out; second, and more fundamentally, because, Fénelon and Mentor notwithstanding, sincerity, virtue, and truth telling have less to do
with the relationships between human beings which are structured by
politics than with those between men and objects structured by semiotics
and epistemology. In other words, Usbek attempted to communicate
with a language that, by his definition, was arhetorical and thus apolitical. To understand better the implications of Usbek's conflict with the
court of Ispahan, it is necessary to explore the linguistic analogy, reminiscent of *Télémaque*, that he himself invokes in referring to his activity as
speaking "a hitherto unknown language."

The symbiotic relationship between courtiers and king, adorers and
idol, at the heart of the despotic system is disrupted when Usbek speaks.
His unknown language, in stark contrast to the vicious language of
flattery, is unornamented and seeks to lay bare the actions of others with
naked truth, instead of masking those of the speaker. It is what Usbek
calls "sincérité," a type of discourse to which the young Montesquieu had
dedicated an *éloge* in 1717. There, too, sincerity was contrasted with
flattery: "By what characteristic can one thus recognize the ministers of
the true God? By the sincerity with which they speak to princes; by the
liberty with which they proclaim to them the most annoying truths, and
seek to bring back to the fold those souls seduced by phony priests and
flatterers."[23]

In the *Lettres persanes*, the reader, through Usbek, learns the consequences of using this sincere language within the despotic political system, which has its own type of discourse: flattery. *Flatter*, according to
the *Dictionnaire de l'Académie Française* of 1694, means "to deceive by
disguising the truth, either through weakness, or through a wrong-
headed fear of displeasing."[24] Flattery is not only false discourse but one
that disguises the truth, masks it. It is also a language based on fear and
weakness, two terms that describe the basis of power in a despotism.

[22]Similar language was used by contemporaries to describe the court of Louis XIV:
"Earlier one spoke only of the interests of the state, the needs of the state, the upholding
of the state. Today it would be *lèse-majesté* to do so. The King has usurped the place of
the state, the King is everything, the state nothing. He is the idol to which the provinces,
the towns, finance, the great and the small—in short, everything—is sacrificed" Jurien,
Soupirs de la France esclave (1691), quoted in Elias, *Court Society*, p. 118.

[23]Montesquieu, *Oeuvres complètes*, ed. Daniel Oster (Paris, 1964), p. 45.

[24]*Le Dictionnaire de l'Académie française [DAF]*, 2 vols. (Paris, 1694; rpt. Lille, 1901),
1:462.

Flattery is false rhetoric, the corruption of political language. As rhetoric, flattery aims to produce conviction through the creation of a sense of community and the use of a highly charged language; as false rhetoric, it does these things willfully and without regard for any truth.[25] The figures of rhetorical discourse, what the eighteenth century saw as ornament or embellishment overlaid onto simple language,[26] are used in flattery not simply to convince but to convince the listener of a falsehood. In fact, the type of conviction produced by flattery is false as well, for in flattery one tells the listener what he wants to hear, what he already believes or is predisposed to believe. In this case, it is not the rhetor whose demagogic power controls the relationship, but the listener whose power lies in the willfulness of his own pleasure or displeasure.

Who then does ultimately control flattering discourse? I would say that the flatterer's aim is to gain control over the listener but that he does so by denying that end. Flattery is that denial. Put otherwise, the flatterer temporarily concedes control of the discourse to the listener in order to regain that power over the listener himself through the use of the community of trust established by the successful rhetorical ploy. Flattery is not an end in itself but a means to one. Rather than power itself, the

[25]In focusing less on the conviction produced by rhetoric than on the sense of community between speaker and hearer that it creates I follow such twentieth-century Aristotelians as Wayne C. Booth, "Metaphor as Rhetoric: The Problem of Evaluation," *Critical Inquiry* 5 (Autumn 1978): 49–72; and Ted Cohen, "Metaphor and the Cultivation of Intimacy," ibid., pp. 3–12.

[26]"Thus when one speaks of figures embellishing discourse one means only that, on those occasions when figures are not removed, the same basic thought will be expressed in a manner either more lively, more noble, or more agreeable by the aid of these figures than if it were expressed without them" César Dumarsais, *Des tropes* (Paris, 1757), pp. 11–12.

According to Oswald Ducrot and Tzvetan Todorov,
During the twenty subsequent centuries [after ancient times], rhetoric has undergone several essential modifications. First, it has lost its immediate pragmatic aim: it no longer teaches persuasion, but rather production of "beautiful" discourse. Thus it has been increasingly disinterested in the deliberative and judiciary genres, for example, and has shown a predilection for taking literature as its object. It has also increasingly cut back its field. . . . Rhetoric now finds itself reduced to *elocutio* or the art of style. The later rhetorics (in the eighteenth and nineteenth centuries) often, though not always, present only a simple enumeration of figures. [*Encyclopedic Dictionary of the Sciences of Language*, trans. Catherine Porter (Baltimore, 1979), p. 74.]
See also Gérard Genette, "La Rhétorique restreinte," *Communications* 16 (1970): 158–71, and Peter France, *Rhetoric and Truth in France: Descartes to Diderot* (Oxford, 1972), pp. 15–16. The twentieth century's rediscovery of Aristotle and the subsequent recovery of rhetoric in its fullest sense reverse this trend and are, as should be obvious, the necessary premises of the present study.

struggle for power is instantiated in flattery. The listener's control is never stable, never permanent, since it is acknowledged only in the interests of undermining it. If all language is rhetorical to some degree, determining a particular community or, more strongly, a political or power relationship, then flattery is the type of language that defines despotic relations.[27]

Despotic relations, however, are not confined to the purely despotic political systems of the Orient. At the same time that Montesquieu, through Usbek, presents the reader with a representation of the structure of one despotic system through its political discourse, familiar elements of that discourse cause the Frenchman to look critically at his own political system. He is reminded perhaps of *De la flaterie*, a popular little work by Amelot de la Houssaie, written in 1686, not long before Fénelon began his critique of flattery in *Télémaque*. There the author introduces his subject as follows: "Everyone is so convinced that FLATTERY pleases great men, that these same people who condemn it in public, court it in private, just like the others: and this civic contagion is so widespread, that there is hardly anybody today who does not wish to be either a flatterer or himself flattered. Self-interest *[l'intérêt]* makes the flatterers speak, and self-love *[amour-propre]* makes them listen."[28] While letter VIII is dedicated to the definition of oriental despotism, the reader is already beginning to make connections between that system and his own in the West. By analyzing despotism into its component elements, Montesquieu allows the reader to discover the despotic elements of the French monarchy.

In our own day, no one has analyzed the "social figuration" of French court absolutism under Louis XIV better than Norbert Elias. *The Court Society* reads as if written by a latter-day Usbek. Under the heading "The Art of Dealing with People," Elias analyzes the structure of court discourse. "The prince," he observes, "can always break the rules of courtly conversation; he can, if he likes, break off the discussion and the relationship for any reason he chooses without losing much." On the other hand, it is the successful courtier who controls the conversation, for "to lead one's higher-ranking interlocutor almost imperceptibly where one

---

[27]Ricoeur finds an opposition between rhetoric and flattery at the very basis of Aristotle's project in the *Rhetoric*. "The question that sets this project in motion is the following: What does it mean to persuade? What distinguishes persuasion from flattery, from seduction, from threat—that is to say, from the subtlest forms of violence?": *Rule of Metaphor*, p. 11.

[28][Abraham-Nicole] Amelot de la Houssaie, *La Morale de Tacite: De la flaterie* (Paris, 1686), p. ij. Hegel also associates flattery with absolute monarchy. See G. W. F. Hegel, *The Phenomenology of Mind*, trans. J. B. Baillie (New York, 1967), pp. 533–35.

wishes is the prime requirement of this courtly manner of dealing with people." It is because conversation, like everything else in this society, is an expression of and attempt to maintain unequal power relations that the formal dimension of discourse is privileged. "The form and tactics of the encounter," furthermore, "require a constant testing of the power-relationship between the partners." The symbiosis of the relations that define the court society is revealed in these reversals between the king and the courtier, and between the form of discourse and the form of power.[29]

In the common understanding of figurative discourse and in the subsequent decision to accept or believe in the figures as a way of grasping reality lie the bonds of a community of discourse.[30] The community produced by flattery, the closed world of the courting and the courted, is what Usbek, in his naïveté, disconcerts; but the language he uses to do so, the naked language of truth, does not, in its turn, create a new community. Serving the interests of representation rather than communication, it isolates the speaker with his personal knowledge of the truth, separates him from the community, makes of him an outcast. Philocles, cast away in Samos, in hermit-like retreat, is again the model for Usbek's plight.

In his notion of sincere discourse, Usbek assumes both that a language can function without concern for the necessity of communication and that it can represent truth transparently. The naïveté of this conception is exposed in the course of the *Lettres persanes* along the two axes that define language: the rhetorical and the semiotic. The possibility of a nonrhetorical language is undermined in the very flight from Persia that gives occasion for the *Lettres*: Usbek cannot remain within the community and polity of Persia if he refuses to speak its common language. The progressive distancing revealed in letter VIII, as Usbek retreats from the court to the country ("I became involved in no more intrigues and withdrew to my country house"), and then from the Orient to the West, does not end there. When spatial distance has been maximized, temporal distance begins to take effect. The result is that Usbek gradually discontinues his correspondences with old friends who remain in Persia and writes only to those others who, like him, have left it. His correspondence with his wives also drops off over time until it is reopened by the crisis in the harem. Then, Usbek's letters to both wives and eunuchs become wholly despotic and rhetorical, as he attempts to reconstitute the domestic despotism through his written commands and reprimands.

[29]Elias, *Court Society*, pp. 108–9.
[30]See Booth, "Metaphor as Rhetoric," p. 65, and Cohen, "Metaphor and the Cultivation of Intimacy," p. 8.

(letters CXLVII, CL, CLIII, CLV). Usbek is reduced to silence if he is unable or unwilling to speak the language of his community.

When Usbek naively ignores the necessary rhetorical aspect of language, he reveals a functional problem: for language to work, it must be accepted by both speaker and hearer according to mutually acknowledged conventions. (This is why Idomeneus had to choose to listen to sincere advice before it could be given.) The assumption that language is semiotically transparent presents a different problem, one that is epistemological rather than functional. Whereas the rhetorical problem is demonstrated in Usbek's distance from the Eastern community, the semiotic one arises in his confrontation with the ideas of the West. Beginning with his letter XVI to the mullah Méhémet-Hali, Usbek reveals his doubts about the ability to know absolute truth. The result of this questioning is an investigation into the basis of ethics. The undermining of dogmatic ethics is effected by showing the polysemy of ethical and relational terms and the resultant instability of the community defined by and revealed in its language. In chapter 3, below, I will trace the path of this undermining of language and community through the decomposition of one term crucial to them both, *fidélité*. For now, I want only to emphasize that Usbek's naïveté is undermined in the course of the text as the rocky foundations of the social world are revealed. The quest of the *Lettres persanes* leads away from the false Fénelonian ideal of transparency and toward a more complex understanding of the epistemological and rhetorical problems posed in terms of language.

Flatterie is one of the key despotic terms in the *Lettres persanes*, and *jalousie* is another. After Usbek has explained his virtuous activity in the despotic court as truth telling in opposition to flattery, he goes on to reveal the consequences of this activity. "I realized," he writes, "that my sincerity had made enemies for me, that I had drawn on myself the jealousy of ministers without having won the favor of the prince" (letter VIII). Turning once again to the *Dictionnaire* of 1694, one finds the following definition of *jaloux*: "He who fears that some competitor will snatch from him something he possesses, or to which he aspires. It is used principally to refer to husbands and wives, and to lovers."[31] As with flattery, fear is at the heart of jealousy. Whereas flattery was seen to be based on a fear of displeasing, jealousy is rooted in a fear of losing something one possesses. Since it is the favor of the prince that the ministers fear to lose in the relationship between the despot and his courtiers, the two types of fear merge in this situation. Both flattery and jealousy are manifestations of a relationship where power is at the pleasure of one of the members. In failing to transform this relationship,

---

[31]*DAF*, 1:579.

Usbek has simply become prey to one of its characteristic manifestations. It is because he has failed to change the despotic relations of the court that he attracts jealousy and does not gain favor, for the favor of the prince is the obverse of the despotic coin that has jealousy as its reverse. In contrast to Fénelon, who identified the weakness of the prince as the basis of the despotic court, Montesquieu shows the individual sincere counselor to be weak in the face of a despotic system of which the prince is simply a part.

The *Dictionnaire* of 1694 also defines *jalousie* as "a latticework made of wood or iron, through which one sees without being seen," and gives as an example: "He watches through the *jalousie*."[32] Although this is clearly not the sense in which Montesquieu is using the word *jalousie* here, the points of reference that it evokes in the reader are significant. First, there is the obvious connection of the *jalousie* with the harem. If, as the definition of *jaloux* notes, jealousy is most often associated with relationships between men and women, either as man and wife or as lovers, the *jalousie* is associated with a particular type of relationship between the sexes that is identified as both despotic and oriental. Much later in the text, in the "Histoire d'Aphéridon et d'Astarte" (letter LXVII), Montesquieu refers to a *jalousie* within the harem, using almost (but not quite) the same expression as that given in the *Dictionnaire*. "Finally I got into his harem," says Aphéridon, "and he arranged for me to speak to her through a jalousie."[33]

The change from *regarder* to *parler* here points up a second important reference of this sense of *jalousie*. Once again, as with the rhetorical or metaphoric aspect of flattery, jealousy here evokes the mask through which one can see without being seen. To say that one speaks behind a mask, or that a mask is placed between the speaker and the listener, as Montesquieu does in letter LXVII, is to signal again the false character of language as a means of defining the corrupt or insincere relations of the society to which it belongs. Thus sincerity, or the unknown language of truth, which was opposed to flattery in the preceding sentence, is here opposed to jealousy. More precisely, sincerity stands in a relationship of opposition to two other relationships, one called flattery and the other jealousy, both of which are based upon fear and describe the political system of the court of Ispahan while evoking numerous other points of reference. This is not to say that jealousy and flattery are simply two words for the same thing, because clearly they are not. Rather, through their multiple constellations of references they both evoke and thus serve

[32]Ibid.
[33]See also letter XXIII, where Usbek writes to Ibben from Leghorn: "Women enjoy great freedom here. They can look at men through certain windows called *jalousies*."

to describe a particular type of society or relationship that is traditionally called "oriental despotism," and that is instantiated in the *Lettres persanes*.[34] The jealousy and flattery that characterize the court of Ispahan reappear in Usbek's harem and in that of Astarte's eunuch husband, but also in France, at the court of Louis xiv and in the salons and boudoirs of Parisian society. Just as Fénelon's reader could see aspects of the absolutist court of Louis xiv in Salente, Montesquieu's reader can see it in Ispahan.

"You must divide your confidence among several," wrote Louis xiv to his son. "The jealousy of one holds the ambition of the others in check. But although they hate each other, they have common interests and can therefore come to an agreement to deceive their lord."[35] Jealousy, Norbert Elias reminds us, was a crucial element in the fragile balancing act upon which Louis xiv's power depended. He not only tolerated jealousy, he cultivated it in order to channel energies that might otherwise be directed against himself. The point was to keep people divided so that he might unify them in his person alone. "Jealousies whirl around the king, maintaining the social balance," Elias writes. "The king plays on them like an artist."[36]

Finally, the *jalousie* that separates Aphéridon and Astarte is associated

---

[34]Franco Venturi argues that although the concept of oriental despotism can be traced to Plato and Aristotle, Montesquieu is the first theorist to synthesize its two major concepts: the master-slave relationship and oriental states. Montesquieu is thus the first to speak of *political* despotism, the slavery of the individual to the political order, rather than a simple breaking of laws. "Oriental Despotism," *Journal of the History of Ideas* 24 (January–March 1963): 133–42.

Alain Grosrichard also credits Montesquieu with transforming the Greek notion of the despotic into a political concept, specifically by inventing the substantive *despotisme*, which politicized domestic power as a form of government. In fact, Grosrichard goes on to argue, all the problems of postclassical political theory can be seen to result from a confusion of the four types of power distinguished by Aristotle in book 1 of the *Politics*: magistrate, royal, paternal, and master. Since the first two are defined as political and the second two as domestic (despotic), the following relation can be inferred: royal is to magistrate (political) as master is to paternal (despotic). However, if (still following Aristotle and Grosrichard) one argues that monarchical power is based upon paternal power, then its abuse is called despotic, analogous to treating children as if they were slaves. With Montesquieu's decisive political transformation of the despotic into despotism, the way is then cleared for the reintroduction of the despotic into the home to describe domestic relations according to a political model. "Strange destiny of meaning," writes Grosrichard, "which becomes 'figured' when one speaks, at the end of the eighteenth century, of the head of the family as a *despot*, when that was, in the beginning, its only proper meaning, all usage of the words *despot* or *despotic* in the political field being only, according to Aristotle, analogical and improper": Alain Grosrichard, *Structure du sérail: La Fiction du despotisme asiatique dans l'Occident classique* (Paris, 1979), pp. 9–12.

[35]Quoted in Elias, *Court Society*, p. 129.

[36]Elias, *Court Society*, pp. 122, 131.

with yet another significant term, *persiennes*, defined in the *Encyclopédie* of Diderot as "jalousies or window frames that open outward like shutters, and on which wooden rods are symmetrically arranged as a kind of shade which serves the same function as blinds, breaking up the light and allowing the air to come in to an apartment."[37] Unlike a regular *jalousie*, which stands between two people, the *persienne* is placed in a window, thus separating inside from outside, or the closed world of a particular society from the rest of humanity. Its function is to break up the light, to figure and filter it, while letting in the fresh air. The impression of patterns of light dancing on floor and walls comes immediately to mind as an image of the *Lettres persanes*. Through the eyes of Montesquieu's Persians, the seemingly stable but dark and closed world of French society is set in motion, figured and refigured, shattered into a million dancing points of light. By placing *persiennes* (*persans*) between the reader and the world in which he lives, Montesquieu shows that world to him in a new light, figured by the tracery that is the subjectivity and individuality of the perceptions of Usbek and Rica.

Usbek has attempted to disrupt the relationship established by means of flattery between the ruler and the ruled; his sincerity has disconcerted a social whole. But in failing to communicate or convince, Usbek has failed to transform the relationship between the king and his courtiers, and in so doing he has managed simply to place himself in active opposition to the members of this symbiotic relationship and the political system they embody. After describing the complementary attitudes of both members of this political whole toward himself, Usbek then sums them up as "a corrupt court." As a social and political relationship, the court is a system of mutual support, in opposition to which, Usbek then says, "I managed to buoy myself up only by an already enfeebled virtue." Whereas the parts of the system support each other, the individual (Usbek) has only himself as a virtuous man for support. Virtue in itself is not weak, but virtue as the action of the individual is when pitted against the combined force of a community that opposes it in its corruption. Instead of supporting virtue, or being supported by it, the political system here opposes virtue.

Usbek's flight from the court of Ispahan results from his realization of his political impotence. Whereas initially he thought only in terms of truth and falsity, virtue and vice, these same terms are now aligned with relations of power—political relations. It is Usbek's weakness as an individual against the community, his inability to transform it by unmasking the words and actions of those who comprise it, that causes him to seek the safety of distance and to abandon his "great plan" to be

---

[37]*Encyclopédie*, 12:428.

virtuous. Restated on the level of language, it is the impotence of the
asocial language of truth to form a community that leaves Usbek the
victim of the political system maintained by the false rhetoric of flattery.
Had Philocles, on his way to Samos, narrated the story of his expulsion
from Crete, the same lesson might have emerged, rather than that drawn
from it by the king from his point of view.

Usbek's flight, moreover, an act conducted within the confines of the
despotic system, is effected within the despotic vocabulary. "I pretended
[*feignis*] to possess a great devotion to learning," Usbek writes in letter
VIII, "and by dint of pretense, such devotion actually came to me." Usbek
borrows the false language of the court, feigning an attachment he does
not have, and does so not in the interest of truth or virtue but in his own
self-interest. The *Dictionnaire* of 1694 defines *feindre* as "to simulate, to
use a false appearance in order to deceive [*tromper*], to pretend."[38] The
similarity to the definition of *flatter* as "to deceive [*tromper*] by disguising
the truth" is striking. The term *déguisement*, as well as the concept of
hiding, is recovered in the subsidiary definition of *feint* as an "artifice by
which one hides something."[39] Instead of removing himself from deceit
in order to expose it, Usbek has decided to act deceitfully in order to
remove himself from the court.

Usbek's feigned attachment for the sciences becomes a real quest for
knowledge, as the narrative of the *Lettres persanes* reveals. Usbek gains
knowledge in spite of himself and his preconceptions, for political circumstances force him to find something that he had only pretended to
seek. In fact, only because Usbek thinks that he can distinguish between
virtue and vice, truth and falsity, do circumstances lead him to realize
that his means are inadequate to make this kind of distinction. Usbek
does not simply progress from ignorance to knowledge, but first, in a
Cartesian process, is stripped of the knowledge he has. It is a process of
questioning, of casting doubt, rather than of building or acquiring. As
Usbek says much later regarding proofs of virginity: "It can be said as
much as one likes that there are certain signs for knowing the truth; this
is an old error that we have gotten over among ourselves these days; our
medical doctors give incontrovertible reasons for the *uncertainty* of
proof" (letter LXXI; emphasis added). It is because Usbek's old certainty is
shattered by the sciences he investigates that his feigned attachment for
them becomes real. This learning process and its end are the antithesis of
those that defined Telemachus' journey, where his travels revealed to
him only the wisdom he had had all along.

Usbek's departure from the court of Ispahan signals a complete break

[38]*DAF*, 1:442.
[39]Ibid., 1:443.

between political and intellectual activity. He claims to have no longer dealt with political affairs, but only to have pursued his growing interest in the sciences. As far as he is concerned, study is now totally divorced from action. To have a real attachment for the sciences is to detach himself from affairs of the court, from political action.[40]

Whereas initially Usbek's sole concern was to unmask hypocrisy and lay bare the truth, it is now he who is exposed, and his concern thus turns toward himself. "I still remained exposed to the malice of my enemies," he writes in letter VIII, "but I had almost completely removed the means of protecting myself from them. Some confidential advice made me think seriously about my[self]." Here the level of language and that of political power are brought together once again, as laying bare the truth is seen to lead to the laying bare of the truth teller. Usbek's powerlessness as truth teller leaves him victim to the power of those who can use language to their advantage and against his. Once again Usbek is forced to flee. To get beyond the reach of vice and, more important, to free himself of the despotic system of thought, language, and action, he must leave Persia altogether.

Using again the now familiar device of the search for knowledge, Usbek goes to his king, and, noting his desire to become instructed in the sciences of the West, he says, "I hinted [*insinuai*] that he might draw some profit from my travels" (letter VIII). Usbek's last act in Persia, his flight from it, is once again accomplished in the terms of the despotic discourse. The key word here is *insinuer*. Like *flatterie*, *jalousie*, and *feindre*, insinuation is a type of false speech, a form of discourse in opposition to the sincere language of virtue. The *Dictionnaire* of 1694 thus defines *insinuation* as: "Action by which one insinuates something: thus in rhetoric insinuation refers to a particular part of speech by which one insinuates oneself smoothly into the audience's good graces."[41] Like

---

[40]Usbek's action, understood within the context of Montesquieu's perception of the duties and responsibilities of the French nobility, must be seen as an abdication of his social and political function. This issue is raised again later in the text in Rica's letter CXXXIX to Ibben. Rica provides no categorical verdict but argues that abdication may be admirable in certain cases when higher motives are involved. Montesquieu's concern in both instances is clearly personal in origin. He too chose his country home (La Brède) over the court; he too as the director of the Academy of Bordeaux, developed an interest in the sciences at the expense of a full commitment to his duties as president of the *parlement* of Bordeaux. The appearance of the *Lettres* in 1721, midway between his accession to that post in 1716 and his sale of it in 1726, can account for the lack of decision on this issue demonstrated in the text. See P. Barrière, "Les Éléments personnels et les éléments Bordelais dans les *Lettres persanes*," *Revue d'Histoire Littéraire de la France* 51 (January-March 1951): 21–22.

[41]*DAF*, 1:599.

other rhetorical forms, insinuation is concerned rather with the effect it produces on the auditor than with conveying truth; like the other forms discussed above, it also has a specifically political connotation, as in the following example: "he insinuated himself somehow into the court."[42] This second sense of the word also underlines the connection between language and action that was found in the other terms: one insinuates oneself through the use of verbal insinuation.[43]

Diderot's definition of *insinuant* in the *Encyclopédie* is telling here, for he too aligns it with the court and with rhetoric: "The *insinuating* man has his own kind of eloquence. . . . It is the art of seizing our weaknesses, of making use of our interests, of creating us; he is owned by men of the court and other unfortunates [*malheureux*]."[44] The word *malheureux* is striking here and recalls once again the terms of the despotic relationship and despotic discourse, where the courtier flatters out of fear of losing what he has (jealousy), rather than from the desire to gain that which he has not. The oriental mode of the *Lettres persanes* is found as well in the sinuosity of the word *insinuer*, which is made graphic in Diderot's reference to the *homme insinuant* as a "serpent" and which is repeated by Montesquieu in the names of Usbek and his wives: Zachi, Zéphis, Zélis.[45] Finally, consider Diderot's warning in the same *Encyclopédie* article concerning *l'homme insinuant*. "Beware the insinuating man," he writes; "he raps softly upon your chest, and he has his ears open to capture the sound it makes. He enters into your home as a slave, but he loses no time in commanding there as the master, whose orders you always take for your own."[46]

Diderot's imagery captures the idea that insinuation, as a form of speech, acts between speaker and listener without concern for the veracity of its reference: it is pure rhetoric. Even more to the point are the implications of this type of speech as a means of reversing political (power) relations. In a relationship where there is no external standard, no point of reference, instability characterizes both politics and language.

When Usbek insinuates that his voyage to the West might be useful to the king, the implication is not that Usbek is an *homme insinuant*, as

---

[42]Ibid., 1:598.

[43]These are precisely the kind of words that Austin, in *How to Do Things with Words*, calls "performatives" because they are themselves actions rather than descriptions of actions.

[44]*Encyclopédie*, 8:788.

[45]Usbek's wives "are described [*dessinées*] by the sinuosity of the letter Z, which rococo fiction associates with all exoticism: the initial letter of their silky names gives body to sensual tension and to the suppleness of apparent obedience": Jean Starobinski, Preface to *Lettres persanes* (Paris, 1973), p. 20.

[46]*Encyclopédie*, 8:788–89.

Diderot later pictures that creature. The point I wish to make here is rather that the word *insinuer* belongs to a family of words that refer to a particular type of discourse and to a corresponding type of political relationship. The four key words found in letter VIII (*flatter, jalousie, feindre, insinuer*) all refer to each other and to this dual system of communication (and false representation) and political relations that corresponds to the oriental despotism of the Persian court and the Persian state. As these four words reappear in other contexts they will evoke the despotism to which they refer.

Like his feint, Usbek's insinuation is successful. In his own words, "I found [favor in the king's] eyes [*je trouvais grâce devant ses yeux*]. I left and thereby robbed my enemies of a victim" (letter VIII). The success of the ploy is once again due to Usbek's acting according to the rules of despotic discourse, as the result reveals. According to the *Dictionnaire* of 1694, "One uses *Trouver grâce devant les yeux de quelqu'un* to mean: give him pleasure, gain his favor. And this is only used by someone who is extremely inferior to the other."[47] Thus the first clause of this sentence, taken as a whole, evokes two aspects of the despotic relationship and its mode of discourse: the necessity of pleasing (flattery) rather than truth telling, and the extreme inequality between the ruler and the ruled. Montesquieu has employed a standard figure of speech that is revitalized by its literal aptness. The phrase gains in depth of meaning as well because of its incorporation of the phrase "devant ses yeux," which emphasizes the partiality of the individual vision. Grace is found only in the eyes of a single person, the king, because within the despotic system it is necessary only to please that one person.

"The king," wrote Saint-Simon of Louis XIV, "used the numerous festivities, walks and excursions as a reward or punishment for those who were or were not invited. As he realized that he did not have enough favours to dispense to make a permanent impression, he replaced real rewards by imaginary ones, by exciting jealousy, by petty everyday advantages, by his partiality."[48] Opposed to the partiality and particularity of grace is the universality of justice, which Usbek later defines as "a true relationship of appropriateness which exists between two things, and this relationship is always the same, no matter by whom considered, whether it be God, or an angel, or finally, a man" (letter LXXXIII).

Within the despotic system, the grace of the king is all that Usbek requires to succeed in his intentions. Thus he leaves Persia and in so doing robs his enemies of a victim. The word *dérober* means not simply to rob but to hide: "To commit larceny, to take and hide that which

[47]*DAF*, 1:531.
[48]Quoted in Elias, *Court Society*, p. 120.

belongs to another."[49] Usbek, it should be remembered, decided to leave Persia because he was exposed to the malice of his enemies; in leaving, he is no longer so exposed. But it must be remembered too that Usbek's safety has been achieved only through deceit: by masking his thoughts and his words he has managed to hide himself.

"Let them talk in Ispahan," Usbek tells Rustan. "Come to my defense only with my friends. Leave to my enemies their evil interpretations. I am only too happy that this should be the only harm they can do me" (letter VIII). In escaping beyond the range of power of the Persian state, Usbek has left behind the battle of words in which he engaged: the project of being politically virtuous. The words of his enemies are as powerless to harm him now as his own were to harm them. But whereas Usbek's speech was powerless because incomprehensible within the despotic system, those used against him have simply been deprived of their object.

When Usbek says, "Let them talk in Ispahan. Come to my defense only with my friends," he is distinguishing between the discourse of his friends and that of his enemies or, more generally, between that of the despotic political system and that of another type of social relationship: friendship.[50] There is no point in trying to convince Usbek's enemies, whose discourse is determined not by an external reference (Usbek's motive) but by the listener (the king), that they have falsely interpreted his action. In fact, the subject of the entire letter, the true and the false motives for Usbek's journey, is outside the system of flattery or despotic discourse because it seeks to substitute a true for a false reference of a predetermined referent.

Consider again the two types of discourse that create the central tension in letter VIII: sincerity and flattery. Flattery has been defined above as false rhetoric, and sincerity as a "naked" or transparent language that is devoid of rhetorical figures and thus of rhetorical power. Flattery is defined further as an act of political vice that in turn defines a despotic relationship, while sincere speech is an act of political virtue that, as nonrhetorical, defines no political relationship or system. If the focus is shifted from the rhetorical relationship between the speaker and listener to the semiotic relationship between the referent and the reference, it is sincerity that has positive value and flattery that is lacking. Since sincerity assumes a simple, transparent relationship between the expression and that which is expressed, the referent determines the

---

[49]DAF, 2:414.

[50]Friendship was impossible in the court of Louis XIV because the cultivation of enmities was at its heart. "What is characteristic of this dominion is the exploitation of enmities between subjects to reduce their hostility towards, and increase their dependence on, their sole ruler, the king": Elias, Court Society, p. 121.

reference. In flattery, on the other hand, the will of the listener, not the external reference, determines the expression. The lack of power of the reference in such discourse, as well as the usurpation of that role by the listener, is perhaps best expressed by Shakespeare in *The Taming of the Shrew* when Katherine, submitting her will at last to Petruchio's, says:

> Then, God be blest, it is the blessed sun:—
> But sun it is not, when you say it is not;
> And the moon changes, even as your mind.
> What you will have it named, even that it is;
> And so it shall be still for Katherine.[51]

It is not a lack of external reference that characterizes flattery, just as there is no lack of a listener for sincere speech; rather, what occurs in flattery is that power in controlling the discourse—and thus the relationship between the people involved and between them and the world—is in the hands of the listener. In sincerity, on the other hand, the external reference functions as a standard of discourse, relieving both parties of possible control and thus depoliticizing their relationship to one another. Letter vIII, then, is Usbek's attempt to establish the correct reference to correspond to the referent: the real motive for his voyage.[52]

The link between epistemology and politics is established here in terms of the semiotic and rhetorical functions of discourse. Discourse can now be defined relative to the four terms: speaker, listener, referent, reference. To generate an epistemological analysis one interrogates a particular discourse in terms of the semiotic function, the relationship

---

[51]William Shakespeare, *The Taming of the Shrew*, iv.5,18–22.

[52]One might argue that the discussion concerns the determination not of a reference but of a meaning. That is, everyone agrees that Usbek left; in question is the interpretation of his action. If the referent is seen as the act and not the motive, then the question is of meaning rather than of simple reference. Even so, the distinction between despotic and sincere discourse remains the listener's (despot's) control of the interpretation versus its objective determination by the external reference. In fact, reference and meaning are identical in both types of discourse because, whether sincere or despotic, it is controlled, determined: either the meaning is what the despot says it is, in the latter case, or it is the "true" meaning in the former. There is no place for ambiguity (disjunction between reference and meaning) in either case.

The distinction between reference and meaning is by no means necessary to linguistic theory, or even generally accepted by its practitioners. For example, the German word *Bedeutung*, whose standard English translation is "meaning," is always given as "reference" or "nominatum" in translations of Gottlob Frege's seminal article, "Über Sinn und Bedeutung," *Zeitschrift für Philosophie und philosophische Kritik* 100 (1892): 25–50. I recognize the distinction simply to show that even if it is admitted, Usbek's project remains the same.

between the referent and its reference. One can then analyze the same discourse politically by formulating the rhetorical question of the relationship established between speaker and listener. In both cases all four terms come into play, and in both cases as well, the ultimate question is of control or determination.

Discourse thus serves as a model of both political and epistemological relations that can be analyzed by means of rhetorical and semiotic functions. Such analyses reveal the locus of control and enable one to arrive at a single definition of the political and epistemological relationships embodied in the discourse. Thus flattery can be called "despotic discourse" because it defines a despotic political relationship when analyzed rhetorically and an equally despotic apprehension of the world when analyzed semiotically, for things are what the despot wills them to be. Sincerity, on the other hand, is epistemologically transparent, representing the world (the reference) truthfully. A rhetorical analysis of sincere discourse shows it to be unable either to define any political relations or to function within the system of despotic relations. Yet sincerity does find an ear in Usbek's scheme of things, and it belongs to those who love him.

When Usbek writes to Rustan, "Come to my defense only with my friends. Leave to my enemies their evil interpretations," he implies the absolute opposition between sincere and despotic discourse and the human relationships in which they function. Although there is no point in telling Usbek's enemies the truth, since truth has no value within the despotic system of the court, there is value in telling it to his friends. Thus Usbek's letter is addressed not simply to Rustan but to "his friend Rustan." It is as a friend that Usbek writes sincerely, and as a friend that he expects Rustan to listen.

Usbek, who is only too happy that his enemies can do no more than talk about him, now that he is gone, then worries that his friends may *cease* to speak of him and thus will forget him. Thus he closes letter VIII to Rustan: "I count on their fidelity as I do on your own." It is in the concept of fidelity that a final link is wrought between the semiotic and rhetorical functions of sincere language and between the two relationships they determine: truth and friendship.

Here is the main definition of *fidélité* from the *Dictionnaire* of 1694: "FIDELITY. Loyalty, faith. Inviolable fidelity. Proven fidelity. To remain faithful to one's prince. To corrupt someone's fidelity. To vow fidelity. A woman must be faithful to her husband."[53] Like *jalousie, fidélité* refers both to a political relationship and to one between husband and wife. Like *insinuer, flatter,* and *feindre,* moreover, *fidélité* traverses the ground

---

[53]*DAF*, 1:485.

between human relationships and language, as the following secondary definition from the *Dictionnaire* shows: "It sign[ifies] also, Truth, Exactitude, Sincerity. This historian writes with great fidelity. This author is translated with fidelity. To make a report with great fidelity."[54] Fidelity to the truth describes a semiotic relationship, while fidelity to a person describes a rhetorical or human relationship.

Usbek's great disillusionment, as he describes it in letter VIII, arose when he discovered that his sincerity made him enemies, that he had "drawn on [himself] the jealousy of ministers without having won the favor of the Prince." Presumably one ought to make friends through acting virtuously and speaking sincerely. Usbek's plan backfired because the system itself was corrupt in which sincerity made enemies and flattery made friends. Within a corrupt system, Usbek's fidelity to the truth did not coincide with fidelity to the prince—or so the prince perceived it, and it was in his perception of things that power lay. In this sense, too, fidelity is like flattery, defined not by the subject (the flatterer, the faithful) but by the object. Unlike flattery, however, fidelity defines not only a relationship between individuals but one of truth between referent and reference, and there lay the problem for Usbek: unless the prince, too, was willing to submit his will to an objective standard, Usbek could not be faithful both to him and to the truth at the same time. By choosing fidelity over flattery, Usbek placed himself in a position of conflicting values that could be resolved only by a change in the political system as a whole, by subordination of the prince's subjective will to an external, objective, standard.

But the court, the political system, is not the only system of human relations in which Usbek lives. If the political system proves to be corrupt, Usbek can still count on the fidelity of his friends. He can do so, it seems, because friendship is not a power relationship, and so the transparent language of truth is made subservient to no rhetorical aim. The connection between sincerity and friendship is not that sincerity makes friends (as Usbek had hoped) but that friendship allows for sincerity— demands it, perhaps; it does not impede it.

From another angle as well the concept of fidelity joins truthfulness and human relations. According to the *Encyclopédie, Fidélité (morale)* is "a virtue that consists in strictly keeping one's word, one's promises, or one's agreements, insofar as they do not demand anything contrary to natural laws . . .; but otherwise nothing can release one from his commitment to another: even less is it permitted, in speaking, promising, or contracting, to equivocate or use other types of obscure language; these

54Ibid.

are nothing but odious artifices."[55] Fidelity here means to keep one's word, and to do so honestly, by speaking plainly. Not only must one hold to one's words, but the words themselves must be free of intentional ambiguity. Thus, beneath the fidelity to the other through fidelity to one's word is a foundation in the unambiguity of the word itself, so that the word is not a barrier between men but a transparent medium that binds them. The *Encyclopédie* article continues:

> [Fidelity] is the source of almost all commerce between reasonable beings: it is a social knot in which resides the sole value of confidence between individuals in society. But if this faith is inviolable between individuals, it is even more so for sovereigns, either amongst themselves, or in relation to their subjects: even were it to be banished from the rest of the world, . . . it would still have to remain forever unshakeable in the mouths of princes.[56]

As opposed to the fear that binds the slave to the master in a despotism, fidelity is the knot that binds reciprocally two reasonable beings, be they partners in a contract, two sovereigns, or—and most important—a king and his subjects. Whereas the despot rules with a changeable will, the monarch must remain faithful to his word in order to remain faithful to his people. Fidelity refers not only to an external standard but also to an internal one: constancy and consistency over time.

Fidelity, by the *Encyclopédie* definition, is a virtue that establishes a social bond. Like despotism, it has its proper mode of discourse: sincere, unambiguous speech that represents transparently its references. It has both an external standard and an internal consistency. A relationship defined by fidelity is thus the opposite of a despotic relationship, which has no external standard, is as changeable as the will of the despot, and engenders masked speech (flattery, feigning, insinuation) that obscures or disfigures the truth in order to conform to the despot's will.

In closing letter VIII with "Perhaps I shall be only too easily forgotten hereafter and my friends . . . ," followed by "I shall always be dear to them. I count on their fidelity as I do on your own," Usbek restates, from the opposite point of view, his closing in letter I: "Farewell, my dear Rustan. Rest assured that in whatever part of the world I may be, you

---

[55]*Encyclopédie*, 6:686. *Fidélité* as keeping one's word appears in letter XXVIII. In a letter to Rica, an actress writes of the abbé who has ravished her: "With such delicacy of feeling, you can be sure that the young abbé would never have succeeded if he had not promised to marry me. . . . Now, however, since his faithlessness [*infidélité*] has dishonored me . . . "

[56]*Encycylopédie*, 6:686. For the centrality of *confiance* to the epistolary form see Altman, *Epistolarity*, pp. 47–86.

have a faithful friend." Since fidelity is a reciprocal relationship, Usbek's avowal of it to Rustan in letter ı is easily reversed in letter vııı as the hope that Rustan will retain it toward him. Beyond this reversibility, which implies a certain equality, Usbek's closing reference to fidelity reveals his idea that it is threatened by a distance between the two parties: it is Usbek's absence that requires the affirmation of fidelity. Usbek's uncertainty in letter vııı, after he had assured Rustan of his own fidelity just a short time before, raises the question of whether such a relationship can be sustained over distance and over time. If Usbek's absence from Persia frees him from the bonds of the despotic relationship of which he was a victim, does it not also free him from the friendship that binds him to Rustan and others? Can their fidelity to him and his to them be sustained? Usbek begins to falter in letter vııı, in contrast to his unquestioning assurance in letter I. In fact, after letter vııı, Usbek writes only two more letters to Rustan: the first before he has reached Europe (letter xıx from Smyrna), and the second, four years later (letter xcı). Clearly the friendship does not stand the test of time and distance. Usbek forgets his friend as he was afraid he himself would be forgotten, thus breaking the bond of fidelity.[57]

Usbek does not forget all his friends. As his letters to friends and family in Persia decrease, those to Ibben (in Smyrna), Rhédi (in Venice), and Rica (in Paris) increase. Fidelity is thus not measured simply as a function of time and distance (although Persia is the farthest away). Rather, Usbek's infidelity can be attributed to the undermining of his values, which makes it increasingly difficult for him to communicate with the world supported by them. The words Usbek uses remain the same, but the ideas that they represent change, such that simple fidelity to the word is no longer adequate as fidelity in either semiotic or human relations (keeping one's word; remembering through speaking).

Usbek's infidelity to Rustan (and the communication problem that underlies it) results from the destabilization of Usbek's moral vocabulary. In contrast to the assurance with which Usbek uses moral terms in his first letters, and especially in the apologue of the Troglodytes (letters

[57]I hesitate to place too much weight on an absence of letters, as I believe others have done (see, e.g., Nivea Melani, "La Structure des *Lettres persanes,*" *Annali dell'Istituto Universario Orientale, Sezione Romanza* [Naples] 10 [January 1968]: 66), since Montesquieu does state that he is presenting here only some of the Persian letters in his possession (see his introduction to *Lettres persanes*, p. 7). Presumably, the correspondence between Usbek and Rustan could have continued but could simply not have been interesting to the compiler. There is, however, good reason to think that it did not, as I hope the discussion below will demonstrate.

xi-xiv), are the first stirrings of moral and epistemological uncertainty in letters xvi and xvii, addressed to the mullah.

"Yesterday we argued the question whether men were happy through the pleasures and satisfactions of the senses or through the practice of virtue," writes Mirza to his friend Usbek in letter x. "I have often heard you say," he continues, "that men were born to be virtuous and that justice is a quality as proper to man as existence. Explain to me, I beg of you, what you mean." Usbek's response reveals the self-assurance of a sage within his society, a man accustomed to being consulted and supply-ing answers. After a display of false modesty, Usbek writes: "To carry out what you have required of me, I did not think it proper to use much abstract reasoning. There are certain truths that it is not enough to impress by rational conviction, that must be felt. Such are the verities of ethics. Perhaps this bit of history will touch you more than some subtle philosophy" (letter xi).

Usbek solves the problem presented him without hesitation, consider-ing only the best means to convey a truth he already knows. As far as Usbek is concerned, moral truths are to be felt rather than analyzed. His attitude toward Mirza is that of a wise man toward a disciple or of a parent toward a child: the attitude of one who knows and seeks only to impress that knowledge upon the other. It is the attitude of Mentor. Not surprisingly, the Bétique of *Télémaque* is generally acknowledged to have inspired the Troglodyte myth.[58]

Considering Usbek's tone, his use of the Fénelonian model, and his assumption that Mirza in asking his opinion is renouncing his own reason (lett. xi), Usbek's uncritical use of moral terms should not be surprising. Thus letter xiii ends: "Such was the battle of Injustice and Virtue. Those cowardly peoples who sought only booty were not ashamed to flee; they yielded to the virtue of the Troglodytes, without even being touched." Letter xiv, and the tale as a whole, concludes on an equally clear note: "Why would you have me afflict them and oblige me to tell them that I have left you here under any yoke other than that of Virtue?"

The Troglodyte series is followed almost immediately by Usbek's first letter to the mullah. (Although the letter to the mullah is written the day after the last of the Troglodyte series, a letter between two eunuchs is placed so as to divide them.) Whereas the Troglodyte letters were insti-gated by Mirza's consulting Usbek's wisdom, the second correspondence

[58]Alessandro Crisafulli, "Montesquieu's Story of the Troglodytes: Its Background, Meaning, and Significance," *PMLA* 58 (June 1943): 376.

is motivated by Usbek's need to know; they mark his own consultation of a higher authority. "Thou readest the Koran upon the breast of our divine Prophet," he writes, "and when thou fallest upon some obscure passage, at his behest an angel unfurls speedy wings and descends from the throne to disclose to thee its secret" (letter xvi). The questioning moves in succession from Mirza to Usbek, from Usbek to the mullah, from the mullah to the prophet through the Koran: if an idea is not clear, one need only move up through the hierarchy of epistemological authority until the one truth is revealed.

In his first letter to the mullah Usbek presents the same problem that underlies (and seeks to undermine) the story just related to Mirza as moral truth. "[Distinguish for me those who are evil], as at break of day, the white thread is distinguished from the black," writes Usbek to the mullah (letter xvi). Usbek cries out for help in making moral distinctions because he now finds himself among "a profane people". In this different social system, the *données* of his own are no longer acceptable simply as such. Usbek still wants to believe in the truths upon which he has based his life, his immediate, felt knowledge of virtue and vice upon which he acted in the royal court. But to believe in them is to believe in their universality, their "givenness," their transcendence of all particular cases, individuals, societies. It is this universality that is called into question with Usbek's departure from Persia.

Already at the court of Ispahan, Usbek had discovered that his concept of fidelity, for example, was not the same as that of his king, for his sincerity there did not meet with favor. He learned that it was necessary to abandon "a hitherto unknown language" if he wanted to communicate. After he has left Persia, Usbek begins an inquiry into the basis of moral decision making. The problem is no longer simply one of who is right—he or the king—but of determining a valid epistemological basis for either (or any) definition of the given moral term. In his second letter to the mullah, written only nine days after the first, Usbek asks him not to distinguish between good and evil but rather to explain how such decisions can be made. "Whence does it come that our lawgiver deprives us of the flesh of the pig and of all the other meats he calls untouchable?" asks Usbek. "Whence does it come that he forbids us to touch a dead body, and that to purify our souls, he commands us to wash our bodies tirelessly?" Such laws, it seems to Usbek, are based on the assumption that impurity exists objectively rather than simply in the mind of the perceiver. "It seems to me," Usbek continues, "that objects in themselves are neither pure nor impure. I cannot think of any quality inherent to the subject which could make them such" (letter xvii). If things are neither pure nor impure in themselves, then one is forced to conclude that the basis of such judgments is in the subject rather than the object. Usbek seeks a standard upon which these seemingly arbitrary "divine" laws are based.

> Our senses, dear mullah, should therefore be our sole judges of the purity or impurity of things. But since objects do not affect men in the same way, since what gives an agreeable sensation to some, produces a disagreeable one with others, it follows that the data of the senses cannot serve here as rule unless one states that each man, according to his fancy, can decide this point for himself and distinguish for his own purposes the pure things from those that are not. (Letter xvii)

The senses, which allow one to distinguish black from white, are not dependable for distinctions between pure and impure. But if there is no external standard for such concepts as impurity, does this not reverse "the distinctions established by our divine Prophet as well as the fundamental points of the law written by the hand of angels?" (letter xvii). Usbek, who only nine days earlier had spoken glibly of virtue and vice as immutable categories, now seeks a standard upon which such judgments are made. The three levels of authority displayed in the two consecutive sets of letters are reproduced in three levels of distinctions: from black and white to pure and impure, and from pure and impure to virtue and vice; or from sensory distinctions to abstract concepts to moral judgments. Before the mullah has even received Usbek's plea to distinguish for him "[those who are evil], as at break of day, the white thread is distinguished from the black," Usbek has exposed the weak link in distinctions between pure and impure that makes the mullah's task impossible.

If Usbek has found a logical flaw in religious law, that is of no consequence to its representative. Rather, the mullah chastizes Usbek for thinking to substitute his own reasoning for the "pure source of all intelligence": the learned commentaries known as the *Traditions*. Just as Usbek undermined his own rhetorical proof (the Troglodyte fable) with a logical inquiry, the mullah would undermine the conclusions of human reason with divine revelation.[59] "Your empty philosophy is the lightning flash that announces storm and obscurity," writes the mullah, and in its place he offers the one truth of divine history. "You do not know the

---

[59]I use here Aristotle's distinction between a rhetorical and a dialectical proof, exposed principally in bk. 2, chaps. 1–2, of the *Rhetoric*. The Troglodyte story, in Aristotle's terms, would be an exemplary proof of the fable type, as defined in bk. 2, chap. 20.

history of eternity. You have not read at all in the books written in heaven" (letter xviii). The one truth, the universal standard for making moral distinctions, exists, says the mullah, but men are incapable of knowing it. The only true knowledge is that revealed to man by God, and that is only a small part of the "divine library."[60]

In seeking the reasoning that underlies the old values, Usbek comes up against a brick wall. No reasoning, no logic lies behind them, but simply their givenness: things are either pure or impure because God made them so. The mullah's reply leaves Usbek with a choice between two radically opposed modes of comprehending the world: human reason and divine revelation. In choosing reason over revelation as he does, Usbek shows his lack of faith, of fidelity toward the word. Already he had chosen to leave, physically, the despotic state of Persia rather than to live by its rules; now he goes one step further, refusing the despotic rule of divine revelation.[61] In rejecting the authority of the word as revealed, Usbek has rejected the despotic principle that underlies his religion and the society whose laws it defines. And in so doing he has rejected once and for all the Fénelonian model of wisdom and counsel, of discovery and discourse.

"He that applies the words of any language to ideas different from those to which the common use of that country applies them, however his own understanding may be filled with truth and light, will not by

---

[60]In his unpublished *Pensées* Montesquieu gives his own historical explanation of the origin of notions of purity and impurity (no. 2147, *Oeuvres complètes*, p. 1076). This historical explanation is purely secular, in contrast to the mullah's. Montesquieu argues with Usbek that such notions derive from a natural aversion to that which is disagreeable to the senses, but he then adds a historical confusion beween body and soul to transform physical soiling into religious impurity. Clearly, Montesquieu did not find such a historical explanation to be appropriate in the discussion of purity and impurity in the *Lettres persanes*, where the only two alternatives presented are reason and dogmatism. This type of explanation rejected by Montesquieu becomes the basis of Rousseau's social critique in the *Second Discours*.

[61]"The Mohammedan religion," writes Grosrichard, "is . . . reduced to an entirely external cult, where the sign [*signifiant*] makes the law. To become a Moslem requires only that one pronounce or write a single stereotyped formula once—whether or not one understands its meaning." This is why, he continues, "the Mohammedan religion agrees so well with a despotic regime. It actually teaches only one thing: to obey to the letter, without discussion or comprehension" *Structure du sérail*, pp. 119–20. Usbek, too, remarks in this context: "In our Koran, on the contrary, we often find the language of God and the ideas of man, as if by some admirable whimsey, God had dictated the words and man had furnished the ideas" (letter xcvii). (The context of Grosrichard's statement is the conception of oriental despotism in eighteenth-century France rather than his own judgment of the Moslem religion.)

such words be able to convey much of it to others, without defining his
terms."[62] So warns John Locke, and in so doing describes (or perhaps
prescribes) Usbek's task. Usbek, abandoning his old friends in Persia by
not remaining faithful to their words, embarks on a project of definition
and redefinition, a task of recomposing the moral terms in common use
in his own country. But Usbek is not alone in this endeavor; Rica, his
young friend and traveling companion, is also constantly questioning the
relationship between names and the ideas they stand for. And beyond
both Usbek and Rica is Montesquieu himself, who, in displaying the
actions, passions, observations, and opinions of these Persians, presents
still more meanings through usage. The result is the decomposition of
the moral terms that seem to bind men and women together in society.

Significantly, *fidélité* itself is a key term whose decomposition is traced
in the course of the *Lettres persanes*. While Usbek hangs on to his dreams
of sincerity and transparency in human and semiotic relations in letter
VIII, the reader is already beginning to learn of the impossibility of that
ideal through the comparative critical method that exposes the polysemy
of *fidélité*.

[62]John Locke, *An Essay Concerning Human Understanding* (Philadelphia, 1856), p. 326.
A discussion of the relationship between Lockean epistemology and Montesquieu's
would go well beyond the scope of this study of the *Lettres persanes*. I introduce Locke
here not to argue that Montesquieu's epistemology is sensationalist but rather to emphasize that the problems of knowledge, judgment, and language that concern both Usbek
and his creator were central issues at that time. The counterpart of Locke's *Essay* in
France was the *Logique de Port-Royal*, which first appeared in 1662 and had gone
through six editions and sixteen printings by the time of the *Lettres persanes*. The
Logique's twentieth-century translators write of its main author, Antoine Arnauld, that
"he was philosophically modern in his distinction between knowledge of matters of fact
and other realms of knowledge on the grounds of acceptability of one kind of knowledge
as opposed to another, on the precise relation between our ideas and the existence of
objects of those ideas, and on the possibility that disagreement in religious and political
matters can rest on disagreements or confusions in epistemological matters": James
Dickoff and Patricia James, Introduction to *The Art of Thinking: Port-Royal Logic*, by
Antoine Arnauld (Indianapolis, 1964), p. xxxvi. The same concerns are evidenced by
Locke in his *Essay*, and the two works together can be said to have launched the
definitional project of the eighteenth century. That project is embodied here in the
Lettres persanes and culminates in the great *Encyclopédie* of Diderot and d'Alembert. And
so, instead of trying to answer the question of whether Montesquieu is a Cartesian
rationalist or a Lockean empiricist, I would simply emphasize the common epistemological concerns that underlie the work of both camps and that together engage Montesquieu
and other eighteenth-century men of letters in a search for acceptable rules of knowing
and judging and a project of defining their social, political, and moral vocabulary.

CHAPTER TWO

The System of Fidelities

The ideal of fidelity that Usbek invokes in letters I and VIII is shattered in the course of the *Lettres persanes*. If Usbek's absence from Persia casts doubt upon the fidelity of, and his fidelity to, his friends, his presence in France places the very notion of fidelity in question. It is not Usbek, however, who confronts this greater problem, but the reader. For although Usbek takes a critical view of what he sees and is able to achieve a degree of objectivity, only the reader is truly outside both Usbek's Persia and his France. Only the reader, moreover, is able to profit from the observations and reflections of Rica and the other correspondents, and only the reader, finally, is able to make connections among the letters and the often conflicting ideas they express.

Fidelity, more than just a moral term or virtue, is a relational term that can describe a relationship between human beings or between a referent and a reference. So much is apparent after a reading of letter VIII. What was only hinted at there and emerges clearly in the course of the *Lettres persanes* is that there is no single, true meaning of the word *fidélité* as Usbek's notion of sincere discourse implied. The combined comparative critical efforts of Usbek, Rica, and (implicitly) Montesquieu and his reader expose fidelity from all sides—that is, in its many different contexts—and in so doing leave in fragments the ideal definition implied in Usbek's use of the term in letter VIII. The reader is led to ask how Usbek *can* count on the fidelity not only of his friends but of his wives and his eunuchs, when the meaning of the word changes each time it is invoked. How, too, can Usbek count on their fidelity when neither his "church" nor his state, neither his god nor his king, can count on his fidelity? Underlying the uncertainty in all these human relationships is the uncertainty of the word itself as a sign, the ambiguity of the verbal referent.

In the *Lettres persanes* conflicting fidelities are shown to be the defining feature of absolutist society. The common ground between the despotism of Persia and the absolutism of France is found here in the notion of fidelity as the social bond that holds society together. From the domestic sphere to the public arena, fidelity is shown to define all social relationships. The critique of society in the *Lettres persanes* thus turns upon this one word. The destabilization of the word *fidélité* exposes the inherent instability in absolutist society and absolutist thinking.

Usbek himself, although limited in his vision and thus unable to see that criticism of any despotic relationship must extend to the system as a whole, initiates the search for a new term that might replace fidelity as the means of unifying a society: a term that, unlike fidelity, is universal, absolute, and undogmatic. The breakdown of fidelity as the defining term of human relationships leads to the introduction, in theory at least, of the new term, justice, to take its place. This chapter thus consists of an investigation of fidelity as it breaks down, first in the private and then the public sphere, through the critical confrontation of East and West. Chapter 3 will take up the next stage of the investigation, with a consideration of the notion of justice and its adequacy as a solution to the problem of conflicting fidelities.

"Farewell, my dear Rustan," writes Usbek in closing his first letter. "Rest assured that in whatever part of the world I may be, you have a faithful friend." In what does this fidelity among friends consist? From what Usbek writes, a faithful friend is one who continues to think and talk about the other even in his absence. Two subsequent references to fidelity between friends establish this meaning, only suggested in letter I by the juxtaposition of "faithful friend" and "in whatever part of the world." There is, first, the now familiar closing of letter VIII: "At the present moment there is talk of me. Perhaps I shall be only too easily forgotten hereafter and my friends . . . No, Rustan, I shall not give myself over to such a sad thought. I shall always be dear to them. I count on their fidelity as I do on your own." To be faithful to an absent friend is to cherish him verbally, to speak of him. It is also to speak to him, though he is absent, through the one means possible: the letter. Letter xxv, from Usbek to Ibben, brings together these two marks of a faithful friend. The first two paragraphs deal with letter writing: the letter Usbek has received from Ibben's nephew, Rhédi, and that which Rica has written to Ibben. The bonds of friendship defined here do not lie between the writer and reader of the present letter (Usbek and Ibben), but touch them through their younger counterparts. These two parallel friendships are bridged in the conversations between Rica and Usbek concerning Ibben. "You are the subject of our most touching conversations," Usbek reports; we cannot say enough about the welcome you gave us at Smyrna and the helpfulness still rendered to us each day by your friendship." It is thus after having described both activities that Usbek concludes: "May you always, my generous Ibben, find friends everywhere as grateful and faithful as ourselves!" And to demonstrate the double sense of his fidelity, Usbek exclaims of his friend in writing to him: "May I see you again soon and rediscover those happy days passed so sweetly between two friends!" (letter xxv). When friends are apart, the letter becomes both the symbol of fidelity and the only means of displaying it: it is both the mark and the means of fidelity between friends.[1]

The Private Sphere: Eunuchs and Wives

The epistolarity of Usbek's conception of friendship provides a ground for the *Lettres persanes* as an epistolary text. Usbek must write letters if he is to maintain his friendships. And although over time he loses the ability to communicate with those who remain in Persia, he continues to write letters to Ibben and Rhédi, and when he is away from Paris, begins a correspondence with Rica. There is, however, a second ground for the *Lettres* as an epistolary text: Usbek's need to administer from afar the private despotism he heads: his harem. Absence, which is at the heart of the harem itself in the relationship between master and eunuch and between eunuch and wives, makes Usbek's correspondence with his eunuchs just as necessary as that with his friends. The contrast between these two sets of letters spurs the reader to his first critical comparison on the basis of a textual concordance.[2]

---

[1]Ronald Rosbottom finds similarly in Rousseau's epistolary novel that "as *La Nouvelle Héloïse* progresses, the letters exchanged between St. Preux and Julie, and eventually between St. Preux and Claire, become symbols of the bonds which unite them as much as messages of love and fidelity" ("Motifs in Epistolary Fiction: Analysis of a Narrative Sub-Genre," *L'Esprit Créateur* 17 [Winter 1977]: 290). In one instance in the *Lettres persanes*, furthermore, letters are shown to be the means of creating a friendship, not just of maintaining one. In letter LXVII, Ibben writes to Usbek of his new friend, the Gheber: "I have spoken a thousand times to him of you. I show him all your letters, and I note that this gives him pleasure. I can see already that you have a friend still unknown to you." Usbek also suggests in letter XXXIV that separation between friends is the rule rather than the exception in Persia, where each household is a society unto itself. In these circumstances letter writing would be a major condition of friendship.

[2]Ouellet and Vachon, *"Lettres persanes" de Montesquieu*, p. 79.

"Farewell, my dear Rustan. Rest assured that in whatever part of the world I may be, you have a faithful friend," wrote Usbek in closing letter 1, and directly follows the opening of his letter 11 to the First Black Eunuch: "You are the faithful guardian of the most beautiful women in Persia." Written by Usbek three days apart, these two letters mark a contrast that strikes only the reader, one determined by their compiler who shows that Usbek uses the same term to describe himself in relation to Rustan and the eunuch in relation to himself. But the relationships are themselves different from each other, and so too are the fidelities that define them.

The letters that pass between Usbek and his eunuchs do not in themselves establish fidelity. The relationship between them is not friendship, but that of master and slave. Further, it is a peculiar type of master-slave relationship because the eunuch, as the representative of the master in dealing with wives and other slaves, is himself a surrogate master. In explaining to the First Black Eunuch his relationship to the master's wives, Usbek defines the fidelity he expects of him: "You command and you obey them; you carry out blindly all their desires, and in the same way, you make them carry out the laws of the harem. . . . You serve them like a slave of their slaves. But, by an exchange of authority, you command as master like myself" (letter 11). The fidelity of the eunuch consists solely in executing the will of his master; in the master's absence, it consists in being the master, in acting as if he were the master. But the master is pure subjectivity, pure will, so to act as the master is to lose one's identity in that of the other. The eunuch's role is further complicated in that the master wills that the wills of the wives also be obeyed— so long as they do not contradict his own: the eunuch plays the man, travestied as the woman. But no matter whose will he is executing (and to be faithful, he must always conform to that of the master), the eunuch himself has no will, no identity of his own: even in commanding he is pure obedience. "Thus the eunuch counts only in what he lacks," writes Alain Grosrichard. "He makes absence positive."[3]

Once again, the absence that makes the *Lettres persanes* necessary as letters is at the heart of the definition of fidelity. But here it is not the letters that serve as intermediary, as the means of remaining faithful; rather, it is the eunuch himself who is intermediary between husband and wives. The fidelity of the eunuch to his master is as transparent as that of the word to the idea in Usbek's naive conception of language.[4] In the absence of the master, there is the eunuch. Like the letter between

[3]Grosrichard, *Structure du sérail*, p. 187.

[4]"The will of the prince," writes Montesquieu of the despot in *L'Esprit des lois*, "once it is known, must have its effect as infallibly as one billiard ball hit against another must have its effect": *Oeuvres complètes*, p. 539.

friends, the eunuch is both the mark and the means of fidelity. He is the mark of fidelity in that this is his one and only virtue, as one of Usbek's French acquaintances points out (letter xxxiv). He is the means of fidelity in that his sole duty lies in retaining the fidelity of the wives toward their husband. "You are the scourge of evil," Usbek writes to the First Black Eunuch, "and the pillar of fidelity." This second reference to fidelity in letter ii must be understood to refer both to the eunuch's fidelity to the master—the embodiment of fidelity—and to that of the wives—the support of fidelity. The eunuch is the very constitution of fidelity, its principle.[5]

Friendship was shown above to be a relationship of equality, of reciprocity; the relationship between master and eunuch can be called a tautology, since the faithful eunuch is one who has negated himself entirely to become his master. If the eunuch is nothing, then the master is everything. However, the master is even present only to the extent that the eunuch is faithful to him. Once the eunuch asserts himself by displaying a will of his own the master disappears. Thus, while the equality that characterizes friendship is entirely foreign to the master-eunuch relationship, its reciprocity is not. Although Usbek may remind the eunuch of the "void from which [he] drew [him]" (letter ii), he must himself remember that his own absence, too, is a void, one from which only the eunuch, in his fidelity, can make him emerge. In the end, the master and the eunuch are mutually dependent in their absolute inequality.

The opposition between the fidelity of a eunuch to his master and that of a friend to a friend is revealed to the reader as early as the transition between letters i and ii, even if Usbek never makes the connection. The term *fidélité*, however, is without ambiguity in both relationships. The properties of each relationship have been presented as they are in the text, as internally stable and uniform. Instability here lies between contexts or relationships, not within them. The next step in the destabilization of *fidélité* is shown in its different meanings within a relationship, and that occurs in the consideration of marriage. The means by which this internal duality is exposed is the cross-cultural comparison of Persia and France. Through this comparison not only are conflicting meanings of *fidélité* exposed, but they are linked to the relative importance of the concept for the relationship. That is, the different *meanings* of *fidélité* within marriage are related to the different *significances* it has to it in each society.

Usbek's noncritical use of moral terms is no better displayed than in the Troglodyte fable, where fidelity in marriage is simply one more

---

[5]*Principe* is the term Montesquieu uses later in *L'Esprit des lois* to signify the basis of action ("ce qui le fait agir") specific to each form of government, "the human passions that make it move": *Oeuvres complètes*, p. 536.

manifestation of natural virtue (letter xii). In writing to one of his own wives, however, Usbek presents an entirely different picture of marital fidelity. No longer a natural virtue, the fidelity Usbek expects of his wife is a strict adherence to a set of laws meant to protect her from her own natural desires. "You will perhaps tell me that you have always been faithful. Come now! Could you have been anything else?" Usbek demands of Zachi. "You vaunt much a virtue that is not free, and perhaps your impure desires have a thousand times over effaced the value and worth of the fidelity of which you boast so much" (letter xx). Fidelity, no longer associated with the natural workings of the heart, no longer springing from within, is simply an external form, an obedience to laws that loses all moral value. The purpose of the laws of the harem is to protect the women from themselves; marital (that is, wifely) fidelity consists solely in obedience to these laws.

In the Troglodyte fable, fidelity was one of several natural virtues. In the harem, virtue and fidelity have become divorced, as virtue is unnaturally protected through fidelity to a set of laws. From a relationship of a part to a whole, fidelity is now to virtue as a means to an end. To be faithful can be construed no longer as being virtuous, but simply as being dutiful, obedient.

Fidelity as natural virtue implied the reciprocity and equality of friendship since it was applied to the union of husband and wife, rather than to one partner alone. In the harem, on the other hand, fidelity refers only to the conduct of wives. Although wifely fidelity, unlike that of a eunuch for his master, is fidelity to a standard, a law, it is a double standard because it measures only the conduct of women. The relationship of fidelity between wife and husband in the harem can thus be defined as unequal, nonreciprocal, and legal.

In contrast to Persian women who demonstrate fidelity through obedience to law are the Parisian women. Although totally disobedient to all propriety, all forms, they still remain ultimately virtuous, and thus faithful. "It is not that I believe, Roxane," writes Usbek to his favorite wife,

> that these women . . . carry debauch to the horrible excess—which strikes terror in the heart—of completely violating conjugal fidelity. There are certainly few women so abandoned as to go that far. They all carry graven within their hearts a certain image of virtue, given by birth, weakened by wordly education, but not destroyed by it. They may quite possibly relax the superficial duties that decency demands. But when it comes to taking the last step, nature revolts. [Letter xxvi]

Unlike Zachi, who was judged unfaithful because she broke the rules (letter xx), Parisian women are measured solely on the basis of whether or not they retain their "virtue" in its most limited sense. The narrowing of the concept of virtue to a specific physical condition narrows equally the notion of fidelity. Whereas in the Troglodyte fable fidelity was one virtue among many, it is here reduced to a technicality, while virtue itself is reduced to a commodity. To retain one's virtue is to be faithful; to be faithful is to retain one's virtue. Virtue and fidelity are two words for the same thing. Fidelity, in this sense, no longer describes a relationship between two people but an attribute of the individual. When virtue loses its moral character, fidelity loses its relational one.

The relationship between husbands and wives is discussed again in Rica's letter xxxviii to Ibben, and the meaning of fidelity once again shifts, along with its significance for marriage. Rica, who has neither a harem in Ispahan nor a wife in Paris, provides a disinterested (although not neutral) perspective, admitting freely that "a wiser man than [he] might find it difficult to decide." The question Rica is considering is "to know whether it is better to deprive a woman of her freedom or let her keep it." The question of liberty is closely aligned with that of fidelity, as Usbek pointed out to Zachi in letter xx. In fact, the same terms are used here in the attack on the forced fidelity of Persian women as Usbek used in his letter to Zachi. "You vaunt much a virtue that is not free," wrote Usbek, while Rica argues: "Let [the Asiatics] object in their turn that Europeans could not possibly be happy with women who are not faithful to them, it could be countered that their much-boasted fidelity [*cette fidélité, qu'ils vantent tant*] does not obviate the disgust that always follows on the satisfaction of the passions" (letter xxxviii).

One finds here in the confrontation of Eastern and Western concepts of marriage an attempt to align a group of crucial moral terms, for Rica's question concerns the relative values of several "virtues" in the relationship between husband and wife. Under fire is the assumption that virtue, obedience, and fidelity are the highest values in the relationship; instead, happiness, liberty, and equality are suggested as the true ends of marriage. Fidelity, whether as obedience to law or as the simple retention of virtue, is shown to be itself of only relative value. While letters xx and xxiv presented an internal analysis of fidelity in the context of the relationship between husband and wife, that relationship is itself analyzed in letter xxxviii, with fidelity one of its constitutive terms that must be given its proper weight with respect to the others.[6]

[6]Starobinski points to this type of calculation in a number of letters and contexts: letter xxxiv, in which the cost of the beauty of Persian women is the castration of men; the depopulation series (letters cxiii–cxxii), where Montesquieu poses the problem arithmetically by weighing the various factors; and letters cv and cvi, which weigh the advantages and disadvantages of cultivating the arts and sciences: Preface to *Lettres persanes*, pp. 37–39.

If the Persian marriage places too high a value on fidelity, to the point where all else is sacrificed—happiness, liberty, equality, even pleasure—the French system, too, has its excesses. In contrast to the polygamy of Persia is the licentiousness of Paris. "Here husbands accept their lot with good grace and consider the unfaithfulness of their wives as a stroke of some inevitable fate," writes Rica in a second letter to Ibben regarding marriage. "A husband who insisted upon keeping his wife to himself would be looked upon as a disturber of the public pleasure, as a madman who would profit by the light of the sun to the exclusion of other men" (letter LV). In contrast to its leading role in Persia, fidelity has fallen out of the constitution of French marriage completely. The equality that results from the liberty of French women is at the expense of fidelity, as already signaled by Rica in letter XXXVIII: "To enable a man to complain with justification of his wife's infidelity, there would have to be only three persons in the world. Things will always be evened out when there are four." The concept of monogamous marriage itself collapses when liberty and equality are placed as its highest values to the exclusion of fidelity.

The polygamous marriage of Usbek also collapses, however, as the last group of Persian letters testifies. If monogamy decomposes with the loss of fidelity, polygamy goes in just the opposite direction, sacrificing everything else simply to maintain fidelity. Thus the eunuch Solim writes to Usbek: "I am aroused by vengeful anger against so many betrayals, and if heaven were to choose that you should judge me capable—the better to serve you—of commanding, I promise you that your wives would be faithful even if they were not virtuous" (letter CLI). Fidelity in the harem, already defined as obedience to its laws, has now become divorced from its stated end: protecting the virtue of the women. It has become an end in itself and in so doing has lost all meaning and all value. Remember, it is the eunuch whose sole virtue is fidelity, and thus marriage degenerates into slavery. Virtue itself displays its double sense, with fidelity both opposing it and embodying it uniquely. A resolution to this contradiction is proposed only in Roxane's last letter to Usbek, with which the *Lettres persanes* ends. "You should continue to be thankful to me for the sacrifice I have made to you," she writes, "thankful that I lowered myself to the point of seeming faithful to you, and thankful because I kept in my cowardly heart all that I should have proclaimed to the whole earth. Finally, you should be thankful that I have dared profane the name of virtue by allowing submission to your fancy to be called by that name" (letter CLXI).

According to Roxane, there is virtue on one hand and what is called virtue on the other. Fidelity to Usbek, she argues, is opposed to virtue but identical to that which is called virtue. But Roxane also denies that what is called fidelity in the harem is obedience to a law, while at the same time she upholds the principle of legality as the key to fidelity. Thus, for Roxane, virtue is retained through obedience to law, just as Usbek had initially argued, but the law itself she defines as the law of nature. It is not natural virtue that is protected by fidelity to artificial laws, but fidelity to natural laws that allows for the free play of virtue. "I might have lived in servitude," she writes to Usbek, "but I have always been free. I have rewritten your laws after the laws of nature, and my spirit has ever sustained itself in independence" (letter CLXI). Not only are fidelity and virtue brought together in this way, but liberty joins them as well. Opposed to both the Persian system of forced fidelity and the French one of faithlessness in libertinism is the third possibility found in obedience to the laws of nature.[7]

"My language, no doubt, seems new to you," writes Roxane to Usbek at the end of her final letter. Like Usbek himself Roxane could say, "I spoke there a hitherto unknown language; I astonished at once both the worshippers and their idol" (letter VIII). She too has disrupted a despotic social system by speaking the language of virtue; like Usbek as well, she assumes an external standard, an objective basis for that language. Whereas Usbek founded his virtuous discourse on a naive, direct knowledge of moral values, Roxane bases hers on a legal conception of nature. In so doing she has done what Usbek asked of the mullah in letter XVI: she has distinguished virtue "as at break of day, the white thread is distinguished from the black." The text thus concludes with this simple solution of its fundamental epistemological problem.

But not really. The *Lettres persanes* ends, in fact, with Roxane's suicide. It is a narrative ending, the representation of an action, and as such functions also as an instantiation of the active and social problematic of the text. Roxane has redefined fidelity as obedience to the laws of nature, but in doing so she is able to be faithful on a human level only to herself. If Roxane has managed to establish a new moral certainty to replace that cast in doubt by Usbek's travels abroad, she has still not succeeded in changing the social order. Her suicide is simply a more desperate, more tragic repetition of Usbek's flight from Persia. Bound by the walls of the harem, weaker still toward Usbek's government than he toward that of the court, Roxane can free herself physically only in suicide. Roxane's solution, like Usbek's before her, is a purely individual one, while the

[7]"The less consent there is, the less freedom of choice in a contract, the more difficult it is to fulfill the conditions, and the less one is guilty of failing to do so in the eyes of reason": *Encyclopédie*, 8:701. From this perspective it is only in liberty that fidelity is possible.

problem, as formulated, is inherently social and political.[8] For the actions of both Usbek and Roxane demonstrate that to live in a society means to live according to its rules. If one is to communicate, one must speak in a language that can be understood; if one is to live virtuously, one must be faithful to a common standard. Just as the function of language is not only to represent (semiotic) but also to communicate, to create a community (rhetorical), so too must virtue be defined as both fidelity to law and as participation in a community. Ultimately, if one is to live in society, one must live according to its rules because society—any society—is a participatory structure. To live virtuously one must act virtuously, by participating in a society that allows for such action. It is not enough to determine a standard for virtue as Roxane has done; rather, if one is to live and die virtuously, that standard must be shared by the community in which one lives.

To summarize, fidelity between friends and between master and eunuch have been seen to be in opposition to one another; the first is impossible in a despotic system, and the second the embodiment of that system. Whereas friendship requires a reciprocal and equal fidelity between the two friends, the master-eunuch relationship is reciprocal only in absolute inequality. In this opposition, the meaning of fidelity is shown to change depending upon the relationship in which it operates.

The relationship between husband and wife, some form of which exists both in the despotic society of Persia and in France, provides an example of a third type of relationship in which fidelity plays a defining role. The opposing despotic and nondespotic definitions of fidelity are here shown to be internal to the relationship itself. The opposition between friendship and slavery is transformed into a parallel opposition between Persian and Parisian conceptions of marriage, neither of which fulfills the transparent ideal of friendship that is reintroduced in the mythic Troglodyte marriage.

The question of the meaning of fidelity, when placed within the context of marriage, is transformed into a question of its significance for this relationship relative to other values. The endpoint of this devolution is the disintegration of both the French and Persian forms of marriage: the first suffers from an excessive reduction of the conception and role (meaning and significance) of fidelity; the second from a false definition of fidelity and the placing of excessive significance on it.

Finally, Roxane's escape from her impossible marriage through suicide demonstrates dramatically the need for a rhetorical as well as a

---

[8]For a parallel reading of the ending of Diderot's *La Religieuse*, see Dena Goodman, "Story-Telling in the Republic of Letters: The Rhetorical Context of Diderot's *La Religieuse*," *Nouvelles de la République des Lettres*, no. 1 (1986), p. 70.

semiotic solution to a problem that is both epistemological and political. The devolution of the term *fidélité* through the three private contexts of the *Lettres persanes*—friendship, slavery, and marriage—demonstrates both that the meaning and significance of the term are unstable and that this instability cannot be eliminated through purely individual means. The instability of fidelity, both within and across relationships, reveals the instability of the relationships themselves as well as of the social and political whole in which they coexist.

The Public Arena: Religion and Politics

"I can see Mohammedanism everywhere," writes Usbek to his cousin the dervish, "although I cannot find Mohammed here at all" (letter xxxv). As opposed to the eunuch who had been described in the preceding letter as "a man who is to be scorned for his very loyalty [*fidélité*] (his sole virtue)," the only virtue the Christian seems to lack is a nominal fidelity to Mohammed. The essence of belief is the same in both religions, Usbek argues; only the name one gives it determines whether one is of the faithful. And since fidelity is defined in relation to the name rather than the essence, the term *fidelity* itself is simply relative to the name chosen by the speaker. "Among Christians," begins the *Encyclopédie* definition of *fidèle*, "it signifies in general him who has faith in Jesus Christ, as opposed to those who profess false religions, like idolaters."[9] Among Moslems, the implication goes, the meaning of *fidèle* would be different. The reference to "false religions" cannot be taken as anything more than relative and conventional either: for wherein lies the objectivity by which the true and the false can be distinguished in this definition of *fidèle*?

The discussion of religious fidelity is cast in public terms in confronting the problem of competing conventional standards to which one may profess faith. The multiple senses in which fidelity can be taken rest here neither upon the kind of relationship in which it figures (as in friendship and masters and eunuchs) nor upon its place relative to other values in a single relationship (as in marriage) but upon the ability to determine a nonarbitrary object of fidelity that can be universally shared. Truth, as universal and universally knowable, is shown to be the opposite of the dogma that gives the name of a religion an identifiable content. Although all religions are essentially the same according to Usbek, they are distinguishable by their dogmas and by their names.

[9] *Encyclopédie*, 6:685.

Usbek and Rica, in casting the problem of religious fidelity in the language of religious toleration, bring together its semiotic and rhetorical dimensions. That is, the reference for the religious referent is shown to be conventional rather than universal. As in language itself, the independence of the two axes, vertical (semiotic) and horizontal (rhetorical), is shown to be an illusion, since the referent connects to the reference only to the extent that speaker and hearer agree on that connection: meaning and communication are mutually dependent in a system, either linguistic or religious, in which the reference or standard is particular and thus conventional rather than universal. The simple distinction that Usbek had maintained since letter VIII between sincere, arhetorical language and the purely (and thus falsely) rhetorical language of despotism and flattery assumed both the independence of these two axes and the existence of a nonconventional reference, or standard. As this simple and naive opposition collapses in the discussion of religious fidelity, the legality of fidelity, its dependence upon an external standard, becomes central. The investigation into fidelity becomes an inquiry into positive law. To arrive at that point, however, we return once again to the level of language.

The arbitrariness of naming undermines the meaning and value of fidelity and is displayed throughout the *Lettres persanes* each time the naming of something is emphasized in referring to it. Usbek, for example, writes: "Doctors and some of these dervishes called *confessors* are always either too well-regarded or too ill-regarded here," while Rica notes: "I have heard people talk about a kind of tribunal called the *French Academy*" (letters LVII and LXXIII). But it is in the discussion of heresy that the arbitrariness of names merges with that of values, and religious fidelity loses all meaning.

"Those who propose some new proposition are called at first *heretics*," explains Rica to Ibben in letter XXIX. "Each heresy has its own name, and this name becomes for those who are involved, something like a rallying cry. But no one has to be a heretic. One needs only to split the difference in half and give some distinction to those who make accusations of heresy, and whatever the distinction—logical or not—it makes a man white as snow, and he may have himself called *orthodox*." A heresy being, according to the *Dictionnaire* of 1694, an "error condemned by the Church in matters of Religion,"[10] the notion of judgment is bound up with naming in the term itself. Thus the metaphor of black and white in this context carries with it the implicit values of bad and good, for "[to make] a man white as snow" is to absolve him of guilt, to reverse one's

[10]*DAF*, 1:560.

judgment of him. A heretic, unlike snow, is what he is not inherently, but according to a conventional definition. If he is able to redefine the standard by which he is judged, he can then change the judgment.

The model of distinguishing between black and white is invoked throughout the *Lettres persanes*, beginning with Usbek's first letter to the mullah (letter xvi). The same distinction is written into the very structure of the harem, where white and black define two different orders of eunuchs, each with its own privileges and responsibilities, as Usbek reminds Zachi in letter xx. This same distinction of orders appears in a letter written by a Frenchman and enclosed in Rica's letter LXXVIII to ***: "Those [Spaniards] in the Indies are no less flattered when they consider that they possess the sublime merit of being, as they put it, *men of white flesh.*" All these treatments of the distinction between black and white speak to the same question: Is there meaning in difference?

Although the words *black* and *white* are conventional, the ideas to which they refer have a basis in the sensory perception of objective reality, and thus the terms themselves are not unstable. Although one may question the significance of a true black-and-white distinction, the distinction itself still holds. Thus Locke condemns those philosophers who "had learning and subtilty [sic] enough to prove that snow was black; *i.e.*, to prove that white was black." Locke sees such philosophical activity as dangerous, for it destroys "the instruments and means of discourse, conversation, instruction, and society."[11]

In the *Lettres persanes*, black-and-white distinctions can be made only if they are objectively based: only because snow *is* white can calling it black be dangerous. Usbek's request in letter xvi that the mullah distinguish for him good from evil as one distinguishes white from black can be filled only if good and evil exist objectively in the world. Rica's letter LIX to Usbek displays the kind of comparative reasoning generated by their trip to the West, which limits the range of black-and-white distinctions. "It seems to me," he writes, "that we never judge of matters except by a secret reflex we make upon ourselves. I am not surprised that Negroes should paint the Devil in blinding white, and their own gods black as coal." Arbitrariness is ascribed not only to giving significance to inherently neutral physical distinctions but also to the very process of naming, once it is removed from the world of objects. The naming of heresies and heretics provides a perfect example of the limitation of black-and-white distinctions. The Church becomes absurd when it attempts to base such distinctions simply upon its own conventions.

Heresy as false discourse would seem to be the opposite of sincerity, or

[11]Locke, *Essay*, p. 320.

fidelity to the truth. Usbek's notion of sincerity, however, was unmediated, transparent, while heresy is not. The opposite of heresy is dogma, for both require the mediation of the Church to determine them. The article "Fidèle" in the *Encyclopédie* shows how faith in a mediated truth (dogma) of the Church replaces the unmediated faith of primitive Christianity: "Jesus Christ himself determined the principal characteristic of the *faithful*. He made it consist in the personal conviction of his power and divinity, trusting in the invariable faith in his word and in his mission."[12] This primitive fidelity, which describes the two fundamental axes of the term—fidelity to the other through fidelity to the word—is replaced by a mediated fidelity as a result of heresies. That is, when this direct knowledge of Christ is undermined through divisive interpretation and criticism, dogma is instituted to determine once again a single standard of fidelity. "It is therefore not enough to have this essential confidence in the power and the mediation of the Savior; the true *fidèle* must add to this primary and primitive faith what one might call faith in dogmas; that is, the adherence pure and simple to the decisions of the Catholic Church."[13] Dogma, determined by the Church, replaces the direct knowledge of the truth (or Christ) as the standard and reference of fidelity in religion.

The process described in the *Encyclopédie*—immediate knowledge of the reference, which then breaks down under criticism into the competing knowledges of a proliferation of standards, to be reconciled finally in the imposition of a conventional standard as a new reference—is repeated in Usbek's confrontation with the West. Usbek, however, pushes this process further when he rejects the dogmatic solution to his epistemological uneasiness provided by the mullah in letter XVIII. The inadequacy of the mullah's response leads him to see in it *merely* convention: a naming with no certain reference outside itself. In his apparent rejection of the mullah's (the Church's) dogma, Usbek takes the step that places him outside the religious community of Islam, just as he earlier left physically the political community of Persia. For a religious community, unlike a political one, is not bound geographically; its boundaries are its conventions, its laws, and a member is one of the faithful, someone who believes in their truthfulness.

Nowhere is the centrality of the law in defining a religious community more apparent than in the case of the Jews. Being of the East and the West, they present Usbek with a third case in opposition to both: "They make show among Christians, just as among us, of an invincible

[12]*Encyclopédie*, 6:685.
[13]Ibid., 6:686.

obstinacy in favor of their religion—an obstinacy that assumes the pro-
portions of folly" (letter LX). Removed from the confines of Moslem
dogmatism, Usbek is able to see each of the three major faiths (the
English term, like the French *foi*, marks the centrality of fidelity) in
relation to the other two. And this relativism takes shape because one
church's orthodoxy is another's heresy: "The Jews consider themselves,
therefore, as the well-spring of all holiness and the origin of all religion.
They look upon us, in contrast, as heretics who have changed the law, or
rather as rebel Jews" (letter LX). It is the law that defines the community,
and he who changes it is no longer one of the faithful.

For Usbek, the identity of dogma with truth can no longer be assumed. And although Montesquieu writes in his "Réflexions" that if Rica
and Usbek "sometimes find our dogmas unusual, such feelings of the
unusual are always stamped with their complete ignorance as to the real
connections between those dogmas and our other verities,"[14] the connections that strike the reader are rather those between Catholic and
Moslem dogma. The result is an equivalence between them as equally
arbitrary. The critical process of comparison substitutes a parity of dogmas for an assumed unique identity between a single dogma and truth:
the opposition between orthodoxy and heresy gives way to that between
conventional dogmas and universal truth. "And discovering the relativity
of the absolutes that are revered in different epochs," writes Jean Starobinski of the reader of the *Lettres persanes*, "he will have felt aroused in
him the cosmopolitan solicitude which desires the happiness and prosperity of all peoples. The groundwork has been laid for the triumph of
universal concepts—Reason, Justice, Nature—in the name of which it
will be possible to condemn all particular fanaticisms and all regional
intolerance."[15]

The groundwork is laid, but the process is slow. In Usbek's case, four
years of discovery and reflection lie between his first doubting letter to
the mullah (letter XVI) and that to Mirza in which he argues for religious
pluralism: "If I must reason straightforwardly, Mirza, I'm not sure that

---

[14]*Lettres persanes*, p. 4.

[15]Starobinski, Preface to *Lettres persanes*, p. 22. The reference is to letter LXXV, in which
Usbek writes: "Truth in one era, falsehood in another." Spatial and temporal distance are
interchangeable in the *Lettres persanes*, as they are also in the *Second Discours* and the
Supplément. Already in the seventeenth century Racine had explained the validity of such
an assumption in his second preface to *Bajazet*: "People make scarcely any distinction
between that which is . . . a thousand years distant from them, and that which is a
thousand miles away . . . . We have so little contact with princes and other people who
live in the harem, that, if I may say so, we think of them as people who live in another
century" (quoted in Grosrichard, *Structure du sérail*, pp. 153–54).

it wouldn't be a good thing for a state to have several religions" (letter LXXXV).

Usbek's reasoning in letter LXXXV centers primarily on the utility for the state in tolerating different religious groups and turns upon the question of whether it is in the interest of the prince to exercise religious toleration. Nonetheless, the final argument resets the problem in the relativism that makes possible a discussion of religion in purely political terms: for only if one religion is as good (i.e., as true) as another can different faiths be seen simply as parts of the political whole within a state, or of competing power structures in and between states. The problem of intolerance leads to the question of proselytizing, and here the complete interchangeability of religions is demonstrated in the reversibility of the perspectives of their faithful. "The man who wants to make me change my religion is doing so only because he would most certainly not change his own, even if someone tried to force him to," reflects Usbek. "Thus, he finds it strange that I should not do something he would not do himself, even perhaps for the mastery of the whole world" (letter LXXXV).

Usbek's doubts about what he really knows—doubts born of his confrontation with the West—lead him to toleration and relativism. His inability to find in dogma a criterion of moral judgment consonant with reason causes him to reject the Church's authority. This dissociation of the absolutes of his religious community from an external standard beyond it leads him to the relativism he comes to share with Rica, who arrives at this position simply through direct comparison. But even in relativism Usbek retains his faith in God. What he rejects is the role of the Church in mediating between the faithful and his object, and particularly the Church's authority to establish dogma, which, asserted as the truth, brings it into conflict with other communities, religious and political.

In choosing relativism over dogma, Usbek must continue the process that began in the undermining of direct knowledge of God, truth, and moral values. He is led to ask the following questions: (1) In what does fidelity to God consist if no one church can be trusted to represent the true God exclusively? (2) If, for epistemological reasons, no one church has the right to assert its authority over others, what should be the relationship between any one church as a legally defined community and other such communities with which it and its laws may come into conflict? How are conflicting fidelities to be reconciled?[16]

---

[16]Louis XIV's revocation of the Edict of Nantes in 1685 had clearly not laid to rest the question of how to reconcile politically the religious divisions brought about by the Protestant Reformation. In addition, within French Catholicism itself, Louis continued

Usbek presents his solution to the first problem in letter xLVI. "Under whatever religion one lives," he writes to Rhédi, "the observance of laws, love for fellow men, and piety towards one's parents are always the first acts of religion." In contrast to religious ceremonies, which "contain no degree of goodness in themselves" because "they are good only with reference to and in the supposition of the knowledge that God has commanded them," both natural morality and civic virtue derive their meaning and value from their reasonableness. Testimony, like the sacred history recounted by the mullah in letter xVIII, is not entertained here as a viable proof but rather is subjected to the criticism of reason and rejected because it does not accord with what may thus be called "sovereign" reason.[17]

In the hierarchy of knowledge, the proofs that support revealed religion are subordinated to reason as the ultimate arbiter of truth: reason replaces the Church as mediator between man and God and as the means of knowledge. But Usbek assumes rather than proves that reason is more valid than dogma. He asserts the supremacy of reason in subjecting dogma to the critical process, just as Montesquieu himself does by endowing Usbek, Rica, Rhédi, and Ibben with the critical spirit. The supremacy of reason is at the very heart of the text, asserted through its universality, not on the level of the characters or their story, but on that of the text itself. It is the critical use of reason that unites author and reader.[18]

The explanation of reason's supremacy can be found in an essay on natural laws written by Montesquieu just before the *Lettres persanes*. Montesquieu begins the essay by asserting that human reason rather than divine revelation is the means by which God communicates with men. "And while [the Divinity] has never spoken to me personally, it could be that it speaks to me through the medium of my reason. I will thus listen to this interpreter, the only one that I know at this point, and

---

to try to impose his will with the closing of the Jansenist center at Port-Royal in 1709 and the support of the papal bull *Unigenitus*, by which Jansenism was condemned in 1713. On the transformation of Jansenism from a religious to a political cause in the eighteenth century, see Dale Van Kley, *The Jansenists and the Expulsion of the Jesuits from France* (New Haven, 1975).

[17]In his attack on the *Lettres persanes*, the abbé Gaultier uses testimony as proof of the unique truth of Christianity. "As if the proofs of false religions could be put in parallel with those which establish the truth of the Christian religion, of its dogmas, its sacraments, and its sacrifice," he writes. "The Christian religion begins with the world itself, and proves its descent to us by innumerable testimonies": [Jean-Baptiste Gaultier], "*Lettres persanes*" *convaincues d'impiété* (n.p., 1751), p. 68.

[18]See Ronald Grimsley, "The Idea of Nature in *Lettres persanes*," *French Studies* 5 (October 1951): 293.

whatever of God's will it discloses to me, that I will call natural law."[19] Reason is valid not only because it is universal (as opposed to the particularity of religious dogmas and ceremonies) but also because it is the true medium of God's will. And just as reason replaces the Church as mediator between God and man, natural laws replace dogmas as the expression of God's truth. Natural laws serve as the standard of moral decision making. For, as Montesquieu continues, "It is clear that if there really is such a law, or such a will of God, there will be a real difference between good and evil, just and unjust, virtue and vice."[20] Montesquieu has answered Usbek's question to the mullah of how to distinguish good from evil in the same way as Roxane will in letter CLXI: by reference to a direct, personal knowledge of the laws of nature.

To the man who tells God, "When I would lift up my prayer to you, I don't know in what language I should speak to you. Nor do I know what position I should assume" (letter XLVI), Usbek suggests the universal language of reason, the universal posture of virtue.[21] And virtue must be understood here to refer to both the positive, moral sense of fulfilling "all the duties of charity and human kindness" and the negative political sense of "never violating the laws" of society (letter XLVI). For man, according to Montesquieu and Usbek, is not only naturally reasonable but naturally sociable as well.

Montesquieu presents two major and complementary proofs of natural law in his essay, both based upon the reason given man to guide his conduct: "But of what use will the light of reason be, if it is not to enlighten one's conduct?"[22] Both proofs also figure in the *Lettres persanes*, but there is a crucial shift in emphasis from one text to the other. The first proof in the essay, which is the more important one there, is limited to the Troglodyte fable in the *Lettres*; the second proof, however, defines a primary critical project of the later work as a whole.[23]

The first proof of natural laws is based in man's natural self-interest

---

[19]*Oeuvres complètes*, p. 175.
[20]Ibid.
[21]"Virtue would be a disposition to practice that which [natural] law ordains": ibid.
[22]Ibid., p. 176.
[23]A third argument presented in the essay on natural laws also figures in the *Lettres* but is equally subordinate in both texts. Montesquieu's argument in the essay that nature "has made us in such a way that we are led mechanically to certain actions" is identical with Usbek's claim in letter XXVI that French women "carry graven within their hearts a certain image of virtue." Yet this is a minor argument in both texts because, as Montesquieu explains, there are just too many factors that can obscure and hinder the workings of instinct (*Oeuvres complètes*, p. 181). Although instinctive virtue may be a proof that natural laws exist, it is not dependable as a guide of conduct and so figures only minimally in both texts.

and moves to an affirmation of mutual interest: "It is in our interest for men to do what we want, and in order for this to happen, we must do the same for them." This proof is confirmed in the notion that God wills the happiness and conservation of mankind. Thus, "God . . . has inseparably joined together the happiness of the human race with virtue."[24] The argument of the Troglodyte fable is easy to recognize here.[25]

In the *Lettres persanes* the Troglodyte proof of natural law based on the mutual interest of human beings, the good will of God toward mankind, and the resulting identity of happiness and virtue precedes the comparative critical process in which Usbek's confrontation with the West engages him. Like the essay on natural laws itself, the Troglodyte fable and the argument it presents both precede the *Lettres persanes* and are enclosed within it. The critical process, however, does not simply disprove the argument for natural virtue; rather, it indicates the inability of such an argument alone to provide the necessary guide to conduct for people living in a society. The dual premise of the *Lettres persanes* is both the oneness of humanity and the variety of human societies. The place-ment of the Troglodyte letters between Usbek's departure from Persia and his arrival in France subordinates the question of humanity to that of society and shows the universals of natural morality to be both prior to and inadequate as the rule of conduct in modern political societies.

The form of the Troglodyte fable is also in contrast to the negative function of criticism embodied in both the satirical and the philosophical or reflective letters that follow and serve to undermine it. As Sheldon Sacks argues, the apologue is a positive form, "a fictional example of the truth of a formulative statement," while satire is negative, "ridiculing particular men, the institutions of men, traits presumed to be in all men, or any combination of the three."[26] The positivity of the apologue can be further identified with the universality of the proposition it instantiates,

[24]*Oeuvres complètes*, pp. 178–181.

[25]In light of the essay on natural laws, Mirza's initial question and his reference to a familiarity with Usbek's position on the matter take on a new resonance: "Yesterday we argued the question whether men were happy through the pleasures and satisfactions of the senses or through the practice of virtue. I have often heard you say that men were born to be virtuous and that justice is a quality as proper to man as existence" (letter x). This connection between the two texts is stressed by Vernière, *Lettres persanes*, p. 27, n. 1; p. 34, n. 1.

[26]Sheldon Sacks, *Fiction and the Shape of Belief: A Study of Henry Fielding with Glances at Swift, Johnson and Richardson* (Berkeley, 1964), pp. 7–8. Sacks defines a third form, "represented action," which would seem to describe the novelistic framework as a whole, the overall story of the voyage. "In any work which belongs to this class, characters about whose fates we are made to care are introduced in unstable relationships which are then further complicated until the complications are finally resolved by the complete removal of the represented instability" (p. 15).

while satire, in its negativity, focuses on the particulars of individuals and the institutions they have created.

Montesquieu's second proof of natural law starts not from the individual and his self-interest but from the inherent sociability of men. "Man was not made to live alone," he writes, "but to be in society with those like himself. This is why he was given language, in order to communicate his thoughts to others." But society can achieve its end—providing the mutual services required by individuals—only if it is ruled by law. "Consequently, Society, to which the Creator has destined us, assumes laws, which are as its basis and foundation." One can say that God wills men to obey the laws of society to the extent that those laws are constitutive of the society itself, which could not exist without them. Crimes like murder, theft, fornication, even drunkenness, when considered as crimes against society, "are no longer things which depend upon the caprice of legislators. They are fixed and as distinct as the good or evil they cause in Society. In a word, all law, without which [society] could not subsist, becomes for that reason a divine law."[27] The critical project of the *Lettres persanes* consists, at least in part, in determining those laws without which society—any society—could not exist.

To answer the first question posed by Usbek's relativism, fidelity to God can be achieved only through fidelity to one's own reason and the natural laws it defines. These laws must be obeyed on the universal level of humanity through a natural morality expressed in the principle of mutual interest; they must also be obeyed on the particular level of the positive laws of society to the extent that those laws are constitutive of the society itself. Reason, taking the place of the Church, mediates between man and God such that fidelity to God is not simply personal but legal. Reason also mediates as the arbiter among conflicting modes of proof. This second type of mediation is the model for the role of positive civil laws in arbitrating disputes among conflicting social bodies. When conflicting fidelities are to be reconciled, it is reason, embodied in the essential laws of society (those without which it could not subsist), that must mediate among them. Reason also provides the key to Usbek's second problem, setting its solution politically.

Usbek is strangely silent concerning the political fidelity that binds a prince and a subject. His first of only two references to this domain of fidelity is in letter CIV. This is the last of three letters to Ibben that form a short series on the limitations of monarchy. In closing the letter and the series Usbek relates the following anecdote: "The English recall that one of their kings, having conquered and imprisoned another prince who lay

[27]*Oeuvres complètes*, p. 180.

claim to his crown, was desirous of reproaching the latter for his perfidy and lack of fidelity. 'It was only a moment ago,' replied the unfortunate prince, 'that it was decided which one, of the two of us, is the traitor.'" Although this anedcote indeed refers to political infidelity, the meaning of that infidelity cannot even be approached here, since it depends upon the more fundamental identification of ruler and ruled, here also put in question. At the point where the reader would expect a restabilization of the term *fidélité* through the unifying force of the political order, the very identification of the polity in terms of the ruler and the ruled is placed in question. The political rug is pulled out from under us, so to speak. Why does this happen?

To remain first within letter civ, Usbek himself provides a commentary on the anecdote he has just recounted. "A usurper calls rebels all those who have not oppressed the country as he has," he argues, "and believing there can be no laws where he can see no judges, he causes the caprices of chance and fortune to be revered as if they were judgments of heaven." Without a recognition of the fundamental laws of society, a prince is simply a usurper and the conception of fidelity itself becomes absurd. Law must precede any notion of fidelity.

The two subsequent references to political fidelity also serve to undermine the validity of fidelity as a political bond. In letter cxxi of Usbek's series on depopulation, he writes to Rhédi of the problems involved in colonization. "The Spanish, despairing of ever holding their conquered nations by devotion [*fidélité*]," he explains, "chose the expedient of destroying the natives and sending faithful citizens from Spain." The particularity of fidelity as a political bond is demonstrated here as the Spanish find themselves unable to extend it to the colonial natives. The relationship between the prince and his colonial subjects is a travesty of a true polity, since fidelity binds ruler and ruled only if the ruler can choose his subjects from among those already deemed faithful. The faithful can thus no longer be conceived of as those defined by a relationship of fidelity. Rather, it is fidelity that has been frozen, bound to a particular group of people who are termed "faithful." As the faithful Spanish settle the colonial lands, replacing the unfaithful natives, they impart fidelity to the political entity, the colony.

Fidelity still describes the relationship between ruler and subject, but the fidelity of the colonists as Spaniards precedes the relationship between colonist and king. As a relational term, fidelity is limited politically by the traditional cultural boundaries of the nation. The same limitation of the relational status of fidelity was seen to occur in the context of marriage after it was identified simply with a physical attribute ("virtue") of the wife. In fact, the three references to political fidelity retrace the steps by which the investigation of fidelity arrived at politics: from the epistemological questioning of religious fidelity (who is the ruler, who is the ruled?), back to the relational limits of the terms here described (as in marriage), and, finally, to the despotic fidelity that defined the relationship between master and eunuch. The examination of the concept of fidelity, from a simple definition to a cultural comparison to an epistemological inquiry, leads only to the failure of that term to transcend the relationships in which it operates. Fidelity can demonstrate the need for an overarching, universal means of defining relationships, but it cannot be that means.

Rica's final reference to political fidelity illustrates this failure. "I should like to talk to kings as the angels speak to our Holy Prophet," he writes to Ibben, and then explains what he means by describing his own conduct at the court of Ispahan.

> You know that in the holy feasts when the Lord of Lords descends from the highest throne of earth to communicate with his slaves, I have made it a strict habit to enslave an unruly tongue. I have never been known to loose a single word that could prove bitter to the lowliest of his subjects. Whenever I had to cease being discreet in speech, I did not in any way cease being an honorable man, and in this proof of our fidelity, I have risked my life but never my virtue. [Letter cxxvii]

By assuming himself to be a slave and the king his master, Rica was able to withstand the test of fidelity. Refusing to betray himself through flattery, or his king through criticism, Rica defines fidelity as silence. This letter only too clearly recalls Usbek's letter viii, as the silence chosen by Rica repeats the absence chosen by Usbek. Fidelity loses meaning as the relationship between ruler and ruled is reduced to that between master and slave, where there is no positive bond but simply an absence, a silence, which makes of political fidelity too a tautology.

Looking to the narrative level of the text, one finds another way to explain the breakdown of the polity in terms of fidelity and Usbek's subsequent silence on political fidelity. If one puts the last fifteen letters back into the chronological order otherwise faithfully maintained, the first of these "harem letters" appears directly after Usbek's letter civ to Ibben. It can then be seen that Usbek's reflections on political fidelity are interrupted by the breakdown of his own polity (the harem) through the destruction of its ties of fidelity. Although the term *fidélité* does not appear in the letter from the Grand Eunuch which first informs Usbek of the crisis in the harem, what is described are a series of infidelities committed by the wives: Zélis broke the rules by letting her veil fall; Zachi was found in bed with one of her slaves, "a thing so strongly prohibited by the laws of the seraglio"; a young boy was found in the garden, evidence of yet another wife's (Roxane's, it turns out later) infidelity. "Add to that all that has not come to my attention, for without any doubt you are betrayed" (letter CXLVII).

Unlike the case of the two kings of England, here the laws are recognized and affirmed (by the eunuch and subsequently by Usbek in letter CXLVIII) and the traitors clearly identified. Usbek and his eunuch-shadow simply maintain the definition of wifely fidelity established in their first letters. In order to enforce the laws that determine fidelity among the wives, however, the eunuch demands to be given powers that would substitute his own will for that of the master. And Usbek grants them: "Receive with this letter unlimited power over the entire seraglio," he writes. "Command with the same authority as myself" (letter CXLVIII).

Maintaining the fidelity of the wives not only requires the overt naming of a despot whose unlimited power gives lie to the supposed legalistic character of their fidelity but, even more significantly, eliminates the object of the fidelity of both wives and eunuchs: the master himself. As Montesquieu implies in summarizing the Grand Eunuch's letter as "disorders that Usbek's absence produces in the seraglio," it is Usbek's absence that forces the harem system beyond its own limits to the point where it collapses.[28] When the system is seen as political, the concept of fidelity cannot hold its members together. And as Roxane's suicide note indicates, the seeds of destruction lie not only in the personal rule of the master but in the arbitrary character of the laws, which are neither transcendent (above both prince and subject) nor universal (natural and reasonable). Fidelity does not work as a means of uniting or creating a body politic, for two reasons: first, because fidelity to law and fidelity to the ruler are not necessarily compatible; second, because fidelity is not an overarching, universal concept: it cannot create a whole that is greater than its parts. The collapse of Usbek's harem is due to the internal, structural tensions that rack it. Conflicting fidelities, in other words, cannot be reconciled simply through the imposition of another kind of fidelity.

Roland Mousnier argues that Louis XIV attempted just such a project of unifying France and the monarchy through the imposition of a new

---

[28]*Lettres persanes*, p. 419. Once again it must be emphasized that Usbek's absence is defined in the epistolary form by spatial and temporal distance. As Laurent Versini notes, "Montesquieu is the first [epistolary novelist] and remains for a long time the only one to date his letters precisely . . . and to take account of the very long delay which separates the sending and receiving [of letters], and which resounds in the drama: the distancing of Usbek renders him powerless to quell the revolt in his harem": *Laclos et la tradition* (Paris, 1968), p. 275. See also Rosbottom, "Motifs in Epistolary Fiction," p. 283.

kind of fidelity: a direct, personal bond between prince and subject. When he took the throne in the seventeenth century, Louis found himself ruler of a nation that was bound together, from top to bottom, by particular ties of fidelity. This fidelity between master and *fidèle* Mousnier defines as "a bond of sentiment, based on mutual affection, which links two men together totally, by their free choice, independently of duty toward nation, king, law, or society."[29] During the Fronde, Louis learned to appreciate the importance of fidelities, as those who rose up did so with the support of thousands of their *fidèles* among the nobility. But the king had his own *fidèles*, and it was they who furnished the officers for his army that eventually put down the rebellion. Having thus witnessed the strength of these bonds, Louis sought not to break them, but to co-opt them, to make himself the object of all fidelities. A liberal and judicious use of royal and personal favor was turned to the creation of *fidèles* whose only allegiance would be to the king, their master. When Louis, speaking of himself in the *Mémoires pour l'instruction du dauphin*, writes that "his favors are seen as the exclusive source of all good things," he makes of himself the master of a nation of *fidèles*.[30]

Absolutism in practical politics and the *Leviathan* of Thomas Hobbes in political theory were both responses to the civil wars of religion that ravaged France and Europe as a whole in the wake of the Reformation.[31] While Usbek's fable of the Troglodytes was meant to demonstrate the inadequacy of Hobbes's explanation of the disharmony of the social order,[32] the *Lettres persanes* as a whole displays the inadequacy of political absolutism as a means of effecting social unification. In the *Lettres persanes*, Montesquieu displays the internal conflicts, the instability of the social whole which absolutist practice and theory sought to overcome through the imposition of an absolute political authority based upon fidelity.

In the treatment of political fidelity as well as in the ultimate dissolution of Usbek's own despotic polity (the harem), the inadequacy of absolutism as a solution to the problem of conflicting fidelities is exposed. The problem, as Mousnier states it, is that in a nation of estates and orders,

> an organ of coordination and direction is needed, expressing and imposing the common will of living together in uniting efforts for the welfare of all.

[29]Mousnier, *Institutions of France*, p. 104.
[30]Quoted in ibid., p. 107.
[31]See Reinhart Koselleck, *Le Règne de la critique*, trans. Hans Hildenbrand (Paris, 1979), pp. 19–33.
[32]See Crisafulli, "Montesquieu's Story of the Troglodytes," p. 373, and Henry J. Merry, *Montesquieu's System of Natural Government* (West Lafayette, Ind., 1970), p. 11.

This organ is the absolute monarchy. And what is needed is a bond which unites all the orders to the king who incarnates the monarchy, and the members of the orders to each other, within the orders according to the hierarchy of estates; between the orders according to their own hierarchy. This bond is fidelity.[33]

Louis xiv's monarchy may have been the high point of absolutism, but it was fragile nonetheless, a delicate balancing act based upon a contradiction. On the one hand, the king asserted himself as necessary to and representative of the nation as a whole. This claim allowed him to rise above and take power from the traditional corporations whose competing interests he alone could resolve for the good of all. But social hierarchy was the necessary support of political absolutism, and thus the egalitarian implications of the king's role as king equally to all had to be combated in order to protect his power from those below him. "For kings," writes Leonard Krieger, "their position at the apex of the divinely constructed social ladder called for obedience even when the benefits of their government were not in evidence, and they never dreamed of destroying a support which linked their own preeminence with the general constitution of human society."[34]

The obedience required of Louis's subjects was a function of the web of fidelities that bound individuals together in a system of hierarchies that culminated always in the king himself. It supported his position as representative of the nation, but it also threatened it in challenging the practice of uniformity by means of which alone the king was able to govern that nation. "Thus," Krieger continues, "peoples were related to their kings in two different ways, one primarily political and uniform, the other primarily social and pyramidal."[35] Fidelity was the key to both these relationships. Fidelity to the king was simply overlaid on the particularistic fidelities that it was meant to supersede but had to maintain.

This investigation of the term *fidélité* in the *Lettres persanes* demonstrates that one term is not adequate to express these two conflicting types of relationships. While fidelity may be invoked to create particular social bonds, it cannot form that overarching, uniform political bond that binds the nation to its ruler and the ruler to the nation. While Montesquieu accepts the ideal of uniformity that the absolute monarchy tried to impose on the hierarchical social order, he then questions the validity of

[33]Roland Mousnier, "Les Concepts d'"ordres,' d'"états,' de 'fidélité,' et de 'monarchie absolue' en France de la fin du xve siècle à la fin du xviiie," *Revue Historique* 247 (April–June 1972): 303.
[34]Leonard Krieger, *Kings and Philosophers, 1689–1789* (New York, 1970), p. 11.
[35]Ibid.

the principle of that social order as a principle of uniform political relations. Absolutism, as a relationship of direct fidelity between subject and prince overlaid on a network of particularistic fidelities, fails to solve the problem of political unification because, while it is indeed absolute, it is not universal. Fidelity—and with it absolutism—must be replaced by another bond, one that is both universal and transcendent, and that new bond, according to Montesquieu, is justice.[36]

[36]Starobinski, focusing on *honneur*, rather than *fidélité*, also arrives at Montesquieu's condemnation of absolutism:

> With the advent of the absolute monarchy, honor, as a supreme and unconditional value, has become the exclusive attribute of the sovereign. The noble class, passing to the rank of a courtesan class, no longer has any honor except in the service of the king. The noble is no longer called so by his own conscience, but at the satisfaction of the king, from whom he awaits recompense. If Montesquieu renounces the heroic ideal which asked a man to surpass himself in the sacrifice and the deed, it is because that ideal can no longer be lived authentically. [Introduction to *Montesquieu par lui-même* (Paris, 1953), p. 48]

CHAPTER THREE

Justice as an
Alternative Social Bond

"Justice is a true relationship of appropriateness which exists between two things, and this relationship is always the same, no matter by whom considered, whether it be God, or an angel, or finally, a man" (letter LXXXIII). Usbek gives this now famous definition of justice in a letter to Rhédi near the midpoint of the *Lettres persanes*. As compiler, Montesquieu has privileged this letter, whose topic is justice, and so has privileged the notion of justice displayed in it.[1] Like *fidélité*, the term *justice* runs through the text as a whole, but it describes its own pattern as it unfolds.[2] Whereas *fidélité* was seen to decompose as it appeared in different contexts, from friendship to politics, the concept of *justice* displays a process of refining and abstracting that leaves it free of particular contexts by the time it reaches its purest form in letter LXXXIII. From that point on, Usbek uses the term with a new confidence, as he then reinserts it into the world of politics as a sure guide to problem solving and decision making in conflicts both domestic and foreign. This process of redefining politics (and through it both domestic and international order) is arrested, however, as news of the crisis in Usbek's harem wrenches him from a theoretical polity based on justice to a real one based tragically on a dogmatic concept of fidelity. The last two letters in

---

[1]"Probably the most telling characterization of man in *Les Lettres persanes* is in the analysis of justice and interest. Clearly justice is the highest value in that work and in what we know of Montesquieu's writing until he began preparations for *L'Esprit des Lois*": Merry, *Montesquieu's System of Natural Government*, p. 8. See also Starobinski, Introduction to *Montesquieu par lui-même*, p. 69.

[2]As *fidélité* was taken to extend to the related terms *infidélité* and *fidèle*, *justice* is here extended to include *injustice* and *juste*.

which justice figures (CXLI and CXLVI) suggest Usbek's opportunity to transform his harem from one system to the other. He misses the opportunity, however, for the reordering of the last part of the *Lettres persanes* gives the final word to the collapse of the system of fidelities rather than to the introduction of a new system of justice.

As opposed to the scattering effect produced by the decomposition of the term *fidélité*, the term *justice* gathers its definitional forces together in universalizing abstraction and then turns downward as a sure guide through the complex relations of the political world, only to be cut short, stopped cold, when it meets head on an actual crisis of the system of fidelities that requires immediate action. Thus, while *justice* reaches the apex of its trajectory in Usbek's letter LXXXIII, any discussion of the term cannot begin or end there. Rather, it will end in the failure of justice to transform the world of fidelities, and it will begin with Usbek's first treatment of it—in the fable of the Troglodytes.

"I have often heard you say," writes Mirza to Usbek in letter X, "that men were born to be virtuous and that justice is a quality as proper to man as existence. Explain to me, I beg of you, what you mean." The fable of the Troglodytes is Usbek's explanation in the Fénelonian mode of this "moral truth," as he calls it in letter XI. It is not an inquiry into the nature or meaning of justice but a demonstration of the moral axiom that men have an innate sense of justice. Similarly, it seeks to prove (rhetorically) the axiom that man's end is virtue rather than to define virtue (or virtues), as the earlier discussion of *fidélité* in the fable showed. Like that of *fidélité*, the definition of *justice* is here assumed, rather than questioned or explored.

The apologue or fable form of Usbek's answer to Mirza is exemplary rather than definitional. Mirza does not get the explanation he requests, because example, as opposed to definition, is a direct instantiation that presents rather than explains. The knowledge that results from it, as Usbek tells Mirza in letter XI, is immediately felt rather than critically understood. Example as a means (or perhaps the iconic means) of direct moral instruction is treated in Montesquieu's unpublished continuation of the Troglodyte fable, in which the reciprocal example of the ruler and the ruled constitutes the basis of an education that will preserve natural morality and the sense of justice.[3] Thus, as Crisafulli argues, "the importance of example is evident from the fact that it was . . . a prime factor in the strengthening of the virtue of the Troglodytes as their numbers increased in the state of nature. Example still remained a preponderant

[3]*Lettres persanes*, pp. 336–38.

force in their new society even though other motives of conduct were still operative."[4]

The use of examples can lead to two very different types of knowledge or understanding, depending upon whether the examples given are complementary or contradictory. In the case of *fidélité*, as has been seen, conflicting examples brought about the abandoning of the term as a general principle in any relationship, public or private. It is because the meaning and signification of *fidélité* are unstable, inconsistent within and between relationships, that examples of it had to be spread throughout the whole of the *Lettres persanes*, appearing and reappearing in each human relationship that the text treats in its representation of life's social complexity. The particular examples of fidelity and infidelity are a clash of discordant notes rather than the strains of a transcendent harmony. Such a harmony, on the other hand, is produced by the many examples of justice and injustice presented in the fable of the Troglodytes. Whereas the use of contradictory examples is destructive of a nominal whole, the use of complementary examples is constructive: the first step beyond a nominal whole and toward the constituting of a universal and transcendent one. Such a universal whole is transcendent in that it is greater than the sum of the particular examples of it.

If justice is consistent, and if all human beings have an innate sense of it, as Usbek's exemplary tale sets out to demonstrate, why need the concept of justice be explored at all? Why is the Troglodyte fable only a first step in an inquiry into justice and not the final word on it? The introduction of the term "the most just" in letter xiv of the Troglodyte series hints at an explanation. Whereas all earlier references are to *justice* as an absolute term, and people are described as either just or not just, here it appears that although the absolute and consistent quality of justice remains intact, individuals may not be absolutely just or unjust, but may be more or less so. Although people have the capacity to know justice, they do not always act justly. The most just is thus he who knows justice the best and acts upon it most often.[5] Since the first obstacle to justice is ignorance of it, the first task is to learn what justice is. But since man is free to act justly or not even when he knows what justice is, it is also necessary to understand the forces that influence his actions. After the

---

[4]Crisafulli, "Montesquieu's Story of the Troglodytes," p. 389.

[5]In a passage from his unpublished "Pensées" originally destined for the unfinished *Traité des devoirs*, Montesquieu writes: "The means of acquiring perfect justice is to make it such a habit that one observes it in the most minor things and bends one's very way of thinking to it": *Oeuvres complètes*, p. 938. Thus, one could say that the more (often) one acts justly, the more just one becomes.

Troglodyte fable, the next four letters in which the concept of justice appears relate it to these other forces: positive and divine laws, natural law, tyrannical power, rhetoric, and custom.

In letter xxxiii, Usbek writes to Rhédi concerning the use of wine among monarchs in the East and West. "If anything has dishonored the life and reputation of our monarchs," he writes, "it has been their intemperance. It is the most envenomed source of their injustice and cruelty." According to Usbek, drinking to excess dehumanizes the kings of the East, and along with their humanity they thus lose their sense of justice. But Usbek sees a more complex problem in the observation that Persian kings, who are forbidden by law to drink, do so to excess, while Christian kings, bound by no such law, commit no faults as a result of their intemperance. What then is the relationship between law (positive and divine) and justice in this case? "In licentious debauch, people rebel with fury against precept, and the law, established to make us more virtuous, often serves only to make us more blameworthy" (letter xxxiii).

Earlier, the most just of the Troglodytes had argued that the rule of law, when compared to that of natural virtue, allowed people to act less than absolutely virtuously (letter xiv); it contained people legally somewhere between absolute virtue and absolute vice. In letter xxxiii, law is compared not to natural virtue but to vice, and it is shown not to be an effective means of keeping people from vice or injustice. The role of law in relation to justice and virtue is thus neither to make people more just (virtuous) nor to make them less unjust (vicious), since it is shown to function in precisely the opposite way. What ought to be the relationship between law and justice is left unresolved.

If the relationship between positive law and justice is still to be defined, that between natural law and justice is given quite clearly in Rica's letter xxxviii to Ibben.[6] Here Rica asks whether natural law submits women to men. The Frenchman's argument, he writes, is that only because men are stronger than women are they able to exercise a tyrannical empire over them by force. And this, he says, is "a true injustice." Justice is directly opposed to tyrannical power based on strength, because strength is itself a product of unequal education. The injustice lies in that man's empire over woman is based upon a strength that is imposed tyrannically rather than based in nature. Justice is thus not simply equality, but it is based on a definition of equity that allows for natural

---

[6]This letter was discussed above in the context of marital fidelity. It is one of only six letters in which both *fidélité* and *justice* figure, out of a total of thirty-three *fidélité* letters and twenty-nine *justice* letters. On the whole, the two issues are kept separate, each describing its own path, but with the paths occasionally crossing.

inequality. If, for example, with equal education women turned out to be the stronger because endowed with more natural talents, their empire over men would be just. Justice, then, is dependent upon natural law and is directly opposed to tyrannical power.

"As soon as an exalted person dies," writes Usbek to Ibben in letter XL, "people assemble in a mosque, where his funeral oration is delivered. This is a discourse in his praise, and after it is delivered, a man would be hard put to decide precisely as to the worth [*au juste du mérite*] of the dead man." Although the type of rhetoric referred to here is epideictic, (having to do with praise and blame), Usbek links it to the deliberation characteristic of the public assembly. And rhetoric, he argues, does not at all help the listener make a fair evaluation of the subject of its discourse. Like positive law, traditional (ancient) forms of rhetoric do not seem to help one to act more justly but simply add another factor to confuse the decision making process.

In Usbek's letter XLVIII to Rhédi the paths of *fidélité* and *justice* intersect in the forms of their antitheses. Usbek recounts a conversation he has had with a man who says of himself: "I have no other position than to drive a husband mad and bring a father to despair. I like to terrify a woman who thinks she has caught me and allow her to advance within a hair of my downfall." Usbek, shocked not simply by the man but by the society of which he is a part, asks Rhédi: "What have you to say about a country that tolerates such people? Where they let a man who leads such an existence live? Where unfaithfulness, betrayal, rape, perfidy, and injustice lead to reputation?" It is this society itself, its customary means of praising and blaming or giving consideration, that is acting as a force against justice. The *moeurs* of a society, like its laws, like the rhetoric of its public speakers, do not guide men to act justly but rather encourage them to act unjustly.

To summarize what has been learned of justice so far, the Troglodyte fable demonstrated through example that justice is both absolute and knowable and that man has a natural sense of it. The last letter of the series, however, indicated that men are able to act unjustly in spite of this natural sense, for two reasons: first, because they have an imperfect knowledge of justice; and second, because they are free to act unjustly even if they know what justice is. The second series of letters in which justice figures then explores the relationships between justice and the social forces, from positive law to custom, that ought to encourage just actions, but that in fact do not. Only natural law is seen to be necessarily complementary to justice, since natural equality and inequality must be the basis of equity in justice. While there is a first sense in which the opposition of justice to law, custom, tyrannical power, and rhetoric is negative, in that justice is seen to be supported by none of the forces that influence decisions within society, a positive conclusion can be drawn as well. That is, justice is by the same token freed of a dependence upon these social forces for its determination. Consequently, both justice and natural law can now be accepted as prior to social forces and social forms. Justice is transcendent in that it escapes the forms of particular societies.

The next three letters in which *justice* appears affirm both the transcendent universality of justice and the fact that it is not immanent in the positive systems of justice that ought to represent, embody, or at least encourage it. Usbek opens letter LXIX to Rhédi by writing: "You could never have imagined that I should turn more metaphysician than I already was. And yet that's what has happened; you will be convinced of it once you have endured this outburst of my philosophy." As a metaphysician Usbek affirms the transcendence of justice by identifying it with a transcendent God. This identification, however, is only incidental to the discussion, which centers on the seeming contradiction between divine perfection and omniscience on the one hand and divine justice on the other. Divine justice, he argues, assumes human free will, as opposed to the determinism often inferred from the concept of divine omniscience.

Sheila Mason restates Usbek's dilemma as follows:

> How . . . could omniscience and justice be predicated on a being who has created a world where evil and sin appear the inevitable consequences of its organization? Either God must be assumed to have set certain general forces in action, and left them free to combine at random, in which case human will is as free as it could wish to be; or, God's prescience is real in that all phenomena and events are the necessary effects of certain predetermined causes; in which case human actions are no freer than the movements of one billiard ball in collision with another.[7]

Usbek, wanting to preserve both divine omniscience and free will, describes a middle path between the opposing poles he has described:

> Since [God] causes his creatures to move at his fancy, he knows all he wants to know. But even though he can see everything, he does not always use this faculty. Normally he leaves to his creature the faculty of acting or not acting, in order to leave to the creature the possibility of merit or demerit. It is then that he gives up his right of acting upon the creature or determining that action. But when he wants to know something, he knows

[7]Sheila Mason, *Montesquieu's Idea of Justice* (The Hague, 1975), p. 171.

it from all time, for he has only to will that it happen as he sees it and to determine his creatures in conformity with his will. [Letter LXIX][8]

Justice is thus not incompatible with God's infinite prescience, nor is human free will. Solving the metaphysical problem to his own satisfaction allows Usbek to affirm a transcendent divine justice and man's freedom to act in opposition to it. This same affirmation poses the social and political problem left unanswered by the metaphysician.

In letter LXXVI to Ibben, Usbek questions whether there should be laws forbidding suicide. "It seems to me," he writes, "that such laws are quite unjust." Here Usbek questions whether a particular law conforms with justice. Such a questioning is possible because the concept of justice has been set apart from any particular law or set of laws. Once justice is determined to be prior to law, it provides the individual with a standard by which particular laws may be judged. Usbek, however, does not stop with the critique of one law but sees whole legal systems as subject to criticism to the degree that they instantiate injustice.

Letter LXXX deals with the concrete political issue of crimes and punishments and shows just how great the gap is between that transcendent divine justice and the administration of it in both Eastern and Western societies. In this letter to Rhédi, Usbek acknowledges first that in all countries greater crimes are met with greater punishments than are lesser ones. On the whole, however, the scale of the punishments reflects the relative harshness of the government, and the effect of the punishments is also relative to the particular society, such that under a harsh system lighter punishments would have no effect. However, writes Usbek, "I cannot see that civil order, justice, and equity are better observed in Turkey, Persia, and among the Mongols than they are in the republics of Holland and Venice and even in England. I cannot see that fewer crimes are committed or that men, intimidated by the degree of punishment, are more submissive to the law." Here we learn again of a social institution—the penal system—that does not necessarily support justice or influence men to act justly. The theme of this letter, however, is degrees, and it is the relative effectiveness of different penal systems that concerns Usbek. Just as the last Troglodyte letter introduced the idea that individuals can be more or less just, this letter emphasizes that

---

[8]Vernière, following Élie Carcassonne, attributes this conclusion (and most of the content of the letter) to Leibniz's *Théodicée* (*Lettres persanes*, p. 152, n. 1.). See also Alessandro Crisafulli, "Parallels to Ideas in *Lettres persanes*," *PMLA* 52 (June 1937): 773–77, and Mason, *Montesquieu's Idea of Justice*, for discussions of Leibniz's influence here and elsewhere in the *Lettres persanes*.

particular societies and institutions are more or less supportive of justice. As the invariability of justice has been strengthened by its association with divine transcendence, yet another variable is added to the problem of instantiating justice in particular societies. From the identity between justice and just men in letters XII and XIII of the Troglodyte fable, justice has moved progressively upward and away from human societies and institutions; as the latter are shown to be complexly variable and the former to be absolute, universal, transcendent, invariable. The concept of justice reaches its apogee in this sense in letter LXXXIII.

Justice is confirmed as divine justice in Usbek's opening words of this letter. "If there is a God, Rhédi, of necessity he must be just, for if he were not, he would be the most evil and imperfect of all beings." In linking again God's perfection and his justice, Usbek continues the metaphysical speculations of letter LXIX, in which perfection, prescience, and justice were argued to be necessary and nonconflicting attributes of God. Here, moreover, the focus falls squarely on justice, and its attribution to God becomes the introduction to an examination of the concept as transcending God as well. "Thus," concludes Usbek later in this letter, "even were there to be no God, we should always love justice—that is to say, do our best to resemble that being of whom we have such a beautiful idea, who if he were to exist, would be, of necessity, just. Free though we might be from the yoke of religion, we ought never to be free from that of equity." The point of proving that justice is independent of God, however, is to prove once again that it is prior to positive law: "That, Rhédi," writes Usbek, "is what made me think that justice is eternal and not dependent on the conventions of men.[9]

Having determined the transcendent universality of justice, and having freed it from any particular notion of God, Usbek can then argue for what he could only demonstrate by parable and example in the Troglodyte letters: that all men have an innate sense of justice. And as the Troglodyte fable was a response to Hobbes, so too is the latter part of letter LXXXIII, which begins: "We are surrounded by men stronger than ourselves. They could harm us in myriad different ways and three fourths of the time could get away with it unpunished. What a relief to know that in the hearts of all these men there exists an interior principle that fights in our favor and protects us from their machinations!"[10]

---

[9]This direct statement of the priority of justice over law is reasserted by Montesquieu in the summary of his *Traité des devoirs*: "The author, in chapters IV and V, shows that Justice is not dependent upon human laws, that it is based upon the existence and the sociability of human beings, and not on the dispositions or wills of particular beings": *Oeuvres complètes*, p. 181.

[10]In the *Traité des devoirs*, too, the determination of the priority of law leads to an attack on Hobbes: ibid., pp. 181–82.

Although the link is not clearly established, Usbek's reassertion of an innate sense of justice is founded on the transcendence of justice. Only because justice is independent of all human conventions—religious and civil—can it be universally knowable. Because it is not simply divine but exists independently of all conceptions of God (of which it is nonetheless necessarily a part), justice can be known by all men directly, without the mediation of religion. In other words, all men have the capacity to know justice and to know it simply by being human—they can know it innately. And because the justice that they know is the same justice that is also an attribute of God, the objective status (both existential and epistemological) of justice is explicable, and justice itself can thus be given a single definition. That definition, with which this discussion of the concept of justice in the *Lettres persanes* began, is found in the second paragraph of letter LXXXIII: "Justice is a true relationship of appropriateness which exists between two things, and this relationship is always the same, no matter by whom considered, whether it be God, or an angel, or finally, a man." The first clause of the sentence asserts the existential objectivity of justice, while the second affirms its epistemological objectivity.

The objectivity of justice is opposed to the subjective basis of human actions. "Men are capable of doing injustice because it is to their own interest to do so, and because they prefer their own satisfaction to that of others. It is always by reference to themselves [*par un retour sur eux-mêmes*] that they act; no man is evil gratuitously. There must be some determinant reason; that reason is always a selfish one" (letter LXXXIII). Over a year earlier, in letter LIX, Rica had expressed this same idea to Usbek. "It seems to me, Usbek," he wrote, "that we never judge of matters except by a secret reflex we make upon ourselves [*par un retour secret que nous faisons sur nous-mêmes*]." But that relativity of human judgments which Rica attributes even to concepts of God ("It has been well said that if triangles were to create a god, they would give him three sides."), Usbek limits by excluding from it both the concept of justice and that of God. But just because our judgments are relative does not mean for Usbek that there can be no objective standard, no just or unjust. It means, rather, that the objective existence of justice and the individual's ability to know it do not ensure that the individual will choose to act justly. Worse, since people see best what is closest to them, "their own profit [*intérêt*] is always what they see most clearly. Justice raises her voice, but she has trouble being heard amid the tumult of passions" (letter LXXXIII).

Self-interest, the tumult of passions, finally, is what distinguishes man from God, just as the sense of justice distinguishes man from the lower beings. It is man's plight, his greatness and his freedom, to be able to see

the just, as only God and the angels do, but to have that view always
obstructed by the passions and interests of his mortal being. And that
mortal being is Usbek himself, who expresses both the joy and the
frustration he feels as a man in the closing paragraph of letter LXXXIII.
"When a man performs a self-examination, what satisfaction for him to
realize that he has a just heart! This pleasure, sober as it may be, must
delight him. He finds that his being is elevated as much above those
without one as he is elevated above tigers and bears. Yes, Rhédi, if I were
sure of always following inviolably that equity which I have before my
eyes, I should think myself the foremost among men."

Usbek can now say that he knows what justice is, both as it is innately
felt and as it is objectively defined. Knowing justice and acting justly are
two very different things, however, as the last sentence of letter LXXXIII
made clear. On an individual level, passions and interests were said to
keep people from acting at all times justly. But the competition that
justice faces comes not only from the individual; there are also social
structures that are, from the individual's point of view, alternative bases
of action. In the next few letters in which justice appears it is discussed
always in connection with another system of judgment and action that
has been instituted in human societies. In each case, it is shown to be
impossible for the competing system to coexist with justice, unless it be
made subordinate to justice as the only truly universal basis of human
judgment and action. In the last of these cases (letter XCV), justice is itself
the subject of the letter. The discussion of justice leads to a final letter of
this group (letter XCVIII), which allows the reader to test the definition of
a system of justice built up in the preceding letters as a means of evaluating a particular French institution that bears the name of "justice."

"It would appear that families are a government unto themselves,"
writes Rica to *** in letter LXXXVI. "The husband has only a shade of
authority over his wife; the father, over his children; the master, over his
slaves. Justice becomes involved in all their differences of opinion, and
you may be sure that it is always against the jealous husband, the sullen
father, the importunate master." Rica here contrasts the absolute authority of the domestic despot in Persia with the limitation of domestic
authority by the civil authority in France. In France, the public system of
justice is not locked outside the private system of the family, but has
authority over it. Public and private are not mutually exclusive spheres,
each with its own code of judgment and action.

The family is the first of the social structures shown to enjoy a private
authority over its members that can compete with a public system based
on justice as Usbek defined it. What is important here is not whether an
existing legal system is based upon justice but whether a system must be

generally applicable if it is to be just. For a system to be just, it must not simply be a code of just laws, but must be structurally just, that is, public and applicable generally and equitably. All private codes must thus fall under its jurisdiction or be superseded by it. The notion of a private sphere includes all the particularistic corps of which which French society was composed. The nobility, with its code of honor, is the next of these particularistic bodies to be examined.

"In times past, Frenchmen, particularly the nobles, followed practically no other laws save those of this point of honor," Ibben learns from Usbek. "They patterned the conduct of their whole life on these laws, which were so severe that it was impossible, without punishment crueler than death—I do not say to violate them—but even to evade their very slightest intention" (letter xc). The trouble with the code of honor, according to Usbek, was that justice was not served by it. Thus, duels have been strictly forbidden by the monarchy, but to no avail: "Honor, always eager to reign, revolts and recognizes no law." The result is that two competing codes of behavior are in operation simultaneously. Those subject to both have the choice of losing either their life or their honor each time they enter into a dispute that must be resolved. As in the case of the family, the public system of justice is shown to have authority over the private code of honor, but the dilemma with which the letter ends shows that this authority is itself limited by public opinion.

> Thus Frenchmen are in a most extraordinary fix: the laws of honor oblige a gentleman to avenge himself when he has been offended, but, on the other hand, justice punishes him in the most cruel fashion for avenging himself. If one follows the laws of honor, he will die on the scaffold; if he follows the laws of justice, he is banished forever from the society of men. Thus, there remains only this cruel alternative: either to die, or to become unworthy of living. [Letter xc]

A second private system is thus added to that of the family, and both are seen to compete with the public system of justice. The major lesson of this letter is the difficulty of overriding the power of such traditional codes as that of honor, which are rooted in the particular interests that define the corporative groups of traditional society.[11]

---

[11]The elimination of dueling and the code that it represented was central to the absolutist program. Richelieu, in fact, devotes a section of his *Testament politique* to this problem. If, as Mousnier argues, Louis xiv attempted to coopt *fidélité*, Richelieu advocated a similar cooptation of *honneur* through identifying it with public service. See [Armand-Jean du Plessis], cardinal de Richelieu, *Testament politique* (Amsterdam, 1709), pp. 158–64.

Authority is the theme of letter xcii from Usbek to Rhédi, which announces the death of Louis xiv. With the dominating presence of the Sun King gone, a five-year-old successor and a regent are put in his place and out of the shadows come the old *parlements*, themselves shadows of their former selves, as Usbek describes them: "The *parlements* resemble ruins that are kicked about underfoot but that ever recall the idea of some famous temple celebrated by the ancient religion of nations. They perform practically no function now other than to administer justice, and their authority will go on steadily declining unless some unforeseen set of circumstances arrives to resuscitate their strength and life." The one recognized function left the *parlements*, even under the absolute rule of Louis xiv, is the rendering of justice. Problems arise (and did arise), however, when the king and the *parlements* disagree in their competing administrations of justice. No longer is it assumed, as in the two previous cases, that one public authority—the monarchy—is the responsible interpreter of justice.

The question here is not of the laws of the state superseding those of traditional social bodies (the family, the nobility) but of reconciling two legitimate judicial authorities: the monarchy and the *parlements*. And this reconciliation, as Usbek attributes it to the first actions of the regent upon taking office, consists in defining the relationship between monarchy and *parlements* in terms of legitimate authority. "But the Regent," he explains, "who wanted to make himself liked by the people, appeared at first to respect this image of public freedom, and as if he had counted upon reerecting both temple and idol after their fall, he wanted the *parlements* to be considered as the support of monarchy and the basis of all legitimate authority."[12] The question of which institution, the monarchy or the *parlements*, is the official seat of justice is reconciled by the requirement that legitimate authority rest upon them jointly. The definition of a system of justice being built in this portion of the *Lettres persanes* now reads: a system that is public and generally applicable, and whose authority is legitimate when responsibility for it is shared jointly by the king and representative bodies.

Letters xciv and xcv focus on the monarchy and the *droit public*, the law of princes or nations. Once again, two systems of human action are opposed and this duality is presented as untenable. "One might say, Rhédi, that there exist two quite different justices; one that regulates individual affairs and that reigns in civil affairs; another that settles differences between nation and nation and that tyrannizes over public

---

[12]The reference here, as Vernière notes, is to the *parlements'* right of remonstrance, which Louis xiv had suppressed and the regent had reinstated: *Lettres persanes*, p. 191, n. 2.

law—as if public law were not itself a form of civil law, not, in truth, of a particular country, but of the world" (letter xciv). Usbek can proclaim the absurdity of there being two different justices because he has already established the universality of the one justice. If civil and international law do not agree, one (or both) must be contrary to justice, since justice must be one. Usbek finds that in Europe princes are taught to believe that there are two different systems and that justice is only a necessary basis of the domestic one. Of the other he writes, "such as it exists today, [it] is a science that teaches princes just how far they can violate justice without jeopardizing their own interests" (letter xciv).[13] Justice cannot be bent to serve other interests, argues Usbek, just as it cannot be doubled to allow for two systems, both called "justice," but based on conflicting principles. In addition to its other qualities, then, a system of justice must be absolute in reference to all other aims, and it must be universal, such that all systems of justice are in fact one.

In letter xcv, Usbek continues his thoughts on the relationship between domestic and international law. "Magistrates," he writes, "should administer justice between citizen and citizen. Each nation should administer justice between itself and another nation. In this second meting out of justice, no other principles can be used save those obtaining in the first." Unlike differences between individuals, he argues, those between nations are usually easy to resolve since the interests of two nations are in most cases so distinct that anyone who wishes to act justly can do so. A third party, an institution whose function is to administer justice in resolving disputes, is necessary only within a society, where the interests of the parties involved are all tangled up with one another. To prove his point that the just course is easily found in differences between nations, Usbek then proceeds to enumerate acts of justice in international relations, from the just war to the renunciation of an unjust alliance.

In a sense, letter xcv is a reprise of the Troglodyte fable. Once again, one need only want to act justly in order to do so; there is no need of an institutionalized system of justice to resolve disputes between parties in conflict. In this case, however, natural, spontaneous justice is restricted to the sphere of international relations, while the need for a third party to resolve domestic disputes is affirmed. Although Usbek's conception of the state of nature is in direct opposition to that of Hobbes, the two theorists do agree that such a state persists between nations even after it has given way to political organization domestically. Just as the

---

[13]The reference to Machiavelli is obvious, as Vernière points out (*Lettres persanes*, p. 194, n. 2). He rightly finds a similar attack in the *Traité des devoirs*: ". . . Nothing is more shocking to justice than what is usually called politics, that science of ruse and artifice": *Oeuvres complètes*, p. 182.

Troglodyte state of nature is one of natural justice rather than of war, so too can nations maintain just relations amongst themselves. And it is because justice is universally knowable through reason that all leaders of nations can know it when, as is usually the case, their view is not obscured by complex and hidden interests. "Here, my dear Rhédi, you have what I call public law. Here you have international law, or rather, the law of reason" (letter xcv).

The definition of a system of justice is now complete. It is a single, public, generally applicable system whose authority is legitimate when responsibility is shared jointly by the king and representative bodies, and it is absolute with respect to all other codes, interests, and aims. It functions properly in the resolution of disputes between members of a particular society. Although its jurisdiction does not extend to disputes between nations, its principles can in no way conflict with those of international law, since both are based upon a single universal justice that is accessible to all men through their reason. The system of justice thus defined is the embodiment of the abstract definition of justice built up in the first part of the *Lettres persanes* and stated in letter LXXXIII. It must be seen too as a description of a specifically French system of justice, since it is clearly a theoretical transformation of French political institutions.

Because the reader now knows not only what justice is in the abstract but how it can be instantiated as a system of justice, he is now able to evaluate those existent institutions that lay some claim to being a part of a system of justice. In letter xcviii, Usbek presents the reader with the opportunity to make such an evaluation of an institution recently established by France's regent. "A tribunal has just been established; it is known as the chamber *of justice* because it is about to take away all their wealth." Clearly, this is not a proper reason for calling something "of justice"; the point here is that Usbek, and with him the reader, now has the analytical tools to determine whether the institution referred to ought to bear the name.

Usbek's inquiry into justice (helped occasionally by Rica) has been extremely methodical up to this point. After establishing the innate sense of justice in the Troglodyte fable, he then moved on to prove that justice is prior to all human institutions and, at the same time, showed that those institutions that ought to support or embody justice often act against it: the critique of social institutions and the definition of abstract justice went hand in hand. This phase of the inquiry ended in the definition of justice in letter LXXXIII. The next phase of the inquiry then set out to define the components necessary to and the parameters of justice as a social institution whose function is to resolve differences, to mediate disputes. This second process of definition was carried out by aligning the system of justice with a single option in each of a series of polarities representing competing systems upon which human action is or can be based. The result was a composite of definitional components that could be used as a basis for evaluating the existing French system "of justice," to see whether it merits the name, as demonstrated in letter XCVIII. One would expect that the next step would be to embark on a methodical project of analyzing and evaluating the entire system of French justice, or even a comparative evaluation of French and Persian systems based upon the definitions of abstract justice and of the structure of justice as a social institution. Such a project is begun in letter XCVIII, but it is immediately abandoned, and the reader must surely ask why, just as he necessarily sought the extension of the inquiry into fidelity in the sphere of politics. Why, for example, does Usbek, who wrote sixteen of the first nineteen letters on justice, write only three of the last eight?

Although one can only guess why Usbek stops his inquiry into justice so abruptly at this point, it seems probable that, as in the case of fidelity, developments in the harem have something to do with it. Letter XCVIII is the last letter on justice that Usbek writes before receiving the first crisis letter from the harem (CXLVII). Were that letter in its proper place chronologically, it would be between letters CIV and CV; Usbek's next mention of justice is in letter CXIX. Of Usbek's last three references to justice, two appear in the series on depopulation (letters CXIX and CXXI) and neither adds anything to our knowledge of justice or to Usbek's critique of the French or Persian systems of justice. (The first refers to "the unjust right of the eldest son among the Europeans, a right unfavorable to propagation," and the other to a purely fatalistic notion of divine justice that might imply the futility of Usbek's efforts in developing a theory of justice.) Instead of being the subject of a methodical investigation, justice is of merely occasional importance here in the examination of the more neutral problem of the depopulation of the world. I say more neutral because the problem of justice and its systematization in human institutions becomes extremely personal for Usbek when he takes up again his political role as despot of the harem.

Only in the last letter he writes (CXLVI) does Usbek seem painfully to consider justice again, and by then it is perhaps too late, since the harem, as the reader will soon find out, has already fallen into ruin. For the crisis in the harem is Usbek's opportunity to utilize the principles of justice, not simply as a critique of an existing system but as they are meant to be used: as a means of resolving disputes and of ordering society. Instead of transforming the practical project inaugurated in letter XCVIII into a different kind of practice by turning it away from France and onto the harem, Usbek drops it altogether. He is unable or unwilling to turn from theory to practice, from criticism to action for political change.

In the letters of Rica and Rhédi, which take up the question that Usbek has left off, Montesquieu the compiler makes clear to the reader that this is indeed Usbek's opportunity to act upon his newly acquired knowledge of justice. Usbek is even given the chance to see himself and his fading opportunity in two of these letters, since they are addressed to him. And the "justice" letters that follow Usbek's receipt of letter CXLVII from the Grand Eunuch are really "injustice" letters, since it is in the negative that the term generally appears. When Rica uses the positive form, it is in a satirical letter (CXXXII). As satire, the letter serves to negate the term by showing the absurdity of attaching the name "justice" to a court system that, in this case, is shown to be so costly as to be useless. It is also significant that in this letter and in Rica's letter c to Rhédi, the term *accabler* appears in conjunction with *justice*: in letter c, justice itself is overwhelmed by an overabundance of laws; in letter CXXXII, Rica's French acquaintance speaks of the futility of trying to collect the rents he is owed because, as he says, "Try as I may to push my farmers and weigh them down [*accabler*] with costs of lawsuits, I manage only to make them less solvent." The notion of competition that emerged from Usbek's analysis of justice gives way here to the sense of being overwhelmed, of losing the battle.

In letter cv, as well, this sense of being overwhelmed comes through, as Rhédi writes to Usbek: "You know that since the invention of gunpowder, there is no impregnable city, which is to say, Usbek, that there is no asylum on earth against violence and injustice." Similarly, in letter CVII, Rica reports that within France injustice is pervasive: "there is nobody with some post at court in Paris, or in the provinces, who hasn't some woman through whose hands he dispenses all the favors and sometimes all the injustices of which he is capable." In letter CXXXI, Rhédi locates injustice in the ancient Roman republic. Injustice is not simply a problem of the Orient or of its despotic organization; it is neither a geographical problem nor a historical problem, though geography and history can explain the particular injustices that plague individual societies. Justice being itself universal, injustice cannot be written off as simply a local problem, particular to one time or place. To recognize it, know it, and eradicate it requires the type of critical, metaphysical and analytical approach that Usbek had been refining. But to this philosophical analysis must be added the willingness to look for injustice everywhere, especially in the work of one's own hands. With the desire to know justice in general must go the will to face injustice in all its particular manifestations: any action to bring about change, to eliminate injustice and institute justice, depends upon this mediating step of converting the general to the particular. It is this step that Usbek fails to take.

There is no place left on earth safe from injustice, Rhédi has written, and so it is in a fantasy fable introduced as a travesty that injustice is vanquished in the *Lettres persanes*. We encountered the theme of travesty, which runs through the text, first in letter III, where the eunuch was seen to play the master travestied as the wife in obeying both their wills. The first explicit reference to travesty is in Usbek's letter XCI to Rustan. Here Usbek reports on the appearance in Paris of "a person disguised [*travesti*] as an ambassador of Persia." In letter CXLI, Rica explains to Usbek that he has translated a story from the Persian at the request of a lady of the French court. "This I did, and several days later I sent her a Persian tale. Maybe you will be glad to see it travestied." And the story travestied is itself the story of a travesty, for it is a woman's dream of paradise as the reversal of the world below, a travesty of the lived world where men take the woman's role, and women the man's. Moreover, the *Lettres persanes* as a whole, particularly Rica's series of letters on his visit to a Parisian library (letters CXXXIII–CXXXVII) can be read as a travesty of France and its learning, which Usbek had naively sought at the beginning of his journey. For travesty, according to the *Encyclopédie*, "is used . . . in reference to an author whom one has disfigured by translating him into a burlesque style, different from his own, such that one has great difficulty in recognizing him."[14]

If, as Vernière argues, Rica is touring Montesquieu's own library in letters CXXXIII–CXXXVII, presenting to the reader a catalog of the library of La Brède at the moment when its owner was beginning an inventory of it in 1720, then this series serves as an elaborate footnote to the text, giving its references.[15] At the same time, however, the *Lettres persanes* appears as a travesty of these same sources, as a translation of them into a burlesque style that makes them almost unrecognizable. If Rica's trip to the French library travesties Usbek's search for knowledge in the library of France, the *Lettres persanes* as a whole travesties the library that Rica exposes. And Western learning is travestied yet again when it is translated from the realm of knowledge to that of cure in the recipes attached to letter CXLIII.

In letter CXLI, Rica recounts the story of Anaïs and Ibrahim, in which paradise is revealed to be a place where sex roles are reversed and a

---

[14]*Encyclopédie*, 16:572.
[15]*Lettres persanes*, p. 283, n. 1.

virtuous woman's fantasy of instituting justice in the harem is realized.[16] In the tale, Anaïs sees her only escape from the oppression of the harem in death, and so, taking her own life, she arrives in a paradise where, for more than a week, she immerses herself in sensual pleasure. "But Anaïs, whose mind was truly philosophic, had passed almost her whole life in meditation. . . . It was that force of mind that had made her scorn both the fear that obsessed her companions, and death, which was to signal the end of her troubles and the beginning of her felicity." Because Anaïs was not only virtuous in life but wise and learned as well, a philosophical compassion for her old companions leads her away from "the intoxication of her pleasures" and into action to right the wrong situation of the harem she has escaped. One of Anaïs's heavenly lovers is sent to earth in the image of her old husband, Ibrahim. When the wives have to decide which is their real husband, they choose the false but good one because, as they put it: "If you are not Ibrahim, it is enough for us that you have so well deserved to be. You are more Ibrahim in one day than he has been in ten whole years." And so they swear fidelity to the new Ibrahim.

In swearing fidelity, however, the wives reveal (to the new Ibrahim, to Usbek the reader, and to Montesquieu's reader) that the change in Ibrahim is still simply a change in masters, since the relationship between wives and husband is still that of fidelity. When the new Ibrahim tells them that they do not even know all the wrong that has been done them, they reply: "We judge [the true Ibrahim's] injustice by the magnitude of your vengeance." Knowing nothing else but despotism, they can measure justice only in terms of vengeance, a word from the despotic lexicon. They are virtuous, but unlike Anaïs, they are naive, unlearned, ignorant of ways of thought and life different from the despotic. The tale thus does not end with a simple changing of masters. When the new Ibrahim is absent chasing away his predecessor, the old despotic order returns, commanded by the middle men whose only function in life is to perpetuate it. And so the first act of the new master on his return is to get rid of the eunuchs. Further reforms follow, and it is these reforms rather than the simple change from an evil to a good master that make possible the happy ending to the tale.

Letter cxli, in which the story of Anaïs and Ibrahim is enclosed, is as complex in its relationship to the rest of the *Lettres persanes* as is Usbek's letter viii with its explanation of his flight to the West. I will not here attempt a full analysis of letter cxli, although it deserves one, but will

[16]Sex roles in this case are, of course, also roles in a power relationship, since in the *Lettres persanes* the relationship between men and women in marriage is shown to be not only that between husband and wife but also that between master and slave and between ruler and subject. The story of Anaïs and Ibrahim brings this point out most clearly.

limit myself to its position and implications relative to the problem of justice and the system of fidelities. In this context, the letter serves as a premonition of Roxane's suicide and the collapse of Usbek's harem, which that suicide symbolizes, and, more important, as a vision of what Usbek might do to avoid that outcome. The happy ending of the tale of Anaïs and Ibrahim is the alternative to the tragic ending of the story of Roxane and Usbek.

Anaïs, in fact, represents both Roxane and Usbek, for she is both the virtuous and wise victim of despotism and, travestied as the new Ibrahim, the virtuous and wise enlightened master who reforms that despotism. And this transformation from victim to reformer, it should be remembered, is dependent upon the philosophical spirit shared by Anaïs and Usbek (and, perhaps, by Roxane, but neither Usbek nor the reader can know this yet). It is as Usbek, then, rather than as Roxane that Anaïs is important to the question of justice. Or rather, it is Anaïs as Ibrahim as Usbek who is important. After reflection, in which she is equivalent to Usbek, Anaïs's first act toward righting the wrongs of Ibrahim's harem is to send away the false Ibrahim; that is, to translate, to transform a bad master into a good one. As in the fable of the Troglodytes, good and bad are here shown simply to be qualities of individuals. Bad Troglodytes destroyed themselves, however, while the bad Ibrahim is replaced by a good Ibrahim through the good will of Anaïs. Bad Troglodytes and good Troglodytes, that is, were mutually exclusive categories, while Anaïs, the new Ibrahim, and the old Ibrahim can be read simply as transformations of the same person, made possible through virtue and wisdom. Usbek, as a model for both Anaïs and the old despotic Ibrahim, can transform himself into the new, enlightened reformed Ibrahim. The transition from thought to action or from reflection to reform is dependent upon Usbek/Anaïs's realizing that he is also Usbek/Ibrahim and effecting the transition as the new Ibrahim.

The problem of reform only begins with this first step. Just being good is not enough if the system itself is corrupt and despotic. Usbek claimed to have learned this lesson in letter viii; it is the lesson learned always by victims, as the suicides of Anaïs and Roxane reveal. As this investigation into the meaning of justice and the obstacles that hinder just actions has shown, however, being virtuous also does not ensure that one is able to recognize and know justice or to act justly. As the example of Ibrahim's wives demonstrates, knowledge of the just cannot be acquired within the linguistic and institutional confines of a despotic system. Unless that system is changed structurally, the victims can do nothing but swear their personal fidelity to a new master. And since that new master is just the old master transformed by goodness, nothing has really changed except his expressed will to be good. As in Usbek's own case, the absence of the master demonstrates that the despotic system rather than the despot is the real oppressor. The personal assurances of the master, which are the complement of the personal fidelity sworn by his wives, are effective only as long as there is direct personal contact: the absence of the master is the absence of all rulers who cannot rule directly and personally. It is in the gap created by this absence that laws must be instituted to ensure the equity that must govern all relationships: justice. In the place of eunuchs, who are a direct substitute for personal rule, there must be a form of rule that is not dependent upon the personal assurance and presence of a good man. In place of fidelity between men of honor there must be justice embodied in law.

To a great extent, these are, of course, my own conclusions about fidelity, justice, and law, but they are my conclusions as the reader of the *Lettres persanes*. Ibrahim, even the new Ibrahim, is no legislator. His polity, which consists of himself and eleven wives, needs only to be released from the constraints of despotic walls and veils for its members to be free. A larger and more complex society, like that of eighteenth-century France, requires social institutions to ensure the freedom that depends upon justice. Usbek himself reveals that need as early as the last Troglodyte letter and continues to develop his thinking on what the properties of such institutions ought to be in the letters that immediately follow the definition of justice (letter LXXXIII).

The lesson of the tale of Anaïs and Ibrahim, a timely lesson that Usbek does not learn, is that the reform of an unjust system requires three major transformations: of the philosopher into an agent of change in his own society; of a bad into a good ruler; and of the institutional structure, of the system itself. Where the story of Anaïs and Ibrahim leaves off is precisely at the point where, were the polity as large and as complex as France, Usbek's analysis of the properties of just social institutions would become relevant. Were the polity France rather than a harem of twelve, the first and last transformations would entail a knowledge both of justice and of just institutions and the application of that knowledge to this concrete, particular society. It is up to the reader to make the connection and in so doing to effect his own transformation of the written text into one that is only implied.

The last of Montesquieu's Persian letters in which the term *justice* figures is the last letter that Usbek or anyone else writes. In it there is no sign that Usbek has any awareness of the transformation required of him as the Anaïs and Ibrahim of his own harem. The subject of this letter (CXLVI, to Rhédi), in fact, is neither the philosopher, nor the monarch, nor the victimized subject; rather, it is the minister. Further, Usbek's theme is the responsibility of the minister. If Usbek is expressing a personal uneasiness in this letter, it is not as despot of the harem but as minister of the court of Ispahan in self-imposed exile. It is the Usbek of letter VIII who fled a corrupt court, disillusioned, in a half-hearted search for knowledge, who speaks again here to close the story of his voyage. This is the Usbek who defines himself politically and who sees virtue as the activity of the responsible member of the polity, the Usbek who, in his frustration with the unstable conditions of power and language, expressed the need for a transcendent principle that would stabilize rhetorical relations between human beings.

The Usbek who recounted the fable of the Troglodytes is also present in letter CXLVI, for here the first responsibility of a minister is to be a good example to both prince and people. The minister, unlike the private citizen, is always in the public spotlight: "An individual can enjoy fully the obscurity of his position; he can lose face only with a few people. He dissimulates [se tient couvert] before others. But a minister who lacks integrity [probité] has as many witnesses and judges as there are people governed by him." The example that the minister must provide is based in his own transparency. For he is neither opaque to those who view him nor lacking in the probity that sees through all the passions and interests of men to the principle that ought to govern all human action. That principle, of course, is justice, which can now be recognized as the transcendent principle that stabilizes all human relations, linguistic and political. The transparency of the minister is such that those above and below him—the monarch and the people—do not see him, but see through him the principle of justice. To be an example is, after all, to be seen through, while probity is the capacity to see through—both examples and masks. If the minister, in his words and his deeds, represents without distortion the principle of justice, then he has achieved the ideal of sincerity posited by Usbek in letter VIII. And so transparency, the unobstructed view, does not require a highest tower or mountain peak, as Starobinski argues;[17] rather the responsible minister stands in the very thick of things, transforming obscurity into transparency through his probity and his example.

Letter CXLVI itself provides an example that must be seen through, for in it Usbek discusses a nation he once visited in the Indies, "a nation, noble by nature, perverted in the flashing of an eye, from the lowliest of her subjects right up to the greatest, and by the bad example of a minister." In this country, Usbek saw a people known for their natural generosity, probity, candor, and good faith transformed into "the basest

---

[17]Starobinski, Introduction to *Montesquieu par lui-même*, pp. 35–39.

of nations." He saw, he continues, "the most virtuous of men do shameful things and violate the prime principles of justice on the vain pretext that they had been first violated to their detriment by others."

Like the example of a good minister, the example of this unnamed country must be seen through to the France that it reveals. And Usbek the teller of the tale must be seen through as well, because behind the mask of Usbek is revealed his creator, Montesquieu. This second revelation must take place and must lead to a third, as behind Rhédi, the reader of the letter, are revealed the external readers of the *Lettres persanes*. The revelation/transformation of writer and reader must take place, because only then does the revelation of France behind the Indian example make any sense: Usbek has no reason to use the Indies as a figure for France when he writes to Rhédi; only between "Frenchmen" can the example become transparent, since only "Frenchmen" could know that which stands behind the example, waiting to be revealed: the contemporary French finance minister, John Law, and the catastrophic effects of his monetary system. I put "Frenchmen" in quotation marks because anyone who shares the knowledge of Montesquieu and his French contemporaries can recognize France behind the anonymous nation and Law behind the anonymous minister.

Rhetorical possibility and rhetorical intention must not be confused, however, since even though Americans of the twentieth century can interpret the example, see its meaning, we are not the primary objects of its intention. This distinction is extremely important because in it lie the different responses that can result from the reading of this letter: any "Frenchman" can understand it, but only a contemporary Frenchman can act upon it. An understanding of the concrete particulars that stand behind the example makes possible its interpretation; only a participation in that particularity, a participation that defines the reader as particularly so, makes possible action upon it. For that action, any action, depends not simply upon understanding but upon participation in a particular and concrete situation.

Rhetoric, which in Montesquieu's own time had been narrowed to the study of figures, functions fully in letter CXLVII: the interpretation of the figure does not simply produce aesthetic pleasure (although it does that too); more important, it leads to action in the world. But it does so only if the reader recognizes the particular world revealed by and behind the figured example as his own. The story of Anaïs and Ibrahim was also an example, a figure presented to Usbek, behind which stood his own world, his own harem. There it was also Montesquieu, rather than the writer of the letter (Rica), whose rhetorical intention directed the letter, but it was still Usbek, and not the outside reader, who was the direct object of that intention. Toward the outside reader, Montesquieu (the implied author of the letters and their compiler) had yet a second level of intention: to use Usbek's failure to act on the example of the story as itself an example behind which stood, once again, contemporary France.

As this case makes especially clear, the rhetorical situation of Montesquieu and the implied outside reader is established both within each letter and between letters. Usbek's failure to act upon the example is not located within the story of Anaïs and Ibrahim (letter CXLI) but in the connection between that letter and those by means of which Usbek's harem collapses (letters CXLVIII–CLXI). That connection is part of the network created jointly by the compiler of the letters and the outside reader. As Rousset argues, the primary role of the writer of an epistolary novel is not to narrate but to compile or compose.

> Here, the event is the words themselves and the effect to be produced by means of these words; it is the manner in which they are said, then read and interpreted; the event is also the exchange and the disposition of the letters, the order given to items in the file. . . . Thus, the author, who seems to disappear because he no longer narrates, because he leaves the talking to his characters, the author takes his revenge as arranger and composer; if he effaces himself as writer and narrator, he appears in broad daylight as an author in the strongest sense of the term, as he who makes the book, who gives it its form and its order . . .; the novelist ceases to be a narrator apparently subjected to the facts he narrates, in order to be promoted to author, that is to say, master of the work.[18]

Usbek's failure lies in his inability and his unwillingness to recognize his own harem behind that of Ibrahim; the failure of Montesquieu's readers would lie in the same inability and unwillingness to recognize their world behind that of the anonymous nation of letter CXLVI, and behind the *Lettres persanes* as a whole. As men of reason they can follow and accept the elaboration of the abstract principle of justice, the need for it as a transcendent, universal principle capable of guiding human action, and even the characteristics definitive of a system of justice. This acceptance, however, is only a first step. The readers of the *Lettres persanes* must recognize themselves and their world behind the many examples of which the text is composed in order to act upon their knowledge of universal principles and general properties. They must recognize themselves in those who "called forth odious laws as guaranty of the most cowardly actions and gave to injustice and perfidy the name of *necessity*" (letter CXLVI). It is they who have read this far and thus know that

---

[18]Rousset, *Forme et signification*, p. 72.

nothing can be put above justice, they who wrongly—and now know-
ingly—call injustice a necessity.

What exactly is the reader being asked to do? That is, what is he being
asked to do outside the book in that concrete world behind the example,
the France in which he lives? For one thing, he is being asked to act
upon the principle of justice that he has learned and to put nothing above
it: he is asked to be a just man and to act justly, or to transform himself
from the old to a new Ibrahim. That he can and must do, because he is a
human being. To the extent that he identifies with Usbek the minister,
as a public person, the reader is also asked to take responsibility for his
actions in their effect on the nation as a whole. Only the reader who
identifies himself with Usbek the despot, however, is asked to reform the
laws and institutions of his society. Since the harem is both a public and a
private social system, the reader can perhaps implement limited reforms
in his household, but even here the reforms must be limited by the extent
to which the greater structure of society controls marriage and other
seemingly private relationships. And, since the private is simply one
aspect of the social whole, instituting a just order in the household will
simply bring it into conflict with the greater order in which its members
participate. Once again, the problem lies in competing systems. In the
end, even if the reader were the king of France, there is nothing he alone
could do to establish the principles of justice as the basis of society, for he
would also have to be the Church and the *parlements*, and perhaps public
opinion as well. The interrelatedness of all aspects of society, so graph-
ically manifested in the *Lettres persanes*, prevents any one individual, any
single reader, from doing anything to reform it. By directing his critical
attention away from the monarch and to the constitution of society,
Montesquieu has stymied any possibility of reform arising out of his
criticism.

Certainly a bad minister can do much to undermine and pervert a
nation, but what can a good minister do? In the principle of justice
Usbek has found the transcendent absolute that can stabilize society and
its discourse. His travels in the West and his travels as metaphor for
philosophical reflection have allowed him to solve the semiotic problem
posed in letter viii; the rhetorical problem, however, remains. The reader, the minister, the enlightened man of learning and good will, has no
more power to affect society than did Usbek in the corrupt court of
Ispahan. What makes this impotence all the more frustrating is that the
reader, like Usbek, like Montesquieu, now knows the proper basis for
society (justice), its definition, and the properties necessary to institute it.
It is this impotence that has caused some modern readers to argue that
the French nobility, with which Montesquieu as president of the *parle-*

ment of Bordeaux identifies himself, is instantiated most boldly in the eunuchs of Usbek's harem.[19]

Knowledge is not power, and sincerity or good will is not action. If these are the tools at the reader's disposal, then he will not be able to rebuild the structure of society, to refashion social institutions on sound principles. Not only Usbek but Montesquieu as well has failed to bridge the gap between knowledge and action, criticism and change. The basis of this impotence can be found embedded in the epistolary form of the *Lettres persanes*, whose unity is based not on narrative development but thematic echoes, parallels, and antitheses.[20] The complex network of relations created by Montesquieu imposes a static image of the society that he criticizes and would like to change—or, perhaps, would simply like to have be different than it is. This network and this static image are the effects created by the use of the polyphonic form of the epistolary novel, which Montesquieu invented.[21] The full potential of the epistolary genre capitalizes upon the correspondence as a network of relations, but this development forces the epistolary text out of the linearity of the univocal model, the seventeenth-century *Lettres portugaises* and its followers. The overriding static effect of the polyphonic form results from an emphasis on the relationships displayed in and created by the correspondence as a whole, rather than on the dynamics of the action narrated from letter to letter.

To Montesquieu's choice—or, rather, to his creation—of the polyphonic form is attributable much of the literary greatness of the *Lettres persanes*. This same form, however, projects the impotence of the critic, his inability to change that which he criticizes. For although change does in fact occur in the *Lettres persanes*, notably in the collapse of the harem, in the ideas of Usbek and the other expatriate Persians, and in France as Louis xiv dies and the regent takes over, it is overshadowed by the superhuman, complex structures that the individual has no power to affect. Thus, although Usbek's perception of what a society is and how it ought to be structured changes greatly in the course of his travels, his helplessness relative to society does not. The changes that occur in

---

[19]See, e.g., J. L. Carr, "The Secret Chain of the *Lettres persanes*," *Studies on Voltaire and the Eighteenth Century* 55 (1967):337, and Aram Vartanian, "Eroticism and Politics in the *Lettres persanes*," *Romanic Review* 60 (February 1969): 32. For a discussion of the thematic importance of the eunuch in the *Lettres persanes* see Roger Kempf, "Les *Lettres persanes*, ou le corps absent," *Tel Quel*, no. 22 (1963), pp. 81–86, and Michel Delon, "Un Monde d'eunuques," *Europe*, no. 574 (1977), pp. 79–88.

[20]Patrick Brady, "The *Lettres persanes*: Rococo or Neoclassical?" *Studies on Voltaire and the Eighteenth Century* 53 (1967): 66.

[21]Versini, *Laclos et la tradition*, pp. 272–74.

Usbek's harem are actual changes, but the collapse is due to the internal mechanisms of the harem itself, its inherent structural instability in the absence of the master. The final act recounted in the *Lettres*, Roxane's suicide, is testimony to the impotence of the subject individual in and upon the social system, as well as of Usbek's blindness as ruler of such a system. In fact, both "final" letters of the *Lettres persanes*—Usbek's letter CXLVI on ministers, which is written last, and Roxane's suicide note, with which the text ends—assert the closed circularity of the text on the level of the individual's effect on the social system of which he is a member and a victim. As letter CXLVI restates the apolitical ideal of ministerial transparency from letter VIII, so does Roxane's letter CLXI reenact Usbek's flight from the sociopolitical system of Persia recounted in that letter. Whether the individual is inside or outside that system, he is powerless to affect it. The elaborate, complex social systems, the images of which were constructed out of the very web of epistolary exchanges, remain impervious to the critic whose power is limited to the generation and manipulation of these multiple images of them.

PART II

ROUSSEAU

Posing Criticism Historically

CHAPTER FOUR

Chance and Necessity

The question of the source of inequality among men, posed by the Academy of Dijon in 1754 as the topic of its annual prize-essay competition, provided Jean-Jacques Rousseau with an opportunity to formulate an overwhelming critique of modern society. For inequality, as presented in his *Discours sur l'inégalité* (*Second Discours*), becomes the defining feature of the social, political, and economic world in which he lives: to understand modern society is to understand it as a condition of inequality.

While Montesquieu had rejected the king as the subject and object of criticism, had seen the king as one player among many caught within the complex relational web that defined the constitution of French society, Rousseau went even further. His search for the source of inequality among men took him deep into the jungle of the past, further than anyone had gone before. Though he pushed back further, he did not, any more than Montesquieu, open a path for the reform of society. And in transforming criticism into a historical inquiry, Rousseau also deprived the reader of that critical activity which had at least made of him a fellow critic, if not in the end a reformer. Rousseau's achievement in the *Second Discours* was to reshape the constitutional criticism inaugurated by Montesquieu, taking it to radically new depths through the use of a narrative historical form and method, but in so doing to immobilize the reader still further, to make of the actively critical reader a passive spectator of the narrative of human history set before him.

Bronislaw Baczko has suggested that "the evolution of Enlightenment thought is shown in the multiplication of questions about 'origins' and

their progressive extension to the totality of social reality."[1] He argues
further that "the interrogation into 'origins' is equivalent to putting
[something] in question." In fact, he concludes, "the thinkers of the
period more or less identify the question of origins with the question of
the 'meaning' of the institution, or of the existent moral norm."[2] If it was
the aim of the Academy of Dijon to place in question the inequality
found in their society, only Rousseau extended this questioning to modern society as a whole, or "the totality of social reality." But if the
Academy sought as well the meaning of inequality, or the reason for its
existence (as the second part of the question concerning the relationship
between inequality and natural law would imply), in that Rousseau
disappointed them, for the form of his discourse demonstrates the lack of
meaning, of reasons, for the origin of inequality. In fact, what Rousseau
demonstrates in the *Second Discours* is that inequality—and the society
characterized by it—is the result of a meaningless combination of chance
events whose occurence goes against all reason.

Unlike the abbé Talbert, who won the Academy's prize in 1754,
Rousseau does not present the origin of inequality in history as the
manifestation of God's will, nor does he agree that the society of ranks
and orders is in accordance with the laws of nature.[3] Rather, it is because
Rousseau cannot accept the constitution of his society but does believe in
the inherent goodness of both man and God that he seeks to account for
the origin of inequality without assigning a cause for it. Rousseau finds
this type of explanation in a historical narrative that is activated by
neither the hand of God nor the will of man, but the blind working of
chance. Its explanatory power lies in the form of historical narrative, a
form that depends upon internal narrative coherence alone as its mode of
explanation, and on the hindsight of its historical perspective for generating the rhetorical conviction that it is true.

Rousseau's purpose in the *Second Discours* is not to demonstrate either

---

[1]Bronislaw Baczko, *Rousseau: Solitude et communauté*, trans. Claire Brendel-Lamhout
(Paris, 1974), p. 61. The actual wording of the question is: "Quelle est la source de
l'inégalité parmi les hommes et si elle est autorisée par la loi naturelle?" Rousseau
changes the word *source* to *origine* in his discourse, but there seems to be no significance
in the substitution. The *Dictionnaire* of 1694 gives as the relevant definition of the word
source: "figur. The principle, the cause, the origin, the first author of something, from
which something proceeds"; it defines *origine* as "principle or beginning of something":
DAF, 2:498, 160.

[2]Baczko, *Solitude et communauté*, p. 61.

[3]For this and nine other extant entries for the competition of 1754, see Roger
Tisserand, *Les Concurrents de J.-J. Rousseau à l'Académie de Dijon pour le prix de 1754*
(Paris, 1936). A tenth entry has recently been found at the Bibliothèque Municipale of
Bordeaux and is published by Charles Porset in "Discours d'un anonyme sur l'inégalité
1754," *Studies on Voltaire and the Eighteenth Century* 182 (1979): 7–27.

man's natural goodness or the evil character of modern men, since these are the premises that reason, in the first case, and experience, in the second, make obvious to him.[4] Instead, Rousseau explains how the conditions of man's existence have changed in order to account for the change in man. The moment of the change in man's condition is shown to be that of the origin of inequality, and the explanation of that origin is found in the blind workings of chance. But what follows the institution of inequality in property, in politics, and in social status is not the work of chance; rather, it is the working out of the tension inherent in the imbalance that the term *inequality* suggests.

The *Second Discours* goes beyond the limits of a response to the question posed by the Academy of Dijon. It begins at a point outside history where inequality cannot originate and extends not only past the moment when inequality is instituted but beyond history again and into the future. Although it has been suggested that in this way Rousseau is able to transcend the temporality of history and present a mythical past as the model for a mythical future, quite the reverse will be argued here. That is, although only the contingent events that lead from man's origins to the origin of inequality fall properly within the bounds of the historical narrative of the origin of inequality, Rousseau integrates the boundaries themselves into his narrative, and in this way he lends them historical credibility even as they ground the narrative in ahistorical logic. Put another way, Rousseau's "hypothetical history" is different from other histories because it is culled directly from life, not from the intermediary of documents (*SD*, p. 133; 103–4). As such, it is grounded in the atemporal (that is, ahistorical) facts that bound it: the natural goodness of man and the experienced or demonstrated evil of men. But by transforming these atemporal premises into the endpoints of a historical chronology, Rousseau historicizes them.

The implications of the historicizing of natural goodness and demonstrated evil go beyond the loss of the state of nature as a hope or a model for the future. Indeed, Rousseau extends his criticism of the present into the future by inserting a chain of logical deductions that constitutes the progress of inequality into the narrative historical framework and pushes it beyond the temporal limits of historical knowledge. Put another way, by answering the question of the origin of inequality with a historical narrative, Rousseau is able not only to avoid "the confrontation of con-

---

[4]Jean-Jacques Rousseau, "Discours sur l'origine et les fondements de l'inégalité parmi les hommes," in *Oeuvres complètes*, ed. Bernard Gagnebin and Marcel Raymond, 4 vols. (Paris, 1959–69), 3:202, n. IX. All further references to the *Second Discours* (*SD*) appear in the text, followed by the page reference to Jean-Jacques Rousseau's *The First and Second Discourses*, edited by Roger D. Masters and Judith R. Masters, copyright © 1964 by St. Martin's Press, Inc. Reprinted by permission of St. Martin's Press.

flicting truths" through a "temporal displacement"[5] but also to criticize the particular society of his time as a historical creation and to extend this critique into a prediction of even greater woes in the future. And thus he tells the reader in the preface to the *Second Discours* that he is unhappy in his present state "for reasons that foretell even greater discontents for your unhappy posterity" (*SD*, p. 133; 104).

The Formal Division of the Text

The form of historical narrative is crucial to an understanding of the *Second Discours*, and central to the historical narrative is the concept of chance. The following exposition begins with Rousseau's formal division of the body of the *Second Discours* into two parts. This initial division will be shown to break down, however, with a new dividing point signaled by a clear shift in modes of historical change from chance to necessity in the middle of part 2. Throughout the following discussion, the terms *necessity* and *contingency* will frequently appear. Although the meaning of *contingency* found in the *Discours* is consistent and definable, that of *necessity* is more complex. The necessity that characterizes the state of nature is different from the historical necessity that allows Rousseau to identify a particular sequence of events as leading to the origin of inequality; it is equally distinct from the necessary deductions that constitute the last portion of the text. To distinguish among these three types of necessity, and to place each in relation to historical contingency as Rousseau defines it, is also a task to be handled here.

The relationship between the state of nature described in part 1 of the text and the development that constitutes part 2 is thus the starting point of this discussion of the *Second Discours*. As the artificiality of the distinction between the two is exposed, however, the focus shifts to the actual mechanisms of change that bring man from the state of nature to the condition of inequality, and from there into the future. It will then be possible to rediscover the relationship between stasis and change, and that between contingent and necessary change, in the structure of the text.

Part 1

Rousseau begins part 1 of the *Second Discours* by defining where, between the animals and civilized man, he locates the original or natural

[5]John Spink, "Rousseau and the Problems of Composition," in *Reappraisals of Rousseau: Studies in Honour of R. A. Leigh*, ed. Simon Harvey et al. (Manchester, 1980), p. 168.

man of whom he will speak. He then goes on to describe in some detail
this primitive man, the life he leads, and the world he inhabits. Rousseau
discusses natural man first as a physical being, and second in his "moral
and metaphysical" aspects. In the latter context Rousseau distinguishes
man from other beings in two respects. First, man is a free agent to the
extent that he makes choices freely, whereas animals do so only by
instinct. The spirituality of the soul, Rousseau argues, is based in man's
consciousness of this liberty. The second, and definitive, quality that
distinguishes man from the animals is that which Rousseau terms "perfectibility." This is the faculty which, residing in man on the individual
and the species level, makes possible both biography and history. In
contrast, Rousseau points out, "an animal is at the end of a few months
what it will be all its life; and its species is at the end of a thousand years
what it was the first year of that thousand" (SD, p. 142; 114–15).

The introduction of the notion of perfectibility brings with it the first
wave of Rousseau's critique of modern society. Whereas up to this point
primitive man was contrasted with the beasts, Rousseau now compares
him to modern man. The result of this comparison is the central conundrum of the text: "Men are wicked; sad and continual experience spares
the need for proof. However, man is naturally good; I believe I have
demonstrated it" (SD, p. 202, n. ix;193, n. i). Perfectibility introduces the
possibility of change, of modern man's differing from primitive man; it
does not, however, make such change inevitable. In the next section of
this part of the Discours, in fact, Rousseau seeks to demonstrate the
extreme improbability of human development.

In one of the most rhetorically powerful passages of the text, Rousseau
expresses his inability to conceptualize the history that the reader has
taken for granted. "The more one meditates on this subject," he writes,
"the more the distance from pure sensations to the simplest knowledge
increases in our eyes; and it is impossible to conceive how a man, by his
strength alone, without the aid of communication and without the stimulus of necessity, could have bridged so great a gap" (SD, p. 144; 117–18).
What follows is a litany of wonderment couched almost entirely in the
interrogative. Question follows unanswerable question as Rousseau im-
presses upon the reader his own awe at the impossible accomplishments
of the human race. "How many centuries perhaps elapsed," he asks,
"before men were capable of seeing another fire than that from heaven?
How many different risks did they have to run to learn the most common uses of that element?" (SD, p. 144; 118). From the discovery of fire
Rousseau passes on to the development of agriculture, then pauses at
length over the problem of how language could have been invented
without society, or society developed without language.

Having demonstrated that "only after many centuries could man have had the desire and opportunity to leave [the state of nature]" (*SD*, p. 152; 127), Rousseau reasserts his argument that primitive man, a being without vices or virtues, could have been neither miserable, nor evil, nor good. At this point, in disputing Hobbes's claim that natural man, not being good, must be evil, Rousseau introduces the concept of *pitié*, "a natural sentiment which, moderating in each individual the activity of love of oneself, contributes to the mutual preservation of the entire species" (*SD*, p. 156; 132–33). This premoral sense, he argues, is the basis of all the virtues that develop in man only in society, such as generosity and goodwill. In contrast to *pitié*, Rousseau finds the passions to be weak in natural man, and he concludes his discussion by arguing that "love itself, like all the other passions, has acquired only in society that impetuous ardor which so often makes it fatal for men" (*SD*, p. 158; 135).

Rousseau has described the life of an individual man, silent, alone, without ambition, without passions or desires beyond those easily and physically satisfied. Rousseau's natural man is also a being dependent upon no other, unless that other be the physical world itself. And this lone individual who is endowed with the unique faculty of perfectibility will, chances are, remain an animal among animals for the duration of his existence. Without language, without human intercourse beyond the momentary and the physical, "art perished with the inventor" (*SD*, p. 160; 137). Rousseau has already shown that the development from natural to social man must, because of its extreme improbability, have been a process lasting centuries upon centuries. Now he goes still further, stopping human time altogether: "There was neither education nor progress; the generations multiplied uselessly; and everyone always starting from the same point, centuries passed in all the crudeness of the first ages; the species was already old, and man remained ever a child" (*SD*, p. 160; 137).

Finally, Rousseau raises the question of the origin of inequality, only to dismiss it entirely from the state of nature. Even natural inequalities of, for example, intellect or strength, he argues, could have had little effect among men whose contacts were fleeting at best. The origin of inequality among men cannot be found in man's nature but must be sought in his later development. To this end—having already shown that the social virtues, perfectibility, and the rest of man's faculties could not have developed by themselves—Rousseau turns to his next task: "to consider and bring together the different accidents that were able to perfect human reason while deteriorating the species, make a being evil while making him sociable, and from such a distant origin finally bring man and the world to the point where we see them" (*SD*, p. 162; 140).

Part 2

"The first person who, having fenced off a plot of ground, took it into his head to say *this is mine* and found people simple enough to believe him, was the true founder of civil society" (*SD*, p. 164; 141). The celebrated opening sentence of part 2 of the *Second Discours* provides a dramatic but false beginning to the history Rousseau is about to recount. He is starting in medias res, capturing the reader's attention with a glimpse of what is to come. More important, Rousseau is at the same time marking a midpoint, introducing what he calls an "intermediate fact." The first section of this history will end with "the first person who . . . fenced off a plot of ground," but it will begin with "man's first sentiment" and "his first care" (*SD*, p. 164; 142).

The static image of man in harmony with his physical environment, all his needs easily fulfilled, is quickly swept away. Soon, Rousseau explains, difficulties must have arisen, physical obstacles to the satisfaction of man's needs that he had to learn to surmount. Through his first struggles with the physical world, man developed swiftness and agility, and for the same reason he made use of rudimentary arms and tools. As the human race began to spread over the earth, obstacles increased, as in each region the inhabitants were confronted with a climate and terrain that drew forth a new industriousness to replace man's natural idleness. Although in part 1 of the *Discours* Rousseau wondered at great length about how people could have learned to make fire, now he simply acknowledges the fact, attributing it to chance: "Lightning, a volcano, or some happy accident introduced them to fire, a new resource against the rigor of winter. They learned to preserve this element, then to reproduce it, and finally to prepare with it meats they previously devoured raw" (*SD*, p. 165; 143). Rousseau also resolves the chicken-and-egg problem of the relationship among the origins of language, thought, and society. From casual encounters between men came both relative concepts such as strong and weak, and a universal language of cries, gestures, and imitative sounds. At the same time, Rousseau argues, particular languages (defined as articulate and conventional sounds) must have emerged, but he admits that this phenomenon is still "not too easy to explain" (*SD*, p. 167; 145).

The beginnings of thought raised man considerably above other beings; they also generated the first stirrings of pride in his consciousness of his superiority. Man's relationships with others of his own kind were still temporary, however, directed only toward immediate ends. Even so, a sense of mutual interest began to emerge.

Man's first slow steps brought him, according to Rousseau, to the gates of "a first revolution": the establishment of families, and with them, of "a sort of property" (*SD*, p. 167; 146). Property, even at the rudimentary level of family huts, stimulated the first acts of human aggression, while, at the same time, communal living gave rise to the first stirrings of sentiment, of conjugal and paternal love. Luxury, too, in the form of the first unnecessary inventions, had its origin at this time.

From the establishment of the family, Rousseau moves swiftly to the origin of nations, prepolitical units that share a common language, *moeurs*, and character deriving from a common mode of life and climate. Families began to intermingle, and more permanent relations among people elevated the level of conceptualization. Concepts of merit and beauty gave rise to preferences, and preferences to jealousy and fury when thwarted. "Discord triumphs," Rousseau writes, "and the gentlest of the passions receives sacrifices of human blood" (*SD*, p. 169; 149).

The simple prepolitical society that Rousseau describes at this point, where music and dance have their origins along with civility, offense, and vengeance, is what he considers to be the happy midpoint between the stupidity of brutes and the fatal enlightenment of modern man. Noting that this is the stage attained by most known "savage peoples," Rousseau claims that it "must have been the happiest and most durable epoch. The more one thinks about it, the more one finds that this state was the least subject to revolutions, the best for man, and that he must have come out of it only by some fatal accident, which for the common good ought never to have happened" (*SD*, p. 171; 151).

Having described this state of happy tranquillity, Rousseau moves on to the origin of civil society. The revolutionary role played by the establishment of the family in achieving the previous stage is here filled by the arts of metallurgy and agriculture. With them came two crucial divisions: the division of labor and the division of land. We have now arrived at the moment announced in the opening sentence of this part of the *Discours*: "From the cultivation of land, its division necessarily followed; and from property once recognized, the first rules of justice" (*SD*, p. 173; 154). It is at this point, too, that Rousseau marks the origin of inequality among men. With the institution of property and the first division of labor, inequality of talents produces inequality of labor and goods.

The text could end here. Rousseau has answered the question posed by the Academy of Dijon. Moreover, as he himself points out, "things having reached this point, it is easy to imagine the rest" (*SD*, p. 174; 155). Even if Rousseau has solved the Academy's problem, however, he has not finished the task he set out for himself: to fill in the historical gap between original and modern man. In fact, he has reached only that intermediary point introduced at the beginning of part 2. Rousseau must now bring his story from there to the eighteenth-century present. Thus, his "glance at the human race placed in this new order of things" (*SD*, p. 174; 155) will, in fact, occupy more space in the text than does the development that leads up to it.

In this new order of things, rich and poor have become dependent upon each other, the one for services, the other for aid. And, with the land all parceled out, the poor, who have nothing to lose, grab their subsistence from the rich, while the latter, having once tasted the power of wealth, seek to subjugate their neighbors in order to extend their domination. "Between the right of the stronger and the right of the first occupant there arose a perpetual conflict which ended only in fights and murders. Nascent society gave way to the most horrible state of war" (*SD*, p. 176; 157).

At this point, and for the first time, human history is directed by a conscious human decision. "The rich," explains Rousseau, "pressed by necessity, finally conceived the most deliberate project that ever entered the human mind. It was to use in his favor the very forces of those who attacked him, to make his defenders out of his adversaries, inspire them with other maxims, and give them other institutions which were as favorable to him as natural right was adverse" (*SD*, p. 177; 158–59). This was the great deception played upon the poor by the rich, the legitimation of the power of property and of political power through the institution of laws that fixed forever inequality among men with their own consent. It is easily seen, Rousseau continues, how the founding of one society must have engendered the founding of others. This is how political bodies spread over the earth.

By giving up their liberty, however, men did not achieve the sought-for elimination of the state of war. Although the rule of law prevailed within nations, between and among them raged an even worse war of all against all. This state of war among nations, however, was only one among many problems faced by the nascent states. In general, although political society was, according to Rousseau, the immediate result of a conscious decision made by the rich and agreed to by the poor, its imperfections were due to the fact that it was "almost the work of chance, and because, as it began badly, time in discovering faults and suggesting remedies could never repair the vices of the constitution" (*SD*, p. 180; 162). The work of wise legislators and vociferous critics could not overcome a fundamental helplessness.

The imperfections of the early political states led to the selection of magistrates and rulers. A grave move, according to Rousseau, as "inconveniences and disorders had to multiply continually in order that men finally thought of confiding to private persons the dangerous trust of public authority, and committed to magistrates the care of enforcing obedience to the deliberations of the people" (*SD*, p. 180; 163). Rousseau presents arguments against the two main alternatives to his own position: the Hobbesian thesis that men voluntarily submitted themselves to the absolute rule of one man, and the view, attributed broadly to theoreticians of absolute monarchy, that political authority derives from paternal authority. Rousseau's own position, he claims, agrees with the commonly held belief that the establishment of political authority was the result of "a true contract between the people and the chiefs it chooses for itself: a contract by which the two parties obligate themselves to observe laws that are stipulated in it and that form the bonds of their union" (*SD*, p. 184; 169). Every government among men, Rousseau continues, had to have come about in the same manner. The differences in form between the rules of the one, the few, and the many, were incidental, the results of circumstances particular to the localities so ruled.

Rousseau now brings his history up to the present, closing it with the rise of the hereditary monarch, who comes to regard the magistrature and the state itself as family property and who, calling his fellow citizens his slaves, counts them too among his goods. He comes to call himself an equal of the gods, the king of kings (*SD*, p. 187; 172). Having finished his history, Rousseau summarizes the last section of it (from the origin of civil society to that of absolute monarchy), calling it the history of the progress of inequality. Its first term is defined by the establishment of law and right of property, the second by the institution of the magistrature, and the third by the change from legitimate to arbitrary power. He further characterizes the first stage as that of rich and poor, the second as that of powerful and weak, and the last as that of master and slave, the ultimate degree of inequality. The necessity of this development, Rousseau argues, lies in the forms of government themselves, "for the vices that make social institutions necessary are the same ones that make their abuse inevitable" (*SD*, p. 187; 172–73).

Rousseau's history is now complete. From its beginning in the state of nature there has been a clear and steady development to the absolute monarchies of the eighteenth century. As a history, his work must end. It does not end here, however, but continues on into a conditional future, that which would be described in another, greater book. It is in this other work, he says, that "one would weigh the advantages and inconveniences of all governments relative to the rights of the state of nature, and where one would unmask all the different faces behind which inequality has appeared until the present and may appear in future centuries, according to the nature of these governments and the revolutions time will necessarily bring about in them" (*SD*, pp. 189–90; 175). Rousseau deals with the problem of continuing a history into the future by casting his thoughts in the conditional mode, speaking of what he would say if this were that other book. "One would see the multitude oppressed . . . ; one would see oppression grow continually . . . ; one would see the rights of citizens and national freedoms die out little by little." It is in this conditional future that inequality, going beyond its own limits, gives way to a new form of equality, the fruit of despotism (*SD*, pp. 190–91; 175–76).

Here Rousseau's story (no longer history) ends. All that remains is to conclude the work by restating its accomplishments. He has discovered and followed, he says, "the forgotten and lost routes that must have led man from the natural state to the civil state" (*SD*, p. 191; 178). He reiterates how long a time that history must have covered. Finally, Rousseau states clearly the purpose of writing such a history: to explain how it is that "savage man and civilized man differ so much in the bottom of their hearts and inclinations that what constitutes the supreme happiness of one would reduce the other to despair" (*SD*, p. 192; 178–79). In other words, through the construction of a history of the human race from the state of nature to the present, Rousseau claims to have solved the conundrum he posed for himself: how it is that men can be wicked, when man is naturally good. The solution to the problem of the origin of inequality resides within this framework.

The State of Nature

The state of nature, Rousseau remarks before commencing his description of it, is a state "which no longer exists, which perhaps never existed, which probably never will exist, and about which it is nevertheless necessary to have precise notions in order to judge our present state correctly" (*SD*, p. 123; 93). And yet, as more than one critic has pointed out, in practice Rousseau endows the state of nature with a historical (actual) credibility.[6] The apparent contradiction implied here can be resolved by assuming that Rousseau asserts the nonexistence of this state as a simple disclaimer to avoid confrontation with the upholders of Genesis.[7] But while Rousseau was certainly conscious of his vulnerability

[6]See, e.g., Baczko, *Solitude et communauté*, p. 75, and Marc F. Plattner, *Rousseau's State of Nature: An Interpretation of the "Discourse on Inequality"* (De Kalb, Ill., 1979), p. 25.

[7]See, e.g., Leo Strauss, *Natural Right and History* (Chicago, 1953), p. 267, n. 32; Roger D. Masters, *The Political Philosophy of Rousseau* (Princeton, 1968), p. 118; and George Armstrong Kelly, "J.-J. Rousseau: The Land of Chimeras and the Land of Prejudices," in *Idealism, Politics and History: Sources of Hegelian Thought* (Cambridge, 1969), p. 39.

to attack from that quarter, his conception of the state of nature is best understood if one accepts both the claim of nonexistence and the appearance of historical authenticity.

The state of nature described by Rousseau in part 1 of the *Discours* is presented initially not as a world apart but as the totality of the qualities that constitute man's nature. In this sense, the word *state* ought to be understood as having no more physical existence than, for example, the "state of the union," or the "state of matrimony." In an early reference to man's primitive state, Rousseau asks how one is to separate "what he gets from his own stock from what circumstances and his progress have added to or changed in his primitive state" (*SD*, p. 122; 91). In this case, the possessive pronoun *his* implies the dependence of this state on man himself; it cannot be construed as existing independently of him. A few paragraphs later, however, Rousseau refers to "our present state," but he contrasts it with "a state which no longer exists, which perhaps never existed, which probably never will exist" (*SD*, p. 123; 93). All of a sudden, the idea of existence is connected with that of man's state, and the implied meaning begins to change. The ambiguity in the meaning of the word *état* allows Rousseau to make of "man in the state of nature" both an individual and a physical world in which to place him.

The opening of the actual description of the state of nature (Rousseau begins part 1 of the text by stating what he will not describe) conveys the first sense of that term: "I see an animal less strong than some, less agile than others, but all things considered, the most advantageously organized of all." In the next sentence he introduces the other state of nature, that in which man, in his natural state, resides: "The earth, abandoned to its natural fertility and covered by immense forests never mutilated by the axe, offers at every step storehouses and shelters to animals of all species" (*SD*, pp. 134–35; 105).

It is because Rousseau has transformed man's nature into a state of nature that the eternal, unchanging quality of man's nature comes to be attributed to a physical world that takes on an independent existence as a "state."[8] In order to describe man in his purity, Rousseau has placed him in a world "where all things move in such a uniform manner, and where the face of the earth is not subject to those brusque and continual changes

---

[8]Starobinski writes that what began in Rousseau's mind as a simple working hypothesis gains life as the history progresses. Rousseau's intellectual prudence, he says, was overpowered by a kind of creative drunkenness. Although this is an attractive image that accords well with a romantic appreciation of Rousseau, it does not account for the references to a physical state of nature within paragraphs of the beginning of pt. 1: *Jean-Jacques Rousseau: Transparency and Obstruction*, trans. Arthur Goldhammer (Chicago, 1988), p. 14.

caused by the passions and inconstancy of united peoples" (*SD*, p. 136; 107). Such a state of nature must come into conflict with the ever-changing world of natural phenomena to which man is forever adapting himself in part 2 of the text.[9]

The state of nature is a logical construct also in the sense that it is the condition in which man, according to his nature alone, ought logically to be.[10] As such it lies outside time, an alternative to the actual historical development within time that is the product of the contingent action of chance. Rousseau indicates the grounds upon which the state of nature must be viewed as an alternative to actual historical development toward the beginning of part 1 of the *Discours*. At this point he is discussing the lack of clothing and housing in the state of nature and refers to it simply as "the deprivation of all those useless things we believe so necessary." But looking ahead to the historical development to be recounted in the second part of the text he concludes:

> Finally, unless we suppose those singular and fortuitous combinations of circumstances of which I shall speak hereafter and which could very well never happen, it is clear in any case that the first man who made himself clothing or a dwelling, in doing so gave himself things that were hardly necessary, since he had done without them until then and since it is hard to see why he could not endure, as a grown man, a kind of life he had endured from his infancy. [*SD*, p. 140; 112]

There is no reason, Rousseau is saying, that anyone should have ever thought to put on clothes or build a house. The invention of clothes and housing is really at odds with what ought to have happened—according to the nature of man. The state of nature is what logically ought to have happened; actual human history, which is the result of "those singular and fortuitous combinations of circumstances," is what has happened. The "ought" of the state of nature, it must be emphasized, is not normative, but logical, and has as its opposite the contingency by which history is characterized.

To arrive at this logical ought, Rousseau adopts the point of view of the first man, "as he must have come from the hands of nature" (*SD*, p.

---

[9]The conflict that arises here produces the sense of "rupture" that several critics have remarked. See, e.g., Patrick Hochart, "Droit naturel et simulacre (l'évidence du signe)," *Les Cahiers pour l'Analyse*, no. 8 (1967), p. 69; Michèle Ansart-Dourlen, *Dénaturation et violence dans la pensée de Jean-Jacques Rousseau* (Paris, 1975), p. 29; and Jean Roussel, "Rousseau, l'Utopie et Thomas More," *Moreana* 15 (December 1978): 49.

[10]See Starobinski, "The Discourse on Inequality," in *Jean-Jacques Rousseau*, p. 294; Henri Gouhier, "Nature et histoire dans la pensée de Rousseau," *Annales de la Société Jean-Jacques Rousseau* 33 (1953–55): 10–11.

134; 105). By looking forward from that point, instead of back from the perspective of the present, Rousseau shows the state of nature to be a sound, stable structure that has in itself no reason to change. In the absence of rational demonstration, the indefinite continuation of the state of nature, from the point of view of its inhabitant, cannot be certain, but only probable. This is not to say that the durability of the state of nature would not be seen as likely from this perspective. To the contrary, Rousseau's argument depends upon the contrast between the probable and the certain. Seen in this light, Rousseau's contention that history never ought to have happened makes perfect sense. He is simply trying to demonstrate that the chance of external causes or "those singular and fortuitous combinations of circumstances" intervening in the state of nature is something like a million to one, or maybe a billion or a trillion to one against. In all probability, he argues, the state of nature ought to have lasted forever.

The crucial term in Rousseau's mention of what he has left out of this discussion is the adjective *fortuitous*. The intervention of chance introduces historical time into man's world in the irreversible changes by which it is measured. Without change there can be no time, and without chance there can be no change.[11] It is not, however, that Rousseau "stops the clock" of human time; rather, he denies the logical necessity of its ever having started. By describing a state in which man would have lived eternally had not chance intervened, Rousseau is defining an alternative that is necessarily nonexistent, since it contradicts the known (albeit contingent) facts of human history. The timelessness of the state of nature, in which generations multiply uselessly and invention perishes with the inventor, is not at the origin of human history, but in contrast to it. Thus the research into the state of nature produces not historical truths "but only . . . hypothetical and conditional reasonings better suited to clarify the nature of things than to show their true origin" (*SD*, pp. 132–33; 103). Nature and history are thus presented as mutually exclusive categories, distinguished primarily by the opposition of necessity and contingency, and then further by different modes of temporality and means of being known.

Rousseau must reconcile nature with history, however, if he is to solve the conundrum that opposes the natural goodness of man to his historically demonstrated maliciousness. To demonstrate that inequality and

---

[11]Rousseau briefly acknowledges the changing face of nature, of sunrises and sunsets, but considers them not to have any effect on man, presumably because the temporality that is thereby produced is not linear. "The spectacle of nature becomes indifferent to him by dint of becoming familiar. There is always the same order, there are always the same revolutions" (*SD*, p. 144; 117).

the rest of man's woes do not originate in man's nature, Rousseau makes an absolute distinction between nature and history, but in order to show how inequality does arise, he must bridge the gap he has created and put natural man into the historical world.[12]

I cannot agree with Lester Crocker that the contradiction between nature and history is resolved through a "trick" that "makes it seem that there is no break, that the historical man is the logical, actual development of the other, the abstract 'original' man."[13] Crocker's mistake is to equate the logical with the actual, whereas these terms must be placed in opposition, since the actual is the result not of logical necessity but of historical contingency. No, if there is any trickery involved, it is in the way Rousseau takes advantage of the ambiguity in the word *state* to generate a world for natural man to inhabit in the first place. And even here what is artificial about the state of nature that Rousseau generates in this fashion is not the image itself but its designation as static, as outside time. To bridge the gap between the state of nature and human history, Rousseau simply eliminates the artificial character of the first by introducing into it the one crucial term he had left out: the action of chance. No longer an atemporal state, neither eternal nor outside the chronology of man's development, the state of nature is transformed into the first period of human history.

Toward the end of part 1 of the *Discours*, Rousseau writes:

> After having shown that *perfectibility*, social virtues, and the other faculties that natural man had received in potentiality could never develop by themselves, that in order to develop they needed the chance combination of several foreign causes which might never have arisen and without which he would have remained eternally in his primitive condition, it remains for me to consider and bring together the different accidents that were able to perfect human reason while deteriorating the species. [*SD*, p. 162; 140]

The effect of introducing chance into the state of nature is demonstrated in part 2 of the *Discours*. Although Rousseau has leapt dramatically to the

---

[12]Victor Goldschmidt points out that the genetic method used by Rousseau's predecessors in the analysis of civil society was not based on a true opposition between nature and society, since the first term was defined only as a function of the second. Rousseau's problem, as opposed to that of these others, such as Hobbes, Locke, and Condillac, is not to derive one state from the other but simply to pass from nature to society, since the two terms—far from implying each other—are in authentic opposition: *Anthropologie et politique: Les Principes du système de Rousseau* (Paris, 1974), pp. 425–26.

[13]Lester G. Crocker, "The Relation of Rousseau's Second *Discours* and the *Contrat social*," *Romanic Review* 51 (February 1960): 34.

beginning of civil society in the opening sentences of this part of the work, he quickly assures the reader that such an event could not have happened overnight. In fact, "it was necessary to make much progress, to acquire much industry and enlightenment, and to transmit and augment them from age to age, before arriving at this last stage of the state of nature" (*SD*, p. 164; 142). All of a sudden, the state of nature, which had until then been pictured as timeless, can be spoken of as having a final stage. No longer is it simply a logical construct, outside human time. The crucial factor, chance, has been added, and the state of nature is transformed into the temporal beginning of man's existence. "Therefore let us start further back in time," Rousseau says, "and attempt to assemble from a single point of view this slow succession of events and knowledge in their most natural order" (*SD*, p. 164; 142). Part 2 will begin not so very differently from part 1, then. But after a mere paragraph describing man as a physical being, the narrative of his development takes over: "Such was the condition of nascent man; such was the life of an animal limited at first to pure sensations and scarcely profiting from the gifts nature offered him, far from dreaming of wresting anything from it. But difficulties soon arose; it was necessary to learn to conquer them" (*SD*, pp. 164–65; 142). Whereas in part 1 Rousseau had intentionally and artificially distinguished between nature and history by extracting chance, in part 2 he brings them together under a "single point of view" to narrate the history of man and, in so doing, to identify and explain the origin of inequality among men.

To summarize, the state of nature that Rousseau describes in part 1 of the *Second Discours* is presented initially as the natural condition of man, the sum of his attributes. By exploiting the ambiguity of the word *state*, Rousseau transforms a sum of human qualities into a physical environment in which natural man lives. In this sense, the state of nature as an actual physical world is a pure fiction, since it is simply an extrapolation from the definition of natural man. The state of nature also must be viewed as nonexistent because it plays the role of a logical construct. That is, it describes a situation defined by a logical "ought": what man's condition ought to be in a world in which the contingent action of chance does not intrude.

By placing natural man in this artificially created environment, Rousseau is able to throw into broad relief a dichotomy between nature and logical necessity, on one hand, and history and contingency, on the other; the second is characterized by a temporality whose measurement depends upon irreversible change. He is also able to demonstrate that the origin of inequality lies not with nature and logic but with their opposite, the contingency of history. Thus, to the secondary question posed by the

Academy of Dijon, whether inequality among men is authorized by natural law, Rousseau clearly responds, "no," and then proceeds, in part 2 of the *Discours*, to trace the actual emergence of inequality in human history. In doing so he returns to his starting point, man as a physical being, but by immediately introducing chance into man's world, transforms a logical construct into a moment of time, the beginning of human history.

Modes of Change

Change comes about in one of two ways in the *Second Discours*: either by chance or through necessity. These two modes of change operate not simultaneously but consecutively, and the shift from one to the other marks a dividing point in part 2 of the text. It is crucial to distinguish between these two modes of change and to understand how such a shift is possible in order to avoid self-contradictory readings such as the following: "What is proposed, in fact, is a doctrine of *chance*, operating on natural man in such a way to produce inevitable results."[14]

Chance gives way to necessary change as a consequence of the revolution created by the simultaneous inventions of metallurgy and agriculture, which bring with them the complementary divisions of property and labor (*SD*, pp. 171–74; 152–54). The point at which contingent gives way to necessary change is at the same time that of the establishment of inequality among men, defined as that moment when the division of property comes together with the natural inequality of talents. The beginning of this new form of inequality, which property tends to engender (and whose origin the *Second Discours* seeks to explain), marks the discrete point at which contingent is superseded by necessary change as the force that drives history. Since property only tends to engender inequality, instead of doing so automatically, this moment is a conceptual gray area between the two types of change. To understand man's development from his natural state to the states of Europe in the eighteenth century, it will be necessary first to analyze Rousseau's notion of chance and the role it plays, and then to show how necessary change takes over.

Chance

Human history, as Rousseau presents it, is the result of blind chance. In the *Second Discours*, change arises first out of the interaction between

[14]J. H. Broome, *Rousseau: A Study of His Thought* (New York, 1963), p. 39.

man as a potentially perfectible being and the natural (physical) world that he inhabits. However, the responsibility for the particular development that has occurred, or even for the very existence of change, can be attributed to neither one nor the other. There is also an absence of any form of divine will. Rousseau's notion of chance is the product of the contingency of man's perfectibility on the one hand and of "circumstances" on the other. To understand the working of chance as it derives from the double contingency in man and nature is to understand the mechanism of historical change in the *Second Discours*.

Rousseau introduces the notion of perfectibility in the context of the distinction between man and the beasts. Man's one distinguishing quality, Rousseau decides, is "the faculty of self-perfection, a faculty which, with the aid of circumstances, successively develops all the others, and resides among us as much in the species as in the individual" (*SD*, p. 142; 114). In contrast to man's other faculties, perfectibility is a quality not only of the individual but of the species as well. It differs from the other faculties also in preceding them and in making their functioning possible. Just as important as these differences, however, is the fact that Rousseau attributes to perfectibility the status of a faculty. The author of the article "Faculté" in the *Encyclopédie*, in contrast, makes no mention of a faculty of perfectibility. He does, however, provide the following explanation of how man's "facultés intellectuelles" do develop. "If men show very little intelligence in the first stages of their life, this defect ought not to be attributed to an imperfection of their *intellectual faculties*, but only to a deprivation of sensations and perceptions that they have not yet received, and that will later procure for them the knowledge upon which the *intellectual faculties*, which are necessary for regulating the will and for deliberation, are exercised."[15] This sensationalist explanation shows no need for the addition of a separate faculty to enable others to develop, but it also does not account for human development on the species level, which is what makes history possible. In fact, nowhere in the article "Faculté" is a faculty operating on any but the individual level mentioned.

The advantage to Rousseau of claiming that perfectibility is a faculty of the human race is not immediately apparent. Certainly he needs to introduce the possibility of historical change, but he could have done so just as easily by extending the reasoning displayed in the *Encyclopédie* article to the species. In that way he would have avoided creating yet another faculty. Why then should Rousseau involve himself in the slightly suspect business of assigning actions to faculties that have no

---

[15]*Encyclopédie*, 6:364.

definite physical location? The article "Faculté," in which the difference between "les forces" and "les facultés" is discussed, suggests the advantage to Rousseau of giving perfectibility the status of a faculty.

"Some authors inopportunely confuse forces with *faculties*," the author remarks; "but they differ from each other in the same way that causes differ from principles. Force, being the cause of action, implies its actual existence. A *faculty* or power implies only possibility. Thus, as to the *faculty*, an action does not follow necessarily; but all existing force properly carries out an action, as an effect of which it is the cause."[16] By calling perfectibility a faculty, Rousseau is *not* calling it a force. Thus the human race's ability to change over time cannot be construed as a necessary cause of the resulting development, nor can such a development itself be called necessary. In saying that perfectibility functions "with the aid of circumstances," Rousseau reinforces both the notion that, as a mere faculty, it requires an external stimulus and the idea that such a stimulus is neither automatic (as sensations are) nor God-given. By calling man's capacity to perfect himself a faculty, Rousseau maintains the theoretical possibility of a state of nature, while still allowing for the historical development that can explain how man can be both naturally good and presently evil.[17]

All that is required now to swing the balance from nature to history is "the aid of circumstances." Man "as he must have come from the hands of nature" (*SD*, p. 134; 105) entered a world where anything (or nothing) might have happened, and where each event that did occur left its mark. In part 1 of the *Second Discours* Rousseau describes the life man would have led and the world that would have been had nothing happened. The narrative of part 2 recounts the history of what might not have happened, but surely must have if one is to explain the existence of modern society. There is no necessity in any of this, except the nature of man himself. The role of providence is here limited to the initial endowment of man with perfectibility, which keyed the development of the rest of his faculties to immediate needs. "It was by a very wise providence," says Rousseau, "that his potential faculties were to develop only with the opportunities to exercise them" (*SD*, p. 152; 127). The occasions that

---

[16]Ibid., 6:361.

[17]Jean Mosconi argues that "one would have to insist upon the necessity that exists in a state of pure nature, of considering the notion of *perfectibility* as one of a true *virtuality*: perfectibility is the *matter* of culture and history and not its *spring*": "Sur la théorie du devenir de l'entendement," *Les Cahiers pour l'Analyse*, no. 4 (1966), p. 68. The only problem with this formulation is the implication that Rousseau's purpose in defining perfectibility as a "pure virtuality" is to allow for a pure state of nature. I see no reason to privilege the state of nature in this way.

Rousseau has in mind he usually refers to as "circonstances" or "hasards"—"heureux" or "funestes"—but also as (for example) the "chance combination of several foreign causes" (*SD*, p. 162; 140), and as "[*diverses*] particular causes" (*SD*, p. 168; 147).

"Lightning, a volcano, or some happy accident"—one of these, Rousseau says, enabled man to discover fire (*SD*, p. 165; 143). A more complicated case is presented by the origin of language, which, in the first part of the *Discours*, Rousseau admitted himself unable to explain. "For myself, frightened by the multiplying difficulties, and convinced of the almost demonstrated impossibility that languages could have arisen and been established by purely human means, I leave to whoever would undertake it the discussion of the following difficult problem: Which was most necessary, previously formed society for the institution of languages; or previously invented languages for the establishment of society?" (*SD*, p. 151; 126). In the narrative of part 2, however, where purely human means have been given the aid of circumstances, Rousseau no longer sees the need to leave to someone else the task of resolving the problem he has raised. At this point, he concludes, "one catches a slightly better glimpse of how the use of speech was established or perfected imperceptibly in the bosom of each family; and one can conjecture further how particular causes could have spread language and accelerated its progress by making it more necessary. Great floods or earthquakes surrounded inhabited cantons with water or precipices; revolutions of the globe detached and broke up portions of the continent into islands" (*SD*, p. 168; 147–48). As a result of these natural disasters, men were forced to live together, and so developed a common language in each area. Rousseau suggests further that islands formed in this manner may well have been the birthplaces of language, which later spread with the development of navigation.

A third example of the kinds of circumstances that have affected man's development can be found in the origin of metallurgy, which Rousseau was also unable to explain with reference to human nature alone in part 1 of the *Discours*. Now he writes: "There only remains, therefore, the extraordinary circumstance of some volcano which, by throwing up metallic materials in fusion, would have given observers the idea of imitating this operation of nature" (*SD*, p. 172; 152).

The circumstances that have enabled man's faculties to develop, and with them the human race as a whole, are simply what one would call "natural disasters," or, more blandly, "natural phenomena." One could, of course, refer to them as "acts of God," but Rousseau does not do so, even in the case of the "great floods," which clearly recall the biblical flood. These phenomena have no ultimate justification and thus merit the term *hasards*, which Rousseau often applies to them, as well as the modifier *fortuit*.

Rousseau creates an artificially static (and thus unnatural) state of nature for the same reason that he describes an artificially static natural man: to distinguish between the necessary and the contingent. Were he simply to have placed natural man in the world of contingent natural events, he would not have been able to express, as he does through the use of the state of nature, the contingency of the particular history that has developed. Only from the perspective of the state of nature can man's history be understood as unnecessary, since from the other end, the present, it becomes subject to historical necessity. In other words, what did not have to have happened becomes that which must have happened. And if one accepts the perspective of the state of nature, that which must have happened not only need not have occurred, but ought not to have occurred. Here again is the logical "ought" of the state of nature as a logical hypothesis. The grammatical shift in tenses, which coincides in this case with the shift from part 1 to part 2 of the *Discours*, signals a transformation of the contingency of the future into the necessity of the past.

When Rousseau writes, at the end of part 1, "I admit that as the events I have to describe could have happened in several ways," he is still looking from the perspective of the state of nature. When, later in the same sentence, he says, "the conclusions I want to deduce from [my conjectures] will not thereby be conjectural, since, on the principles I have established, one could not conceive of any other system that would not provide me with the same results, and from which I could not draw the same conclusions" (*SD*, p. 162; 140–41), he is assuming the historical perspective of the present. This retrospection, moreover, is not simply a deduction backward through time, since the starting point has been established independently and is both anterior to and in contradiction with the end point. In fact, a crucial element of Rousseau's argument is that the origin of civil society (and thus of inequality) cannot be deduced from man's present condition, as others before him had tried to do (*SD*, p. 124; 94–95). It is in this sense that Rousseau's narrative is historical rather than pseudohistorical.[18]

When Rousseau refers to the "uncertain testimonies of history," he challenges not the facts of recorded history but the idea of necessity implied in the development history describes. Only by ignoring the de facto testimony of retrospective history can one realize that "everything seems to remove savage man from the temptation and means of ceasing

[18]Goldschmidt, *Anthropologie et politique*, pp. 425–26.

to be savage" (*SD*, p. 144; 117). The negativity of so much of the description in part 1 of the text results from Rousseau's constant attempts to counteract the forward pull of historical hindsight. Sentences like the following are typical: "With so few sources of illness, man in the state of nature hardly has need of remedies, still less of doctors. In this respect the human species is not in any worse condition than all the others" (*SD*, p. 139; 110). The description of part 1 of the *Discours* thus counteracts the narrative thrust of the second part almost to the point of antinarrative, so that the text, as it were, stands still only as a result of being forcibly held back.

Just as natural man has always the potential to develop, the volcanoes, floods, and earthquakes that occur in part 2 of the *Discours* must be seen to be always possible in part 1. To go even further, there is no reason that they might not have occurred in the state of nature, since perfectibility, being a faculty of man, need not respond to the first external stimulus it receives. In fact, Rousseau is adamant that a thousand opportunities were missed before man finally learned something as simple as the use of fire and became able to transmit this important skill to his fellows. Chance, then, the motor of human history, cannot be viewed as identical with natural phenomena in general. The particular circumstances that become particular causes are those upon which man (that is, particular men) has capitalized. What is fortuitous is not, for example, the eruption of a volcano, but the coming together of man's potential (perfectibility) and nature's potential (natural phenomena such as volcanoes) at a particular moment. History, by this definition, is doubly contingent. One cannot assume, as Gabriel Gosselin does, that "man carries within him the necessity of *a* history, because he has perfectibility: that which is contingent is *this particular* history."[19] As a faculty and not a force, perfectibility cannot be a necessary cause. By stressing the number of opportunities that must have passed men by, Rousseau shows that perfectibility does not come into play automatically. Thus it is better to say with Raymond Polin that, after Rousseau, "man has neither providence, nor destiny, but that he can have a history."[20]

Man can have a history because he is endowed with the faculty of perfectibility and because circumstances arise of which that faculty can

[19]Gabriel Gosselin, "L'Utopie de l'homme naturel dans le second discours de Rousseau ou la fonction de l'utopie dans la connaissance sociologique," in *Modèles et moyens de la réflexion politique au XVIIIe siècle*, vol. 2: *Utopies et voyages imaginaires* (Lille, 1978), p. 353.

[20]Raymond Polin, *La Politique de la solitude: Essai sur la philosophie politique de Jean-Jacques Rousseau* (Paris, 1971), p. 245. "A humanity without history is not a contradiction, in the eyes of Rousseau," notes Gouhier: "in this sense, history is contingent, with the development of reason and of social life which it implies": "Nature et histoire," p. 26.

take advantage. Over time the probability that these two potentials—the potential of man and that of the physical world—will come together must increase, even if everything acts against its happening. But the probability can never reach necessity, and for that reason chance alone has determined not only the course of human history but its very existence. Here is the double contingency of history, and because of it neither man nor the world he inhabits can be held responsible for the ills that have resulted from it. Chance is an absolute third term that resides in neither of the two potentialities that define it. Not only God but man himself has been absolved of all responsibility for human events. History may have been freed from determinism—both divine and physical—but it has also been released from man's own grasp and set adrift on the proverbial sea of chance.[21]

Necessity

The changes that take man from the state of nature to civil society and that are responsible for the origin of inequality have been shown to be the work of blind chance; those which follow, however, follow necessarily. In Rousseau's terms, "things having reached this point, it is easy to imagine the rest" (*SD*, p. 174; 155). To understand why and how the shift from contingent to necessary change occurs, one must first examine this point from which all that follows can be easily imagined, that is, deduced.

The last revolution attributed to chance in Rousseau's scenario is that

[21]Starobinski argues that because there is nothing inevitable in the passage from perfectibility to "perfecting," "man is free to accept or reject, to hasten progress or slow it down" ("Discourse on Inequality," p. 294). Polin, too, opposes necessity to free will when he says that "the philosophy of history suggested by Rousseau is a philosophy of contingency, a philosophy of the history of liberty and of the history of man in the process of becoming human" (*La Politique de la solitude*, p. 253). This conception would seem to arise from the assumption that what is not God's work must be man's. Starobinski voices this assumption when he writes elsewhere that "the drama of the fall does not precede earthly existence; Rousseau takes the religious myth and sets it in historical time" and then concludes that "if the fall is man's own doing, a mere accident of human history, it follows that man is not by nature condemned to live in a vicious climate of mistrust and opacity. For the flaws in man's condition are the work of man himself, or of society. Hence there is no reason why we cannot remake or unmake history" (*Jean-Jacques Rousseau*, p. 12).

It was not by choice, however, but simply by chance that opportunities to develop were missed. Moreover, Rousseau gives one very clear example of man's inability to undo the damage done by chance. "Despite all the labors of the wisest legislators," he writes, "the political state remained ever imperfect because it was almost the work of chance, and because, as it began badly, time in discovering faults and suggesting remedies could never repair the vices of the constitution" (*SD*, p. 180; 162) caused by the development of metallurgy and agriculture. Metallurgy, according to Rousseau, could have been developed only through the observation of some fortuitous volcanic eruption, and the development of agriculture was contingent upon that of metallurgy. The invention of these two arts established a complex of relationships and institutions from which all that followed will be deduced.

Just as the revolution caused by the establishment and distinction of families produced a constellation of effects that constitute a state or stage of development, so too does the great revolution produced by the inventions of metallurgy and agriculture. The first of these effects is the division of labor, and the second the division of land into property. With the institution of property, Rousseau continues, came the first rules of justice. Taking up again the familiar formulation of the workings of chance, Rousseau then remarks: "Things in this state could have remained equal if talents had been equal, and if, for example, the use of iron and the consumption of foodstuffs had always been exactly balanced" (*SD*, p. 174; 154). But though the formulation resembles those by which each previous step was shown to have been entirely independent of those that must have followed, the context and meaning here are different. Whereas before it was a volcano, a flood, or some other "heureux hasard" that gave man's faculties the opportunity to develop, here it is the natural inequality of men's talents, previously established as the result not of chance but of natural endowment, that forces the next step. And the balance between production and consumption that Rousseau suggests as a means of combating the results of natural inequality is unnatural since it would have to be maintained artificially. For, as Rousseau says, "this proportion, which nothing maintained, was soon broken" (*SD*, p. 174; 154).

This next step in human development is almost necessary, for natural inequality, unlike natural phenomena, must—without self-conscious intervention to counter it—have an effect.[22] In fact, natural inequality has been shown to have been a factor in men's relations with one another for as long as they have had any. The difference at this point is that natural inequality has permanent effects on these relations: "Thus does natural inequality imperceptibly manifest itself along with contrived inequality; and thus do the differences among men, developed by those of circumstances, become more perceptible, more permanent in their effects, and begin to have a proportionate influence over the fate of individuals" (*SD*, p. 174; 155). Natural inequality, which had no effect when men lived

[22]The implications of inequality that arises neither from a double contingency nor from an absolute necessity will be discussed in the conclusion of chap. 5.

isolated lives, and which gave rise to passions, thought, and language in early societies, becomes at last a permanent and defining feature of human life and human history. Natural inequalities, which have been much augmented through the chance development of the faculties, now grounded in property and legitimized by law, become themselves the source of change. Inequality among men, Rousseau argues, is the result of a series of contingent developments, ending in property, that makes the effects of natural inequality permanent and thus a defining feature of all subsequent human relations.

The history that follows records the development not of man's faculties in his interaction with the physical world but of human institutions that are established because of the inequality that now exists permanently among men, an inequality augmented by these efforts. Although the development of man's faculties is not complete, it is superseded in importance in this new order of things when man's dependence on nature decreases as his dependence on other men increases. Thus in one fell swoop Rousseau finds: "Behold all our faculties developed, memory and imagination in play, vanity aroused, reason rendered active, and the mind having almost reached the limit of the perfection of which it is susceptible" (SD, p. 174; 155). Having in this way brought to a close his first history, Rousseau is now able to describe the playing out of the second. Chance has been eliminated, and necessity enters.

Rousseau summarizes the progress of inequality into three stages: (1) the establishment of law and the right of property; (2) the institution of a magistrature; and (3) the change from legitimate to arbitrary power. The relationship of rich and poor is authorized in the first stage, of strong and weak in the second, and of master and slave in the third. The necessity of this progress from property rights to arbitrary power, from rich and poor to master and slave, lies not in the body politic or the motives behind its formation but in the vices that, having made social institutions necessary in the first place, make their abuse inevitable (SD, p. 187; 172–73). And it must be emphasized that the vices referred to here are not inherent in man or apparent at any time preceding the institution of property. "The destruction of equality was followed by the most frightful disorder," Rousseau explains; "thus the usurpations of the rich, the brigandage of the poor, the unbridled passions of all, stifling natural pity and the as yet weak voice of justice, made man avaricious, ambitious, and evil" (SD, p. 176; 157).

Although details here and there may prove wrong, Rousseau asserts the necessity of the broad outline of events that follow one another, from the moment when equality among men is broken, to the final stage of inequality that leaves men once more in the state of war into which inequality first brought them. At times Rousseau is very specific, going so far as to put words in the mouths of actors in the historical drama; at others he allows room for variations, as in discussing the different forms of government that reflect the different circumstances from which they arise. Throughout, however, Rousseau insists that the three stages he enumerates, the relations they embody, and the institutions that give them form arise and follow one another necessarily. It is a question here not of historical particularity, but of the formal outlines of a general truth.

To conclude, there are three types of necessity invoked by Rousseau in the *Second Discours*. The first is the minimal necessity of the state of nature: what man and his life would be without the intervention of chance, or, what characterizes man minimally as man. The second is historical necessity, which depends on retrospection: for example, even though there is no necessary reason for man to have invented language, he must have done so, because experience shows that he does in fact speak. This kind of necessity characterizes the inherently contingent events that lead up to the origin of inequality. The third type of necessity is that of the necessary deduction: a particular chain of deductions (or events) necessarily follows a given condition, as effects follow from a given cause.

The distinctions among these three types of necessity can also be made in terms of point of view (forward and backward) and stasis versus change. Along these axes, the first type of necessity is static and forward-looking; the second is dynamic and depends on hindsight; and the third is both dynamic and forward-looking. More precisely, the necessity of the state of nature exists only if one ignores the facts that inform historical hindsight, whereas historical change is necessary only with the aid of hindsight; both positions are dependent upon and limited by their points of view for their necessary conclusions. Only the third type of necessity, that of deductive reasoning, is independent of the temporality that restrains the other two, requiring neither hindsight nor blindness to that which history teaches. In fact, it knows no difference between the two perspectives. That is, forward and backward are meaningless terms in this case because the logic of change, if not its process, is reversible. Thus, whether Rousseau deduces backward from the present to the past, or forward from an independently established past to the present, makes no difference, since the same chain of reasoning is produced in either case. Even more important, because there is no directionality, the necessary deductions can just as easily be extended from the past through the present and into the future. The human perspective of the present gives way to a God's-eye view, which sees the whole process of human history from a point beyond its limits.

Rousseau is able to extend his argument beyond the temporal bound of the present into a conjectured future because necessary deductions supersede historical necessity. In this future, "despotism, by degrees raising its hideous head and devouring all it had seen to be good and healthy in all parts of the State, would finally succeed in trampling underfoot the laws and people, and in establishing itself upon the ruins of the Republic" (*SD*, pp. 190–91; 176–77). Whereas the first type of necessity determines what ought (logically) to be, and the second type what must have been, the necessity of deductive reasoning allows Rousseau to talk about what will be. Furthermore, by inserting a chain of logical deductions into the historically established chronology, Rousseau is able to introduce necessity into history and to identify logical developments with historical ones.

CHAPTER FIVE

Historical Narrative:
The Form of the Text

The *Second Discours* is structured by a narrative history that extends outward in both directions to enclose its ahistorical boundaries: the state of nature at one end, and the inevitable progress of inequality at the other. In narrow terms, only the first half (roughly) of part 2 of the text is a historical narrative, that section which describes the development of man from his origins to the origin of inequality. These limits of the historical narrative correspond both to the limits of the rule of chance discussed above and to those of the historical perspective, which is confined within the determinate bounds of human temporality. These boundaries are defined formally by probabilistic logic expressed in timeless description, on the one hand, and the pseudohistory of a chain of logical deductions, on the other. And although from one point of view it can be said that the weakness of historical narrative as a means of explanation requires the introduction of nonhistorically defined points to determine it, the strength of the form can be seen in its ability to co-opt these points. By locating the results of other modes of reasoning as historical boundary points, the author extends to them the kind of certainty enjoyed by historical narrative.

For Rousseau, the virtues of the historical narrative form are twofold. First, by allowing the emphasis to be placed on how rather than why change occurs, Rousseau is able to locate the origin of inequality as the last in a series of contingent events rather than as the effect of a cause. In the *Second Discours*, chance makes possible this coherent sequence of events that connects two independently defined points. Rousseau identifies chance as explanation by identifying it with the zero degree of historical explanation: its simple coherence as narrative.

The second aspect of historical narrative that Rousseau makes use of is the unidirectionality of its linear chronology. By integrating the two logical (that is, ahistorical) constructs of the state of nature and the progress of inequality into the narrative as its beginning and end, Rousseau is able to distinguish between them absolutely. The state of nature cannot be viewed as a possible future, not only because a hopeless one has been projected instead but also because, having been transformed into the starting point of history, it is locked in as a particular moment in the established chronology.

Historical Narrative as Explanation

Explanation can exist on various levels in historical writing. Broadly speaking, there are two types of explanation: internal and external. Explanation drawn from outside the historical events themselves can range from a divinely ordained teleology to (in the present day) a Freudian analysis or the dialectic of the human spirit. These are the grand, overarching explanations that, when imposed upon the seemingly random events of the past, transform them into meaningful parts of a comprehensible whole.

The historian, however, need not look to philosophy, theology, or psychology for a means of explaining past events or the present that has followed them. If one thinks of explanation not as cause but as coherence, then the very creation of a coherent narrative establishes its own explanation. The past is in this manner explained to the extent that it makes sense to the reader. Simply getting from one event or one moment in the past to another, in a believable fashion, explains not necessarily *why* something happened, but at least *how* it reasonably could have happened. The emphasis here is on the narrative itself. This type of historical writing does not primarily paint a picture of an age or a moment *in* time descriptively; rather, it narrates a series of events *over* time.

The distinction between narration and description can be traced to Aristotle's definition of tragedy as "a representation [not] of men but [of] a piece of action, of life," and of the plot as the representation of the action, of the "arrangement of the incidents."[1] Aristotle's definition of plot has been taken up in recent years by theorists of narrative and contrasted with a static notion of description. Thus Gérard Genette writes that "every narrative includes two types of representation . . . :

[1] Aristotle, *Poetics* 6.1450a 12, 8.

representations of actions and events, which constitute the narration properly speaking, and representations of objects or people, which make up the act of what we today call 'description.'"[2] Tzvetan Todorov, too, builds a theory of narrative on this basic distinction when he writes: "Description and narrative presuppose different kinds of temporality. The initial description [is] certainly situated in time, but this time [is] continuous; whereas the changes, characteristic of narrative, cut time into discontinuous unities. The time of pure duration is opposed to the sequence time of events."[3] This sequential temporality (chronology) not only characterizes historical narrative but is crucial to it as a mode of explanation. The explanatory power of historical writing is located in its nature as narrative.

Is there no difference, then, between historical and fictional narrative? According to Aristotle, "the difference between a historian and a poet is not that one writes in prose and the other in verse. The real difference is this, that the one tells what happened, and the other what might happen." Thus, while there may be no formal difference between the two types of narrative, the distinction between the definite past and the possible does have important implications. "For this reason," Aristotle continues, "poetry is something more scientific and serious than history because poetry tends to give general truths while history gives particular facts."[4]

Rousseau's hypothetical history lies squarely between poetic and historical narrative, for if history speaks of what has been and poetry of what might be, hypothetical history deals with what must have been. In abstracting the form of historical narrative from the particular contents of histories, both sacred and secular, Rousseau discovers narrative itself, since its very particularity makes a narrative historical. But in discussing what must have been, Rousseau does not simply substitute fiction for fact, universal for particular. Rather, he merges the two in the notion of the scientific hypothesis or conjecture that seeks to explain what is in terms of what is physically and reasonably possible.

The notion of reasonableness, of making sense, is important here as well. Since the historian appeals to no authority beyond the facts as he knows them, no causes either rationally demonstrable or divinely ordered, he can convince the reader of the validity of his narrative only if that reader can himself see the reasonableness of it. Often, a particular narrative gains strength because it is shown to be more likely (and thus

[2]Gérard Genette, "Boundaries of Narrative," trans. Ann Levonas, *New Literary History* 8 (Autumn 1976): 5.
[3]Tzvetan Todorov, "The Two Principles of Narrative," *Diacritics* 1 (Fall 1971): 38.
[4]*Poetics* 9.1451a–b 1–3.

more reasonable) than alternate scenarios. The reasonableness or acceptability of a narrative is what makes following it possible, as W. B. Gallie
points out. In the reader's activity of following the "story," he argues, lies
his historical understanding: "We follow a story through or across contingencies—accidents, coincidences, unpredictable events of all kinds;
yet the story's general direction and continuous advance towards its final
conclusion somehow succeed in rendering these contingencies acceptable."[5]

The differences among possible narrative explanations depend not
only on the selection of relevant facts and their arrangement but also on
the filling in of gaps. If one assumes that there is a past distinct from the
documentary traces of it to which the historian has access, then the
difference between the past and its traces can account for gaps in the
created narrative and justify their being bridged by reasonable hypotheses, hypotheses that may vary from historian to historian.

Michel Foucault has challenged this distinction in our own time. In
the past, he argues, "the document was always treated as the language of
a voice since reduced to silence, its fragile, but possibly decipherable
trace." Now, as a result of a gradual change in the historian's perception
of his task, the document "is no longer for history an inert material
through which it tries to reconstitute what men have done or said, the
events of which only the trace remains; history is now trying to define
within the documentary material itself unities, totalities, series, relations."[6]

Whether or not Foucault is correct in his assessment of twentieth-
century historical writing, his argument points up an important assumption that is implicit in narrative history: the existence of an objectively
defined (but possibly inaccessible) past that the historian tries to recreate.
Such an objective quantity is analogous to that which the physical scien-
tist assumes in his own hypothetical approximations. Significantly, the
origins of this analogy between physical and social reality have been
traced to the Enlightenment.[7] It is on the basis of this analogy between
the physical and social worlds that Rousseau can argue in the *Second
Discours* that his own research is similar to that carried out by contempo-

[5]W. B. Gallie, *Philosophy and the Historical Understanding*, 2d ed. (New York, 1968), p.
29.
[6]Michel Foucault, *The Archaeology of Knowledge and the Discourse on Language*, trans.
A. M. Sheridan Smith (New York, 1976), pp. 6–7.
[7]For the origins of the scientific model for investigations of society see Ernst Cassirer,
The Philosophy of the Enlightenment, trans. Fritz C. A. Koelln and James P. Pettegrove
(Boston, 1955), chap. 1; Peter Gay, *The Enlightenment: An Interpretation*, 2 vols. (New
York, 1977), 2: chaps. 4 and 7; and Keith Michael Baker, *Condorcet: From Natural
Philosophy to Social Mathematics* (Chicago, 1975), chap. 2.

rary physicists concerning the formation of the earth (*SD*, p. 133; 103).

Narrative history, then, provides a particular kind of explanation that is identical with its own coherence. This coherence is accomplished in part by bridging gaps or filling them in. The validity of such a procedure depends first and foremost on an assumption not only of an objective reality that history recreates but also of the coherence of that reality. Otherwise, narrative coherence would be viewed either as a total fabrication or at least as an artistic falsification of that reality.

Louis Mink argues persuasively that the common-sense perception implicit in narrative assumes not only a coherent past but one that is an "untold story."[8] Narrative history is presumed to be transparent, discovering the narrative in, rather than imposing it upon, the past. Significantly, Mink finds the source of this presupposition in the idea of "Universal History," which flowered in the late eighteenth century. Although the idea can be traced back at least to St. Augustine, the eighteenth century saw its secularization and its scholarly prominence. At this point God the author drops out, and what remains is a single story of man, "the idea of a history which is simply *there*, devised by no one . . . but waiting to be told by someone."[9]

Yet narrative coherence, whether consciously or unconsciously imposed upon the past, is, as Mink asserts, "a primary cognitive instrument—an instrument rivaled, in fact, only by theory and by metaphor as irreducible ways of making the flux of experience comprehensible."[10] And the plausibility of the narrative depends not on its ability either to satisfy existing laws or to cover instances beyond itself but simply on its being able to account for itself, on its coherence. (There is an assumption here, of course, that the historian has made critical use of his documents and that the credibility of the facts is thus not in question.)

Historical narrative is both the form of the *Second Discours* and its mode of argumentation and explanation. Although this may appear to the modern reader a naive form in which to couch the answer to a question of origins, for Rousseau it was a conscious choice and a radical one. Historical explanation need depend only upon an internal coherence whose possibility is grounded in a notion of reasonableness shared by writer and reader. Its usefulness, as Rousseau's work indicates, lies in its ability to reconcile opposites through the introduction of historical temporality.

[8]Louis Mink, "Narrative Form as a Cognitive Instrument," in *The Writing of History, Literary Form and Historical Understanding*, ed. Robert H. Canary and Henry Kozicki (Madison, Wis., 1978), p. 135.

[9]Ibid., p. 137.

[10]Ibid., p. 131.

It must be emphasized that historical explanation does not and cannot answer the question "why." Because internal coherence alone constitutes its validity, it provides no overarching metaphysical explanation. The realm of historical narrative is the mechanistic world of "how." Thus, in order to understand the *Second Discours* as an exercise in narrative historical explanation, it is crucial to identify the mechanisms by which change occurs over time in the text.

Rousseau's Use of the Form

Rousseau's exploitation of the narrative form is evidenced first in the way in which he manipulates and controls the relationship between narrative time and historical time. He also takes advantage of the retrospection peculiar to historical narrative by doubling the structure such retrospection entails. In so doing he circumscribes a single moment of historical change that is identical with the origin of inequality and endows it rhetorically with a certainty it would otherwise lack.

This is not to say that in his use of historical narrative Rousseau is not confronted with problems arising from the form as well. The need in narrative to condense historical time in representing it, for example, does not work in Rousseau's favor. And Rousseau's need to establish the state of nature independently of the historical perspective undermines its historicity when, from the historical viewpoint, it becomes the beginning of human development. The following discussion of Rousseau's use of the form of historical narrative (as a special case of narrative in general) will try to account for both the advantages and the disadvantages of the form and how Rousseau confronts them in the *Second Discours*.

Narrative Time and Historical Time

By placing the state of nature in time at the beginning of part 2 of the *Second Discours*, Rousseau transforms an eternity into a passing moment. If this seems an overstatement, it can at least be said that what occupies the entire first section of the text is reduced to a single paragraph in the second. Further, there is a definite correlation between the space allotted to the state of nature in each part of the text and the sense of time that adheres to it in each case. The narrative form of the *Second Discours*— both its virtues and the problems it poses for Rousseau—can be approached through its dual temporality.

"Narrative," writes Christian Metz, "is a . . . doubly temporal sequence: there is the time of the thing told and the time of the narration (the time of the signified and the time of the signifier). This duality not only renders possible all the temporal distortions that are commonplace in narratives (three years of the hero's life summed up in two sentences of a novel . . .). More basically it invites us to consider that one of the functions of narrative is to invent one time scheme in terms of another time scheme."[11]

If it is the function of narrative to convert historical time into narrative time, then a problematic of narrative is that historical time cannot be reproduced without distortion.[12] And, as Genette points out further, there is a definite asymmetry in narrative distortion which privileges summary over elongation. He identifies four canonical forms of narrative tempo. At the two extremes are located the descriptive pause and the ellipsis; in between are the scene (which closely approximates historical time, generally through the use of dialogue) and the summary. The rhythm of a text can be analyzed in terms of the alternation of these four movements and the discrepancy between narrative and historical time of each particular distortion.[13]

When Rousseau places the state of nature within a narrative of the history of man, he is forced to condense the time it constitutes through the use of summary, ellipsis, or both. While a novelist, whose work may span a single year or a single lifetime, is forced to summarize and to utilize the narrative ellipsis, that is as nothing compared to the monumental task of time reduction which the historian of the human race must confront. Thus, Rousseau has no sooner begun his narrative than he interjects: "I cover multitudes of centuries like a flash, forced by the time that elapses, the abundance of things I have to say, and the almost imperceptible progress of the beginnings; for the more slowly events followed upon one another, the more quickly they can be described" (*SD*, p. 167; 146). Rousseau faces a threefold problem. First, like all narrators he must condense his narrative. Second, since his narrative is not only a history but one of the entire duration of human existence, the problem of reduction is maximized. And third, as he himself claims, the more slowly history develops, the more quickly it can be narrated.

The problem Rousseau must solve, then, is somehow to convey the sense of a "slow succession of events and knowledge" (*SD*, p. 164; 142), while condensing, through summary and ellipsis, those thousands of years of human history. Why, we might ask, should it matter? Whether

---

[11]Quoted in Gérard Genette, *Narrative Discourse: An Essay on Method*, trans. Jane E. Lewin (Ithaca, 1980), p. 33.

[12]I am using Genette's pair of terms, *histoire/récit*, which he in turn borrows from Émile Benveniste.

[13]Genette, *Narrative Discourse*, pp. 93–95.

it took a million years or a mere thousand, the order of the events recounted would not change and neither would the location of the origin of inequality. Yet Rousseau repeatedly emphasizes the slowness of the progression in direct statements such as those quoted above.

A brief explanation of the importance of a slow rate of change in the early stages of human history can be found at the end of part 1 of the *Discours*, as Rousseau introduces the narrative that is to follow. One must regret, however, that Rousseau felt he could dispense with his "reflections concerning the way in which the lapse of time compensates for the slight probability of events," because therein lies his need to combat the sense of swift progress conveyed by the condensing action of narrative (*SD*, p. 162; 141). Rousseau must convey a sense of the slowness of human development because the verisimilitude, and thus the believability, of the history he wants to narrate is in direct proportion to the length of time it covers.[14] The believability of the history increases as (and because) the probability of the events' actually having occurred increases. With the improbability of a development out of the state of nature already established in part 1 of the *Discours*, Rousseau must now, through the introduction of temporality, demonstrate its possibility and, through the use of a long duration, its probability. The extension of temporal duration is a key factor in producing the type of conviction born of probability that characterizes the contingency of historical knowledge. As Pierre Burgelin notes in his discussion of this dimension of the text, "by extending the length of time, combinations infinitely varied by chance can be produced."[15]

Rousseau is faced with a difficult problem. In order for his history to be believable (which is, after all, one of the few criteria of validity in historical knowledge), it must convey a sense of almost infinite duration; the closer it approaches infinity, the higher the probability and thus the believability of the history. Yet any one state—the first one included—must respect the limits of the finite in order to be historical at all. In addition, Rousseau is bound by the form of historical narrative, which allows him to introduce chance as explanation, even though the form itself acts against his purposes by its necessary condensation of historical into narrative time.

By stating directly that the succession of events is slow, Rousseau counteracts the force of narrative time to some degree. Rousseau's major weapon in this battle, however, is the use of that one of Genette's four canonical forms of narrative movement which is not narrational, and

---

[14]On the relationship between believability and verisimilitude in the eighteenth century see François Jost, "Le Roman épistolaire," p. 398.

[15]Pierre Burgelin, *La Philosophie de l'existence de J.-J. Rousseau* (Paris, 1952), p. 194.

which he calls "the absolute slowness of descriptive pause."[16] What better way to define the temporality of the state of nature as described in part 1 of the *Second Discours* than this, an "absolute slowness"?

By arresting time at the outset, by not starting the historical clock, Rousseau is employing the most powerful narrative tool at his disposal to convey a sense of long duration. Although when viewed in its own terms the state of nature described in part 1 of the *Discours* is in temporal opposition to any notion of history to come, its summary in the first paragraphs of part 2 allows for its assimilation into narrative time. As such, it would be accurate to say both that the description given in part 1 draws out the narrative moment of part 2 and that the infinity of the first part is reduced to a single moment in the second. In fact, although the opposition between nature and history, or between logic and contingency, is seemingly absolute in the first part of the *Discours*, even here Rousseau introduces temporality into the state of nature through the use of rhetorical questions and conditional suppositions.

While maintaining the eternity of the state of nature, Rousseau also uses a temporal vocabulary to approximate its infinite duration. While asserting that without the intervention of chance men would have remained forever in the state of nature, Rousseau also asks such questions as: "How many centuries perhaps elapsed before men were capable of seeing another fire than that from heaven?" (*SD*, p. 144; 118). In fact, what Rousseau claims to have proved in part 1 of the *Discours* is not that the state of nature is eternal, but that only after "many centuries" could men have had either the desire or the opportunity to leave it (*SD*, p. 152; 127). Thus, even within the context of a logical argument describing an eternal condition, Rousseau conveys a sense of long duration necessary to support the probabilistic argument of part 2. Absolute slowness does not, in this case, equal absence of movement altogether. Thus Michèle Duchet can argue that

> in the "slow succession of things," the first period is that in which Rousseau stops for the longest time: the whole first part of the *Discours* concerns "primitive man" and "the pure state of nature," while in the second part the "intermediate positions" are marked only by rather brief pauses. To the state of happy immobility, to the narcissistic repose of original man, is thus opposed—dialectically and stylistically—the cycle of revolutions that quickly succeed one another.[17]

[16]Genette, *Narrative Discourse*, p. 93. Genette makes the distinction between narrational and nonnarrational elements in a narrative in his essay "Boundaries of Narrative," in which he discusses the relative functions of narration and description in the narrative. See also below, p. 144.

[17]Michèle Duchet, *Anthropologie et histoire au siècle des lumières: Buffon, Voltaire, Rousseau, Helvétius, Diderot* (Paris, 1971), p. 327.

Viewed in its own terms, the state of nature is what Duchet calls that of "happy immobility," and as such it contrasts dramatically with the irreversible and uncontrollable movement narrated in part 2. From the perspective of that linear temporality (or of its relative end in the present), however, the immobility of the state of nature is a narrative illusion, the effect of the use of a descriptive pause. Duchet is exactly right when she says that it is Rousseau who stops at length to describe the state of nature: as narrator, it is he who arrests narrative time in order to approximate the "absolute slowness" of historical time.

In contrast to the lengthy description of the state of nature in part 1, the descriptions found in part 2 of the *Discours* are relatively short. Even so, they do provide momentary pauses, as Duchet points out, and as such they serve Rousseau's purpose in slowing down the narrative. They do so, moreover, not by great ruptures but by steady increments. Thus, although Rousseau's aim is to show how change has occurred, the stages that come between the moments of change play an important role in defining that change, not only through before-and-after comparisons, which the descriptions provide substantively, but also in defining the speed or tempo of historical change.

If the state of nature as described in part 1 of the *Discours* becomes a part of the historical narrative as a pause in it, then the pseudohistory that establishes the other boundary of the narrative can be said to be marked by a refusal to pause. Because the pseudohistory does not depend on verisimilitude for its believability, it can dispense with the complex interaction of extension and condensation with which the narrative tries to convey a specific sense of historical time. Thus Rousseau signals the beginning of the pseudohistory by dispensing with the narrative mechanism of descriptive pause: "Things having reached this point, it is easy to imagine the rest. I shall not stop to describe the successive invention of the other arts, the progress of languages, the testing and use of talents" (*SD*, p. 174; 155).

The descriptive pause of the state of nature and the refusal to pause that signals the pseudohistory surround a narrative composed in two of Genette's four canonical forms of narrative movement: summary and (again) short descriptive pauses. The technique that Rousseau does not use to condense time is the narrative ellipsis, by means of which a portion of historical time is bracketed and omitted, as, for example: "thousands of years later . . ." or "years passed until one day . . . ." Rousseau cannot use this technique because it would create unexplained gaps in the narrative. Such temporal gaps would not serve his purpose. Rather, in order to produce a convincing historical narrative, Rousseau must present it as a continuous whole. As he says at the end of part 1 of the *Discours*, "when two facts given as real are to be connected by a series of intermediate facts which are unknown or considered as such, it is up to history, when it exists, to present the facts that connect them; while it is up to philosophy, when history is lacking, to determine similar facts that might connect them" (*SD*, pp. 162–63; 141). As both historian and philosopher in this case, Rousseau's aim is to fill in the gaps in the historical record, an aim not served by creating gaps in narrative time. Since the use of narrative forces him to condense time in some fashion, Rousseau is left with the summary as the basic style of the history he narrates. The alternation of summary and description creates a slow and steady rhythm that conveys the sense of a development by small increments.

Rousseau takes advantage of one additional technique to control the temporality of this narrative: the use of the authorial intrusion or excursis that comments upon the narrative. Genette distinguishes such digressions from the descriptive pause because they are nonnarrative, as opposed to descriptions which, "as constitutive of the spatio-temporal universe of the story are *diegetic*."[18] Although the state of nature described in the first part of the *Discours* is initially placed outside the temporal framework of the subsequent narrative, when it is summarized at the beginning of part 2 it meets Genette's criteria for descriptive pause. However, the lengthy footnotes, which do not describe but substantiate the state of nature, cannot be merged into the time frame of part 2. They are, for the most part, references to anthropological information gathered from published accounts of contemporary voyages of exploration. There are also numerous references to Buffon's *Histoire naturelle*, as well as to ancient authors (notes v, xiii, xiv) and to modern philosophers such as Locke (note xii). By separating the notes physically from the main body of the text, Rousseau has made possible the subtle assimilation of the description of the state of nature into the narrative time frame in part 2. The notes themselves, however, add bulk to the first part of the work, creating a second level of pause that, by extending reading (narrative) time, adds to the perceived length of historical duration represented.[19]

Rousseau's exploitation of the various functions described here may not be typical of narrative, but it is highly effective. He uses the panoply of narrative functions to combat the necessary condensation of historical time when it is converted into narrative time. He also wants to produce a

---

[18]Genette, *Narrative Discourse*, p. 94, n. 12.

[19]Although Rousseau adds notes to pt. 2 of the *Discours* as well, there are only four of them, compared to the twelve in pt. 1. Of the four notes to pt. 2, moreover, the longest is (in the Pléiade edition) less than two pages, whereas notes ix and x to pt. 1 are both over six pages long. Of the four notes to pt. 2, only one pertains to the historical narrative, and it comments on the "new beginning" whose rhetorical validity rests on being an imitation of the state of nature (see below). This note (xvi) alone in pt. 2 acts as a pause in the narrative, the others being temporally insignificant comments on the pseudohistory.

slow and steady rhythm that will lend continuity to historical change, in contrast to the rapidity with which human institutions rise and fall in the pseudohistory. Rousseau achieves these goals primarily through the use of narrational summary and one long and several short descriptive pauses. The refusal to pause that marks the dividing line between historical narrative and pseudohistory, as well as the nonnarrative footnotes, also work toward a narrative that represents a long, continuous historical duration marked by slow but steady change. In the end, it is Rousseau who is master of the crucial power of narrative, by which it converts historical time into narrative time, and not the form that masters him.

Retrospection

Because the history Rousseau narrates in part 2 of the *Second Discours* does not have the advantage of conventional historical particulars, such as names, dates, and places, to give it the credibility of facts, the author is much more dependent than is the usual historian on the rhetorical power of historical narrative as literary form. In the last section I dealt with the narrative aspect of Rousseau's history: the way in which the author capitalized on the distinction between narrative and historical time to create a particular temporal structure that allowed for both the contingency of historical change and its actual occurrence. In the following discussion I will turn the problem around and focus on the historical aspect of the narrative.

The essential feature of all historical narratives is their inherent retrospection. Whereas a novelist may employ a retrospective point of view to give his narrative the semblance of history, just as he may introduce historical particulars for the same reason, these are borrowings that can only emphasize their value as rhetorical elements of history rather than of fiction. That is, the assumption that retrospection lends credibility to a fictional narrative is at least circumstantial evidence that it is associated in the author's mind (and, he must believe, the reader's) with historical veracity. Louis Mink provides additional evidence in distinguishing between fiction and history as narrative modes of comprehension in terms of the retrospection characteristic of the latter. He argues against W. B. Gallie that historical comprehension cannot be based on the phenomenology of following. Whereas Gallie argues that all stories, including histories, are propelled by the reader's curiosity to know how they end, Mink denies that (in Gallie's words) "it is chiefly in terms of the conclusion—eagerly awaited as we read forward and accepted at the story's end—that we feel and appreciate the unity of a story."[20] Even

<hr />

[20]Gallie, *Philosophy and the Historical Understanding*, p. 29.

the most naive reader of a historical narrative, Mink counters, must know how it all comes out, and the recognition of that knowledge determines the difference in structure between fictional and historical comprehension. We may understand fiction by anticipation, but we comprehend history by retrospection, a fundamentally different process. In a historical narrative, it is not the end that must be acceptable as consistent with the middle, but the middle that must be made to lead to the predetermined and stated conclusion.[21]

Before examining the structure of part 2 of the *Second Discours* to see how the historical perspective operates in the text, we should discuss once again the relationship between nature and history, this time with reference to the historical perspective inherent in Rousseau's choice of form. For, as A. R. Louch notes, "what confers the aura of inevitability on the historical process is that the different episodes that carry the story forward are chosen in such a way as to *lead* to the circumstances with which the historian has chosen to end his tale."[22]

The retrospection inherent in the historical perspective is, first, an obstacle that Rousseau must overcome if he is to make clear the contingency of history in part 1 of the *Discours*. In part 2, however, once the contingency of the history he is about to relate has been established, Rousseau's problem is none other than to determine those events that "must have led" to the endpoint of the historical present: historical necessity takes the place of historical contingency. The historical perspective, which is repeatedly denied in part 1 of the *Discours*, is thus repeatedly invoked in part 2. As stated earlier, the "need not be" of part 1 is transformed into the "must have been" of part 2. Through an intensified

[21]Mink, "History and Fiction as Modes of Comprehension," *New Literary History* 1 (1970): 544–46. Although I believe that Mink has found a crucial flaw in Gallie's argument, I do not agree that it invalidates Gallie's notion of following altogether. As my references to this notion earlier should make clear, following need not be viewed as teleological in the way Gallie describes it in order to function as the propellant of narrative. It is the emphasis on the process, the movement implied by following, that is crucial, rather than the sense of a movement toward some unknown end. Whether or not that end is known, acceptability of the narrative still depends on one thing's following another. In fact, following is more important in historical than in fictional narrative because the end is already known and only the middle—the following itself—is in question. Gallie himself comes close to this perception in the following passage: "To appreciate, and in a proper sense to use, a book or a chapter of history means to read it through; to follow it in the light of its *promised or adumbrated outcome* through a succession of contingencies, and not simply to be interested in what resulted or could be inferred as due to result from certain initial conditions. . . . History, like all stories and all imaginative literature, is as much a journey as an arrival, as much an approach as a result": *Philosophy and the Historical Understanding*, pp. 66–67.

[22]A. R. Louch, "History as Narrative," *History and Theory* 8 (1969): 69.

use of the form of historical narrative, characterized by retrospection, the middle of Rousseau's narrative seeks to produce a level of rhetorical conviction that may approximate two others: that born of logic, which defines its beginning, and that based on lived experience, which defines its end.

"True history follows a *durée* between two fixed points," writes Pierre Burgelin: "The first is attained by a phenomenological analysis of the essence of man, promoted to a hypothetical existence in a propitious environment. The second is experimental: the situation of 'l'homme de l'homme' in the most complex and the most corrupt societies."[23] These two points, it must be emphasized, are independent of the historical narrative and precede it. The present state of man in society, according to Rousseau, need not be proved at all, since it is constantly experienced. The starting point, the natural state of man, is the subject of part 1 of the *Discours*, and is shown there to be not only independent of the historical argument and its conclusion but diametrically opposed to it. Only because the convictions arising from these two certainties are in opposition is the historical narrative necessary at all as a means of reconciling them through the introduction of chance working in time.

One thing still leads to another in historical narrative, as narrative coherence requires, but it does so within circumscribed boundaries that are established independently of the narrative. The historian's task can thus be seen as the filling in of a gap between two known points. As Louch puts it: "What we want to do . . . is fill in the gaps and provide a smooth flow of change where a first glance reveals radical discontinuities."[24] Certainly there is no better term to describe Rousseau's starting and end points as they first appear than "radical discontinuities"; as to filling in the gap between them, this is what Rousseau himself says he must do: "when two facts given as real are to be connected by a series of intermediate facts which are unknown or considered as such, it is up to history, when it exists, to present the facts that connect them; while it is up to philosophy, when history is lacking, to determine similar facts that might connect them" (*SD*, pp. 162–63; 141). Rousseau's narrative can be considered philosophical in these terms because the intermediate events he introduces to connect the two ends are drawn from no historical record, but it is historical in that what is discovered "philosophically" is validated (that is, carries conviction) through the use of a historical form.

In beginning his narrative Rousseau does not simply establish a point

[23]Pierre Burgelin, "Rousseau et l'histoire," in *De Ronsard à Breton: Recueil d'essais, hommages à Marcel Raymond* (Paris, 1967), p. 113.
[24]Louch, "History as Narrative," p. 55.

A and then proceed in linear fashion to the point *B* of the present. Rather, he begins by marking an intermediate point between the two: the moment of the origin of civil society, that moment when "the first person who, having fenced off a plot of ground, took it into his head to say *this is mine* and found people simple enough to believe him" (*SD*, p. 164; 141). This is the most crucial intermediate point in Rousseau's narrative, and, significantly it is placed at the beginning of the narrative, not in its proper chronological position. Rousseau does more than simply establish the historical perspective here; that could have been accomplished simply by invoking the present. Rather, he substitutes for the present an intermediate point that cannot in itself carry the same conviction, since it is not known through experience. In this way Rousseau bestows on a hypothetical (but possible) intermediate point the rhetorical value of the true endpoint. Furthermore, not only has Rousseau placed the origin of civil society in such a position that it seems to need no proof, but in so doing he has reduced the gap that must now be filled. Since the origin of civil society is earlier in time than the present, it is less changed from nature as well, and it is thus easier for the reader to grasp the space that divides them. In other words, Rousseau is giving the reader a smaller bite of time to swallow. This reduction does not eliminate the sense of change or the linear temporality of the "bite;" it simply allows the reader to keep both ends in view at the same time, thus maintaining a constant sense of the historical perspective and the historical necessity it implies.[25]

The creation of "smaller bites of time" makes Rousseau's method (that is, historical narrative) "geometric" rather than "genetic," for it proceeds

---

[25]Mink uses the distinction between anticipation and retrospection as the basis of an argument against the temporality of historical narrative, since its comprehension does not build as the story unfolds but occurs only when the entire complex of relationships that makes up the story has been presented, and everything fits together. Comprehension, he says, "consists in thinking together in a single act, or in a cumulative series of acts, the complicated relationships of parts which can be experienced only *seriatum*" ("History and Fiction as Modes of Comprehension," p. 548). Mink is giving the same argument for historical comprehension as certain linguists give for the comprehension of a sentence: it must be presented temporally but is only comprehended at the end when the listener or reader knows the grammatical role of each word, and thus its sentential meaning. What is lost in Mink's extension of sentential grammar to narrative (and to historical narrative in particular) is that the relationship of parts in a narrative *is* linear to the extent (but not exclusively) that it aims to reproduce or represent the linearity of human (historical or biographical) time—either factual or fictional. In Hayden White's terms, the historical work is "a verbal structure in the form of narrative prose discourse that purports to be a model, or icon, of past structures and processes in the interest of *explaining what they were by representing them*": *Metahistory: The Historical Imagination in Nineteenth-Century Europe* (Baltimore, 1973), p. 2.

by dividing and subdividing a timeline defined and determined by two boundary points through the marking of intermediate points between them. As Goldschmidt explains: "Time no longer appears as an infinitude, impossible to traverse, but as an interval limited by two terms; and the problem is not to traverse it, but to divide an extent by means of a system."[26]

The second well-defined intermediate point that Rousseau marks in his narrative is the "golden mean between the indolence of the primitive state and the petulant activity of our vanity" (*SD*, p. 171; 150–51). This point lies between the origin of man and the origin of civil society, and thus it again reduces the temporal gap by creating two where there was one. This point, however, is introduced in its proper place chronologically and so does not take on the rhetorical validity of an endpoint, as does the origin of civil society. Rather, by attributing to this point the stability of the state of nature, Rousseau makes of it a new beginning. In Rousseau's terms, a beginning is not simply, as for Aristotle, "that which is not a necessary consequent of anything else but after which something else exists or happens as a natural result."[27] For Rousseau, a beginning is something that need not be followed by anything else, but that, in fact, is. The "golden mean," characterized as it is by stasis and not by change, recalls the state of nature, and in that recollection is found its rhetorical validity. As the logical validity of the state of nature is dependent upon a denial of the historical perspective, this new beginning mimics that state by borrowing the language of the denial: "The more one thinks about it, the more one finds that this state was the least subject to revolutions, the best for man, and that he must have come out of it only by some fatal accident, which for the common good ought never to have happened" (*SD*, p. 171; 151). Described in this way, the intermediate point becomes a new beginning not because what comes before it is denied, but because that which follows it need not have; it is the image not of a chronological beginning but of a logical one.

There is another important ramification of the introduction of this second intermediate point. One problem that results from the hypothetical or philosophical character of Rousseau's historical narrative is that, while covering a period of time that is both defined and determined (that is, bounded) by two points, the length of the historical time represented is not measurable because the origin is not datable (or at least not dated). Although the lack of historical dating may be seen as an advantage to Rousseau in terms of his ability to manipulate freely the relationship between narrative and historical time (and also because he thus avoids

[26]Goldschmidt, *Anthropologie et politique*, p. 428.
[27]*Poetics* 7.1450b 4–5.

direct confrontation with biblical chronology), its disadvantage is a diminution of historical credibility. The duration of the narrative being only relatively and not absolutely definable, it takes on a fictional quality. The introduction of a new beginning, the "golden mean," helps reduce the temporal fictionality of the narrative by situating it in real (that is, observable) space.

While in describing the state of nature Rousseau frequently finds analogies in the behavior and conditions of both animals and primitive peoples, there is no identification of that state with any known society. Furthermore, as stated earlier, references to known primitive peoples are relegated almost entirely to the notes, thus reinforcing their role as analogy or commentary rather than as descriptions of the state of nature itself. Such a distinction and such a limitation do not, however, characterize the reference to primitive peoples in the description of the second beginning. In the midst of his discussion Rousseau remarks: "This is precisely the point reached by most of the savage peoples known to us, and it is for want of having sufficiently distinguished between ideas and noticed how far these people already were from the first state of nature that many have hastened to conclude that man is naturally cruel" (*SD*, p. 170; 150).

By equating this intermediate state with that of known primitive peoples Rousseau has given the appearance of grounding his narrative in historical time. What he has really done is introduced a second chronology, since the present (the time of knowing the primitives) is already assumed to be that of the advanced societies in which Rousseau and his readers live. By merging the two chronologies, the present of the known primitive peoples becomes the past of the author and reader, and the certainty that adheres to it as observed fact remains with it when transformed into the shared past.[28] This new beginning, which is acknowledged to be of the same linear temporality as the original one, is created not only in rhetorical imitation of the logical certainty of the state of nature, but with the additional value of providing the narrative with a second anchor point in historical space and time. As a new beginning, the "golden mean" has the rhetorical power of appearing both logical

[28]The interchangeability of spatial and temporal distances has already been encountered in the *Lettres persanes* and will appear as well in the *Supplément*. Anthropology (and the voyages that provide its data) is simply history on a different axis. But as with any common assumption, the particular use of the equation of space and time is of prime importance here. The use of anthropological observation to ground a historical argument is here in the service of historical and not anthropological understanding. The opposite procedure (one that is close to Diderot's purpose in the *Supplément*) is described by Duchet in *Anthropologie et histoire*, p. 15.

and factual, even though it can be described neither as natural nor as historical.

Within the history of the human race from its origin to the present time, Rousseau has inserted a subhistory that begins with primitive societies (that is, savage societies turned primitive) and ends with the origin of civil society. It is within this subset of historical time that Rousseau locates the origin of inequality. Because this period follows the new beginning, it is presented both as contingent and as within historical time and space; because it precedes the new ending (or is cotemporal with it), the amount of change that leads up to it is limited to a single transformation that is easily grasped: that which results directly from the introduction of agriculture and metallurgy. Rousseau has thus situated the origin of inequality precisely and historically (in the double sense of factual and contingent). By subdividing the seemingly infinite duration required by probability, and locating the point he seeks between narrow bounds that mirror rhetorically the certainties of logic and observation, Rousseau has defined precisely (although without dates) a single moment of historical change.

The question of the definition and number of stages portrayed in the *Second Discours* gives way here to its reverse image of moments of change. One finds the diachrony of history not in the stages described but in the change that divides them. Since Rousseau employs historical narrative as a form that expresses change over time, it is the moments of change that stand out against a background of static images. The various stages Rousseau describes or alludes to are important only insofar as they divide change into single moments. The valorization of these stages, and especially of the "golden mean"as a golden age, becomes difficult to support as the stages themselves shrink in importance relative to the changes that divide them. The history of the human race, as Rousseau presents it, is divided not into stages but by them.[29]

The moment of change that defines the origin of inequality is a history within a history; its validity depends on its being inscribed within the larger whole whose endpoints are not rhetorically but logically and factually grounded. The story cannot end here, even though the origin of

[29]See Michèle Duchet and Michel Launay, "Synchrophonie et diachronie: *L'Essai sur l'origine des langues* et le second *Discours*," *Revue Internationale de Philosophie*, no. 82 (1967), p. 434; and Pierre Daguerressar, *Morale et politique: Jean-Jacques Rousseau ou la fonction d'un refus* (Paris, 1977), p. 35. For the valorization of the "golden mean" as a golden age see Burgelin, *La Philosophie de l'existence*, p. 204; Judith N. Shklar, *Men and Citizens: A Study of Rousseau's Social Theory*, (Cambridge, 1969), p. 51; Jean Terrasse, *Jean-Jacques Rousseau et la quête de l'âge d'or* (Brussels, 1970), pp. 59–85; and Marc Eigeldinger, *Jean-Jacques Rousseau: Univers mythique et cohérence* (Neuchâtel, 1978), pp. 85ff.

inequality has been located and defined, since it has not yet fully connected the two points that define it. It does, however, change radically (if almost imperceptibly) in form, since at this point the contingency of chance gives way to the necessity of deductive reasoning, and historical narrative to pseudohistory.

Pseudohistory and Historical Narrative

Rousseau has been accused more than once of creating simply a pseudohistory based on a chain of deductions backward from the present to the state of nature.[30] He is, however, at great pains to demonstrate that modern man, far from being the logical result of natural man, is just the opposite, and that he could have come into existence only through the working of chance over an extremely long period of time. Rousseau does not simply disguise a backward deduction (from modern society to the state of nature) as the forward march of history. This legitimately historical narrative, however, stops at the moment of the joint origins of property, civil society, and inequality, and it there gives way to a chain of necessary deductions. If there is a pseudohistory in the *Second Discours*, it is located here, for Rousseau inserts this chain of necessary deductions into the previously established historical space between the origin of civil society and the present. An examination of the structure of this portion of the text (the second half of part 2) will indicate how it differs from that of the historical narrative that precedes it.

The working of chance depended on the narrative historical structure based upon retrospection; the subsequent chain of deductive reasoning lacks that structure. Not only are no new endpoints generated to reduce the retrospective gap, but the ultimate historical endpoint—the present—becomes itself a new midpoint, as the chain of deductions, unhindered by historical temporality, continues into the future. Although this chain of deductions describes changes in the human world, and although it follows the linear chronology of human history, it is immediately distinguishable from true history by its lack of retrospection. The elimination of the retrospective vantage point does away equally with the limitation it defines.

Because subsequent developments can be deduced from this new starting point, Rousseau is able to alternate narrative and descriptive passages

[30]See, e.g., Ulrich S. Allers, "Rousseau's *Second Discourse*," *Review of Politics* 20 (January 1958): 97; Broome, *Rousseau: A Study of His Thought*, p. 35; Jacques Dehaussy, "La Dialectique de la souveraine liberté dans le *Contrat social*," in *Études sur le "Contrat social"* (Paris, 1964), p. 127; and Pierre Manent, *Naissances de la politique moderne* (Paris, 1977), p. 152.

at will, without concern for their implications for the relationship between narrative and historical time. Chance being eliminated, duration is no longer a rhetorical factor, although temporality does remain. The mimetic effect of narrative temporality is replaced by a regularity of deduction that has its own rhythm of inevitability. This regularity carries the narrative beyond the limits of the historical present into a necessary future described in language recalling the epic: "It is from the bosom of this disorder and these revolutions that despotism, by degrees raising its hideous head and devouring all it had seen to be good and healthy in all parts of the State, would finally succeed in trampling underfoot the laws and the people, and in establishing itself upon the ruins of the Republic" (*SD*, pp. 190–91; 176–77). More than a simple overflowing of language, this passage shows Rousseau to be free at last of the historical bounds he has imposed upon the text to this point.

Pseudohistory is attained through the insertion of a chain of necessary deductions into a historical timeframe; it can be distinguished from historical narrative through its lack of historical perspective. Such a historical perspective is defined by the point at which a historical narrative must end and by the end to which the narrative must lead, which confers upon it historical necessity.

Historical narrative has been seen to be a mode of explanation that, at its zero degree of narrative coherence, is able to attribute change to chance; one can go further and say that if the change described is the result of chance, then the condition that undergoes the change must be inherently static. In other words, the dynamics of change are extrinsic to that which undergoes it. In these terms, pseudohistory can easily be seen as the opposite of historical narrative, because the changes it describes are intrinsic to that which undergoes them. For a reading of the *Second Discours*, this means that not only the state of nature, but man's condition up to the point when inequality characterizes it, is inherently stable, but that inequality destabilizes man's world, making it necessarily dynamic. Staying with this reading, the second state of nature, which follows the last stage of inequality, is thus a new stability. It is the necessary and predictable end of the pseudohistory if one assumes that an unstable condition cannot persist indefinitely but that, like an object in motion, it seeks rest.[31]

Viewed in this way, the *Second Discours* divides not between the stability of the state of nature and the dynamism of history but between the inherent stability of equality—even as man's condition changes con-

---

[31]The similarity in phrasing to a physical law is intentional. It might not be too farfetched to identify the condition of stability (equality) with Newton's first law, in that it remains at rest unless subject to an external force.

tingently—and the inherent dynamics of inequality. It is not in terms of history and nature that the text divides, but in terms of narrative history and pseudohistory.[32] The original state of nature, brought into the narrative as a descriptive pause and in a condensed version early in part 2, shows the division between the first and second parts of the text to be— in retrospect—artificial, just as the state of nature is itself seen to be an artificial construct when viewed from the historical perspective. The pseudohistory, on the other hand, although located chronologically and overlapping the space determined by the vantage point of the present as that of historical narrative, cannot be merged with narrative history, even though it emerges out of it, because the laws of its motion are not controlled by the narrative. The dynamic that propels inequality through its three successive stages is independent of historical particularity (that is, circumstance, and thus chance). Whereas the integration of the state of nature into the historical narrative removes an artificial ahistoricity, the placing of the three stages of inequality into the chronology generates an artificial historicity.

In consequence of the redivision of the *Second Discours* between historical narrative and pseudohistory, the condemnation of history, and of change in general, that some critics have found in the text loses credibility.[33] Stability is no longer opposed to change, since Rousseau's narrative demonstrates that change can be undergone without jeopardizing stability. Stability is now aligned with equality, and instability with inequality. Historical change is itself value-free, and the terms "good" and "bad," if they must be applied, align with stability (equality) and instability (inequality). Figure 1 illustrates how the opposition between nature and history, now seen to be a product merely of point of view, shifts to one between narrative history and pseudohistory, as the crucial terms are redistributed.

Ambiguities in Rousseau's attitude toward change can now be resolved, since change is no longer viewed as a monolithic concept opposed to a static nature. For example, consider the various attitudes toward change that William Pickles attributes to Rousseau.

> Along with Rousseau's belief in both the creative and stabilizing values of time, however, there goes an acceptance of the inevitability of change through time, and a recognition, in both earlier and later works, that

---

[32]See Gouhier, "Nature et histoire," for the clearest statement of the nature/history dichotomy in the *Discours*.

[33]See, e.g., Kelly, "Land of Chimeras," in his *Idealism, Politics, and History*, p. 25; Eigeldinger, *Univers mythique et cohérence*, p. 56; Judith Shklar, "Rousseau's Two Models: Sparta and the Age of Gold," *Political Science Quarterly* 81 (March 1966): 48; Starobinski, "Discourse on Inequality," p. 303.

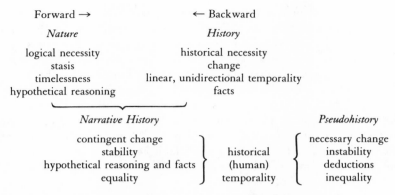

Figure 1. The distribution of crucial terms in Rousseau's *Second Discours*.

change is sometimes desirable. . . . [In the *Second Discours*] we find a conflict that Rousseau never satisfactorily resolves, between acceptance of change on the one hand, and on the other what might be called Platonic pessimism about its consequences in political life.[34]

Leaving aside the idea that time is "creative," we can certainly see that it is stabilizing, since the pseudohistory shows that an unstable situation will eventually (and inevitably) restabilize over time. This kind of change, still following Pickles, is inevitable, but it is not desirable insofar as man's relations worsen because of it. On the other hand, once instability has begun, only through change can a new stability be attained, so in this sense, or, in the long run, change is for the better. In either case, desire does not really have an effect. The only good or desirable changes are those that do not destabilize human relations in the first place. Finally, Rousseau's acceptance of change is attributable both to a historical perspective that sees change as the only solution to the conundrum in terms of which the question of the origin of inequality is posed, and to Rousseau's assumption that an unstable condition will necessarily restabilize.

A final consequence of eliminating the opposition between nature and history is that any formal resemblance between the *Second Discours* and the biblical story of the fall disappears with it. Starobinski, although neither the first nor the last to present the argument that the *Second Discours* is simply Rousseau's version of the fall, is perhaps its most

---

[34]William Pickles, "The Notion of Time in Rousseau's Political Thought," in *Hobbes and Rousseau: A Collection of Critical Essays*, ed. Maurice Cranston and Richard S. Peters (Garden City, N.Y., 1972), p. 377.

influential proponent. "The drama of the fall does not precede man's earthly existence," he writes. "Rousseau takes the religious myth and sets it in historical time, which he divides into two ages: a changeless age of innocence, during which pristine nature reigns in peace, and an age of historical change, of culpable activity, of negation of nature by man."[35] Viewed structurally, the *Second Discours* is completely different from a fall from grace. In Rousseau's text, it is not temporality or change that is opposed to an eternal state of innocence, but a stable, equal relationship among men in and over time that gives way to its opposite: an unstable order that must undergo certain predictable changes so as to leave social, political, and economic relations among men once more equal and stable.

If the opposition of historical narrative and pseudohistory supersedes that of nature and history in the text, it still must not be viewed as the overall structuring device of the *Discours*. The pseudohistory, although operating on a principle that leaves it independent of the retrospective point of view of historical narrative, is significant only in terms of the chronological timeframe established by the narrative. Although it breaks the bounds of the historically knowable, the pseudohistorical chain of deductions is inscribed in the narrative space of historical chronology. Only by placing the first stage of the progress of inequality in the past can Rousseau predict the occurrence of the third and final stage in the future. And although Rousseau calls this final stage a new state of nature, it is qualitatively different from the first because it is temporally removed from it. All those developments, those changes resulting from chance that constitute history (not pseudohistory), remain irreversibly. The image of the closing circle is only an image. In the end, it is the irreversibility of historical narrative and of its chronology, extended into the future, that separates one state of nature from the other. The determinate, linear, narrative historical structure is now seen to reverse on itself, reaching outward to include its nonhistorically defined boundaries within its own structure.

Jean Terrasse argues that "there is no . . . absolute opposition between the past and the future; if the state of nature did not perhaps ever exist, it becomes a goal to realize in the future." This cannot be so, however, since it is the distinction between past and future created by the historical narrative that gives the state of nature its concrete existence in the world. And so Terrasse has again missed Rousseau's point when he says that "time is not linear; history is submitted to an eternal return, and this is

[35]*Jean-Jacques Rousseau*, p. 12. See also Ernst Cassirer, *The Question of Jean-Jacques Rousseau*, trans. Peter Gay (Bloomington, Ind., 1963), p. 78; and Bertrand de Jouvenel, "Essai sur la politique de Rousseau," in Rousseau, *Du Contrat social* (Geneva, 1947), pp. 72–73.

why it is stripped of all meaning."[36] The illusion is not linear history, since only historical narrative can explain the origin of inequality, but the image of circularity to which the reinstatement of equality and stability gives rise.

What does the future hold for Rousseau? With the original state of nature established as man's most ancient past, it cannot return as his future. And the changes wrought by chance on man's constitution—the development of his faculties—cannot be undone either. The future must take account of these consequences of historical linearity, as well as of the necessary progress of inequality to its final stage, now merged into human chronology as the immediate future.

Conclusion

Paradoxical as it may seem, it is the form of historical narrative, itself limited within the bounds of a historical past and the present, that allows Rousseau to extend his critique of civil society into the future. The pseudohistory is inserted into the structure of historical narrative but extends beyond it, and the rhetorical strength of the base in actual narrative thereby supports it. But the pseudohistory, too, is of determinate length, ending at some definite and necessary point in the future when the third and final term of inequality brings men into a new state of nature, a new balance of equality. At that point the future, still holding to the linearity and unidirectionality established by narrative historical structure as human temporality, will again be undetermined. Just as the past divides at the moment when inequality is established, separating history from pseudohistory and contingent from necessary change, so too will the future divide at the moment when equality among men is reestablished. If there is room for change based on human action in the future into which the *Second Discours* projects, it can only be in this second, indeterminate period.

A problem stands in the way of any discussion of the future that would emerge from the *Second Discours*, since it is not at all clear where the present is located in the pseudohistory, and thus where the future begins. If the point at which the use of the imperfect gives way to the conditional mode signals the present, then that moment is the one described as follows: "the chiefs, having become hereditary, grew accustomed to consider their magistracy as a family possession, to regard themselves as proprietors of the State, of which they were at first only the

---

[36]Terrasse, *La Quête de l'âge d'or*, pp. 73, 84.

officers, to call their fellow citizens their slaves, count them like cattle in the number of things that belonged to them, and call themselves equals of the gods and kings of kings" (*SD*, p. 187; 172). In then schematizing the progress of inequality into three stages, Rousseau still uses the imperfect to describe all three, so it would seem that the situation described above, which clearly represents the absolute monarchy of eighteenth-century France painted in its bleakest colors, is indeed the third term, that following the change from legitimate to arbitrary power and characterized by master–slave relations.[37]

Somewhat later, however, Rousseau again discusses the "ultimate stage of inequality," but here he seems to be speaking of the future. This is the passage in which Rousseau writes of the subjects he would discuss in another, larger work, where "one would unmask all the different faces behind which inequality has appeared until the present and may appear in future centuries, according to the nature of these governments and the revolutions time will necessarily bring about in them" (*SD*, pp. 189–90; 175).

But if we have already reached the third stage, what more is there to describe? Anyway, the description that follows this introduction does not continue the one that ended with the magistrates' calling themselves the equals of gods, kings of kings. Here one would see "the rights of citizens and national freedoms die out little by little" and "politics limit to a mercenary portion of the people the honor of defending the common cause"; here the Roman poet Lucan is invoked to speak out against the oppressor; here "one would see chiefs foment all that can weaken assembled men by disuniting them; all that can give society an air of apparent concord while spreading a seed of real division; all that can inspire defiance and mutual hatred in different orders through the opposition of their rights and interests, and consequently fortify the power that contains them all." And finally, "It is from the bosom of this disorder and these revolutions that despotism, by degrees raising its hideous head . . . , would finally succeed in trampling underfoot the laws and the people, and in establishing itself upon the ruins of the Republic" (*SD*, pp. 190–91; 175–77).

---

[37] A manuscript of an earlier version of this portion of the text, now in the Bibliothèque Nationale (Paris), supports this reading. Although the manuscript is in an unknown hand, the corrections are in Rousseau's. In the passage quoted above, Rousseau has crossed out the word *sujets* and substituted for it *esclaves*, as in the published version: ". . . à appeler leurs concitoyens leurs esclaves." By changing *sujets* to *esclaves* Rousseau makes the association of this description with the third stage of inequality more obvious, since that is the key term of that stage (*maître/esclave*); his original use of *sujets* suggests that he was indeed thinking of the monarchy as embodying that description. The manuscript is published in Rousseau, *Oeuvres complètes* 3:1356–58.

This is again the third term of inequality, "the extreme point which closes the circle. . . . Here all individuals become equals again" (*SD*, p. 191; 177). It is not, however, a simple restatement of the first description, a picture with greater detail. Rather, this third stage, cast in the conditional mode proper to the future rather than in the imperfect tense of the past, describes the third stage of inequality in a different historical chronology. The stages of inequality being only pseudohistorical, they are not unique to any one historical chronology, as historical particulars must be. Thus, the same stages can describe more than one set of historical circumstances—as long as the conditions from which they are deduced remain the same. Opposed to the uniqueness of historical narrative ("one could not conceive of any other system that would not provide me with the same results," *SD*, p. 162; 141) is the unity of representation that describes pseudohistory. That is, the generality of the pseudohistory lies in its ability to represent schematically a multitude of particular (unique) histories.

The third stage of inequality is reached twice in the *Second Discours*, because the pseudohistory of the progress of inequality has been historically instantiated twice. Both chronologies necessarily begin at the moment when inequality is established. That moment is historically determined and part of a unique historical chronology; it is also the condition from which the deductions that constitute the pseudohistory necessarily follow. It is thus the end of one history and the beginning of many. Since this point is located in the past, the pseudohistory that follows can describe not only multiple futures but multiple presents as well.

Put still another way, according to Rousseau, all nations have the same history up to the point when inequality is established. Only at this point do particular histories vary on the basis of particular circumstances that give rise to particular institutions. Yet each of these histories necessarily moves through the three stages of inequality until, at last, equality is reestablished. In the *Second Discours*, Rousseau presents two possible sets of particulars that (can) instantiate the pseudohistorical schema. The first is couched in the past tense and refers to France, with the last term designating the consolidation of the monarchy and the beginning of absolute rule. It is a critical representation of the society in which Rousseau lives.

The second instantiation of the progress of inequality is couched not in the imperfect tense of the past but in the conditional mode of the future. Whereas the representation of the French monarchy as the final stage of inequality is a severe criticism, this second representation, projected into the future, is a warning, if not a prediction. But for whom? The clues have already been presented: the references to the rights of the citizens, to the honor of defending the common cause, to the republican poet Lucan, to apparent harmony masking the seeds of division, and, finally, to the republic. When Rousseau says he has brought us back full circle to the point of departure, he means it, because he has brought us back to Geneva.

Rousseau's entry in the Dijon competition is lost. There is no way of knowing how much of the published text was part of that original manuscript. It is certain, however, that the "Dedication" addressed to "the Republic of Geneva" was added afterward, written especially for the published version.[38] I suggest that the "second ending" might have been added at the same time. Were this the case, the whole text could be seen to lie within a Genevan or republican parenthesis that adds to the critique of France and the absolute monarchy a second level of criticism of Geneva and the degeneration of the republic. The juxtaposition of the two polities, placed at different stages of the same schematic pseudohistory, then serves as a striking warning to the Council of Geneva that its system, too, is subject to the inevitable degeneration of which its monarchical neighbor is the grand example.

This is not to say that the "meaning" of the text, or its import, is simply a warning to the Genevans of what is before them. That would be to lose sight of the text for the brackets that enclose it. The critique of Geneva in no way supersedes that of France; rather, the two complement each other and make doubly clear that the evils of man's current existence cannot be laid at the door of one political system or another but arise from the fundamental condition that underlies them both: inequality.

What then of the future? Rousseau has shown that all modern societies—the decaying modern republics as well as the troubled monarchies—are subject to the process of dissolution inherent in the inequality that is their common origin. It matters less that France is more advanced in this process than that nothing can be done to stop inequality in either case. Rousseau has already indicated that reform, which modifies the governmental edifice while leaving the foundations in place, is useless.

> Despite all the labors of the wisest legislators, the political state remained ever imperfect because it was almost the work of chance, and because, as it began badly, time in discovering faults and suggesting remedies could never repair the vices of the constitution. People incessantly mended, whereas it would have been necessary to begin by clearing the area and setting aside all the old materials, as Lycurgus did in Sparta, in order to raise a good edifice afterward. [*SD*, p. 180; 162–63]

[38]In the *Confessions*, Rousseau writes that he composed the "Dedication" in Paris, just before his departure for Geneva, in June 1754: *Oeuvres complètes*, 1:392.

Although this passage has been interpreted as a call to revolution, it should not be, since the state, as Rousseau emphasizes, will destroy itself.[39] And, one could oppose the possibly revolutionary tinge of this passage to the rather strange ending of note ix, in which Rousseau asks: "What! must we destroy societies, annihilate thine and mine, and go back to live in forests with bears?" Certainly Rousseau does not advise a retreat into the past because, as he says, such a retreat is impossible. But the alternative he suggests is not much more satisfying. Speaking of people like himself who have all the social attributes, including a knowledge of the divinity, he says:

> they will respect the sacred bonds of the societies of which they are members; . . . they will scrupulously obey the laws, and the men who are their authors and ministers; they will honor above all the good and wise princes who will know how to prevent, cure, or palliate that multitude of abuses and evils always ready to crush us. . . . But they will nonetheless scorn a constitution that can be maintained only with the help of so many respectable people—who are desired more often than obtained—and from which, despite all their care, always arise more real calamities than apparent advantages. [SD, pp. 207–8, n. ix; 201–3, n. i]

Rousseau seems to be saying here that, once born into society, with all that that implies, one has no choice but to embrace it, since there is no way of escaping it or its consequences in ourselves. Moreover, he seems to be counseling that, as long as one is a citizen—a member of society— one ought to be a good citizen. But third, one must be a good citizen, assisting the state and its leaders whenever possible, in the full knowledge that the state, which depends upon exactly this type of cooperation,

[39]It is not difficult to understand why the *Second Discours* lends itself to a Marxist interpretation. Sergio Cotta, for example, writes: "In order to reverse the course of human degradation, it is enough, according to Rousseau, to destroy the erroneous foundations of the corrupting society and, recognizing the primacy of politics, to bring forth a state renewed *ab imis*, founded no longer on opinion, but on reason" ("Philosophie et politique dans l'oeuvre de Rousseau," *Archiv für Rechts- und Sozialphilosophie* 49 [1963]: 183). Thus, he goes on, "it must be emphasized that it is the Marxist formula of 'overcoming in praxis' which can most adequately express the meaning of the new position and function that society assumes in the constructive phase of Rousseau's thought" (p. 184).

Friedrich Engels fixed on Rousseau's expression "the extreme point which closes the circle and touches the point from which we started" to give the first Marxist reading of the *Second Discours*. "And so," writes Engels, "inequality is once more transformed into equality; not however, into the former natural equality of speechless primeval man, but into the higher equality of the social contract. The oppressors are oppressed. It is the negation of the negation": *Herr Eugen Düring's Revolution in Science [Anti-Düring]*, trans. Emile Burns (New York, 1939), p. 153.

is fundamentally corrupt and does more harm than good. This is certainly not the advice of a revolutionary ready to tear down the state in order to build anew. And so some critics argue that Rousseau is, in the end, a pessimistic conservative who sees man as helpless to intervene as his society collapses.[40]

Rousseau's problem is that in neither the French nor the Genevan chronology will equality be reestablished in his lifetime. Although things are bad in Geneva and worse in France, they must get worse still before they can get better. This is not to say that things will get better, but there is no reason to say absolutely that they will or cannot. The pseudohistorical schema extends only to the point at which inequality gives way to a new, if corrupt, form of equality. It cannot go further because at that point necessity must once again be replaced by chance, and thus the future is not predictable beyond the reinstitution of equality. There is no reason to assume that at that point, when the indeterminacy of a balanced condition is reached, it might not be maintained.

Although nowhere in the *Second Discours* does Rousseau discuss the possibilities this new condition might hold for human action and the direction of a new future, inferences can be drawn. If the future cannot be predicted beyond the limits of the pseudohistory of determined change, the characteristics of change possible under defined conditions can at least be described. To discover what kind of change can occur under the conditions that Rousseau calls a second state of nature, it is necessary, first, to compare these new conditions with those of the original state of nature and the type of change by which it is characterized, and, second, to examine the moment at which the balance of original equality was ruptured and change shifted from indeterminate to determinate.

The state of nature, strictly speaking, is characterized by a lack of change. The condition of equality that it describes, however, and that persists until the division of property and labor, is subject to the type of change that has been defined above as doubly contingent. The potentiality of perfectibility, which may, but need not, capitalize on opportunities randomly presented by nature, constitutes this double contingency. This type of change has also been called historical change because it is not predictable and can be known only from the historical perspective, from which vantage point it becomes historically necessary. As historical change, that which constitutes the original condition of equality is both

---

[40]See Iring Fetscher, "Rousseau, auteur d'intention conservatrice et d'action révolutionnaire," in *Annales de philosophie politique*, vol. 5: *Rousseau et la philosophie politique* (Paris, 1965), pp. 52–53; and Bertrand de Jouvenel, "Rousseau the Pessimistic Evolutionist," *Yale French Studies*, no. 28 (1961–62), pp. 83–96.

linear and irreversible, and its effects are cumulative. Is this kind of change possible in the second state of nature?

Although those changes that may occur under the new condition of equality cannot be determined, it is certain that they cannot be indeterminate in the same way as those that occurred before inequality was established. Doubly contingent change cannot return for the same reason that the original condition of equality cannot be recovered: it is not only history as a narrative of events that is irreversible but the development of man's faculties as well, the potential for which made history possible in the first place. The historical change that brought man out of the condition of equality depended upon the potential inherent in man's undeveloped faculties, a potential that could be realized only through an interaction with the physical world and the opportunities for growth it presented. But this development, perfectibility, though cumulative in Rousseau's terms, is also limited. Once man's faculties have been perfected, doubly contingent change is no longer possible.

The possibility of doubly contingent historical change was lost at almost the same moment as inequality was established (although the relationship between the two events is not clear). In casting an eye upon the human race placed in the new order of things (inequality), Rousseau first takes notice of the progress of perfectibility: "Behold all our faculties developed, memory and imagination in play, vanity aroused, reason rendered active, and the mind having almost reached the limit of the perfection of which it is susceptible" (SD, p. 174; 155). No longer can change come about through the interaction of man and his environment, because man's faculties, being fully and irreversibly developed, are no longer susceptible to that influence. Subsequent change will take place in a new arena, whether in the condition of inequality or in that of a new equality, as the focus of history shifts from nature to man himself.

Change in the second state of nature will have to be contingent, but it cannot be doubly contingent in the way that man's initial development was. It will be contingent in that it need not occur at all but not in that, if it does, it will be the work of pure chance. Because man's faculties have been fully perfected, he will no longer be at the mercy of pure chance, but this development alone does not necessitate change—either in a particular direction or in general. Just as the original state of nature could have lasted indefinitely, so too could this second one: "Everything thus occurs according to the natural order; and whatever the outcome of these short and frequent revolutions may be, no one can complain of another's injustice, but only of his own imprudence or his misfortune" (SD, p. 191; 177–78). These short and frequent revolutions, which occur indefinitely in the second state of nature, define a new natural order that plainly recalls the one inhabited by natural man in part 1 of the *Discours*: "The spectacle of nature becomes indifferent to him by dint of becoming familiar. There is always the same order, there are always the same revolutions" (*SD*, p. 144; 117). But if chance does not intervene to introduce change in the natural order, what will? An answer to this question is suggested by a consideration of how the establishment of inequality might have been avoided in the first place. "Things in this state could have remained equal if talents had been equal, and if, for example, the use of iron and the consumption of foodstuffs had always been exactly balanced. But this proportion, which nothing maintained, was soon broken" (*SD*, p. 174; 154).

The original establishment of inequality, Rousseau suggests, was neither simply fortuitous (since the inequality of talents is not potential but actual) nor necessarily determined. It was almost inevitable, however, since to avoid it would have required men to maintain a balance, the consequence of whose destruction they could not predict. The moment just before inequality was established was thus characterized neither by chance nor by determinism; rather, it was the single point between history and pseudohistory when self-conscious human action might have intervened. This is the moment that stretches into eternity as the new state of nature.

In the new state of nature, three choices will present themselves. Since chance alone cannot act, men can simply choose (or achieve the same effect by refusing to choose) to remain in this miserable state of equality. But if they do decide to act, to do something to ameliorate their condition, they can choose either to reestablish inequality, which will determine their future course along the familiar pattern, or to maintain the fragile balance of equality in the institutions they construct. The latter does not mean establishing a society based upon a deceptive contract that legitimizes and establishes inequality in property, giving rise then to other unequal but equally legitimate social and political institutions; it means instead to form a new social contract that will maintain the balance of production and consumption, of property, and thus will generate social and political institutions to support it.

The two courses of action that will be open to men in the future reflect two opposing elements in man's constitution: *amour-propre*, from which the passions arise, and *pitié*, which is the basis for all men's social virtues. The individual can act on the basis of either one, but the former tends to overpower the latter as man develops. The intellect, which Rousseau does not really discuss in the *Second Discours*, except as one of the faculties that are perfectible and perfected, can, it seems, serve either one of these two aspects of man's constitution. The possibility held out by the future will be to conceive once again "the most deliberate project that ever entered the human mind": to employ the powers of reflection in the service not of *amour-propre* and the establishment of inequality but of devising social and political institutions that will maintain equality in human relations (*SD*, p. 177; 158–59).

Institutions of some kind are necessary because property—the product of irreversible historical development—cannot be abolished. One could as easily do away with property as the family, or any other development that arises out of the initial perfecting of men's faculties. But it is not property itself that makes inequality necessary. The necessary result of property is that, unless people come up with a way to legitimize the relations it generates, these relations will constantly be in flux, endangering persons as well, whose extension is found in property. In other words, a war of all against all will characterize human relations, and it is this situation that, because of the misery to which all parties are subjected, prods men to devise institutions to legitimize property and its relations. But not all institutions man can create are necessarily evil. Those Rousseau describes in the pseudohistory are necessarily corrupt only because they are based on inequality. What are required, then, are institutions rooted in *pitié*, the innate sense each individual has of his similarity to other human beings. Equality is thus maintained institutionally in the service of *pitié* rather than *amour-propre*, in spite of natural inequality.[41]

In the *Contrat social* Rousseau himself has sketched out the institutions he believes would maintain the delicate balance of property and thus the equality of human relations. The problem of how one would go about founding and forming such institutions belongs more properly to that text than to the *Second Discours*.

To summarize, Rousseau extends the contingent historical narrative that ends with the establishment of inequality among men into the future through two separate instantiations of a pseudohistorical schema. The first completes his critique of contemporary French society, and the second adds to it a critique of and warning to the contemporary republic

[41]Although the sense of sameness that *pitié* generates is anterior to the observation of differences, it is difference that language—the work of the passions—first expresses. In the 1782 edition of the *Discours*, Rousseau added a note to his discussion of language in pt. 1 to express this point: "the first idea that one has of two things is that they are not the same; and it often takes a long time to notice what they have in common" (*SD*, p. 149). Since the project of devising social and political institutions must be *réfléchi*, it makes sense that they were initially based on difference rather than sameness. In other words, thought, being based on language, acts first in the service of *amour-propre*, and only later is it able to perceive that which *pitié* sees instinctively; thus only later can it act toward preserving similarity rather than legitimizing differences.

of Geneva. Through these two instantiations of a chain of necessary (nonhistorical) deductions, Rousseau takes the historical chronology beyond his own lifetime twice over. The doomsday tone of the text, the "historical pessimism," as well as the lack of any mention of a role for human action in turning the critique into positive political action, have their origin here. But Rousseau does hold out the hope for some future generation to intervene wisely in the direction of its future. Although such a possibility is nowhere mentioned in the *Second Discours*, it can be inferred from the types of change that are shown to be possible in the conditions of equality and inequality. But a simple oscillation between these two conditions is not adequate to define the change possible in the future. In the end, not only the contingency of historical development but its irreversibility as well allows for the possibility of positive political action in the future for the establishment of a better society.

Lest this picture seem too rosy, let it be remembered that Rousseau's criticism of the societies in which he lives (both France and Geneva) could not be meant to lead to any political action in those societies, since their immediate futures are predetermined. Furthermore, although he has left the door open for the self-conscious construction of a new and better society some time in the future, he does not suggest, in this text at least, the means by which it would be formed. There is still a double gap between social criticism and action toward change in the *Second Discours*, just as there was in the *Lettres persanes*: a temporal gap that leaves the present criticized but unchangeable, and a practical gap between the type of institutions that are required and the means of establishing them.

PART III

DIDEROT
The Dialogical Critique of Society

CHAPTER SIX

The Implied Reader
Reintroduced

The social and political critiques launched against the Old Regime by Montesquieu and Rousseau both went far beneath the surface of monarchical rule. With his comparative critical method, Montesquieu began an exploration of the very constitution of France which he was to continue in *L'Esprit des lois*. Rousseau, too, broke through the surface not only of monarchical rule but of contemporary society more broadly construed. His narrative historical approach led him to the root of the contemporary crisis, buried deep in the past, before the founding of monarchies or republics. Both critiques, but especially the second one, are devastating. Unlike Fénelon's pleasant tale of adventures, whose message of reform based on princely virtue and wise counsel needed only a ruler willing to listen in order to be put into action, the critiques of Montesquieu and Rousseau deny implicitly the possibility of reform by placing the causes of current social and political woes far from the reach of any who would remedy them. And who *is* supposed to remedy these ills? The *Lettres persanes* makes it pretty clear that the king, trapped within his court and the flattering discourse that defines it, is little more than a stooge of the system. But it is not at all clear where the authority or the power to institute a system of justice is supposed to come from. And Rousseau does not clarify the problem in the *Second Discours*. Indeed, he argues that all attempts at reform have been and will continue to be in vain, until some vague future when *maybe* something positive will be done. And this long shot is never spelled out, never made explicit; the question of who is going to create the new institutions that will ensure equality, and how they are going to do so is left wide open.

Rousseau's need to invent a "legislator" in the *Contrat social* merely highlights the problem; it does not solve it.

Critics, of course, are in no way obligated to suggest practical solutions to the problems they set out only to expose. "If you can't say anything good, don't say anything at all" is hardly a fair response to a Montesquieu or a Rousseau. Very true. It is not, however, unreasonable to think that as the eighteenth century wore on, someone might have worried over exactly this issue: was there not some way to go about criticizing the monarchy and the society it represented which would lead out of the impasse reached by the earlier writers? Granted, the impasse may not have bothered these writers, but this does not mean that it was not an impasse, or that it was not a problem that needed to be overcome. Granted, too, that the solution might very well not have lain in the realm of critical writing at all, but only in the realm of overt, maybe even violent, political action. Perhaps the solution lay in administrative reforms, such as those suggested by Turgot and Malesherbes; perhaps it lay in the French Revolution. For Denis Diderot, however, who demonstrated through his dedication to the production of the *Encyclopédie* the seriousness with which he viewed the power of words to transform the "common way of thinking"—and with it the world—the solution lay within criticism itself.

Diderot's *Supplément au Voyage de Bougainville* extended the critical project inaugurated by Montesquieu, but in a direction radically different from the one pursued by Rousseau in the *Second Discours*. While Rousseau had focused on the subject of criticism opened up by Montesquieu—the uncharted terrain beneath the surface of the monarchy—Diderot turned his attention to the rhetorical object of criticism: the reader of the critical text. In Diderot's hands, the dialogue became an extension of Montesquieu's comparative critical method, an extension that transformed criticism into a method for social and political reform. The activity of the reader which had been stimulated by the epistolary text could be redirected into the world through the dialogue. For the dialogue, as Diderot conceived it, became a model of active reading, and reading critically, the model of analysis to be applied to all laws and institutions. Montesquieu's reader had already begun to learn how to analyze his world, and especially the terms by which it was defined; Diderot's reader was now given the responsibility for extending such analysis and making it the basis of legal and institutional reform. By 1772, when the *Supplément* was written, Diderot seems to have decided that it was up to the enlightened critic and his enlightened reader to take matters into their own hands and, through critical activity itself, do something about the injustices and absurdities that fifty years of criticism had brought to light.[1]

In addressing the role of the social critic in bringing about political change, Diderot was less interested in a critique of society—a critique that had changed little since Montesquieu's articulation of it over fifty years earlier—than in the transformation of the *philosophe* from observer into participant. And Diderot located the solution to the problem in a restructuring of criticism: through dialogue it could become at the same time the means of representing, interpreting, and changing society. The solution was not to put criticism in the service of politics but to make of criticism a political activity that could replace absolutist politics, just as Montesquieu had earlier shown that critical reasoning had to replace absolutist reasoning. Criticism, properly structured and properly read, was to be the means of this political transformation.

Diderot's *Supplément au Voyage de Bougainville* is the most experimental of the works considered here, though the *Lettres persanes* is more complex and the *Second Discours* is more profound. Whereas Montesquieu exploited the epistolary form to the fullest to achieve maximum complexity and Rousseau used the full explanatory potential of historical narrative to plumb the depths of social inequality, Diderot refashioned the dialogue form as part of a lifelong effort to expand the possibilities of criticism. The *Supplément* was one in a series of experiments in which Diderot explored the range of dialogue and the range of criticism. The dialogues, each one different, each one a redefinition of dialogue and what it can do, must be seen in the context of a lifetime of literary experimentation, from the *Encyclopédie* to the *drame bourgeois*.

Because the *Supplément* is the most experimental of the three texts examined here, it is the most radical as well. It is most radical not in the depth of its critique but in the way it breaks the boundaries of the critical text to make critical writing a form of political action. And yet the *Supplément* was not itself that political act. It was only an experiment. Ironically, the most radical of these three texts, the one that went furthest in its efforts to reshape the public world of politics through the creation of a critical reading public—the one that demanded the most of readers by bringing them into the political arena with responsibility for reforming it—was the only one that was not read by the public in the eighteenth century. Both the *Lettres persanes* and the *Second Discours* were

[1]Charles G. Stricklen, Jr., describes a parallel politicization of the *philosophes* in the 1770s in their increased participation in the royal bureaucracy. "The *Philosophes'* Political Mission: The Creation of an Idea, 1750–1789," *Studies on Voltaire and the Eighteenth Century* 86 (1971): 158–83.

widely read among the growing literate elite, and both stimulated lively debate among readers; the *Supplément* was read only by Diderot's friends and the handful of people who subscribed to the manuscript *Correspondance littéraire* before it was published in 1796. By then, of course, the relationship between enlightened readership and political change had to take on a new meaning. Diderot's attempt to answer Montesquieu's question about how to write political criticism in the modern age, how to locate and shape a new reader who could effect political change in a world no longer dominated by the monarchy but still enmeshed in the social complexities of the Old Regime, had by then lost its immediacy, and the *Supplément* became merely a curiosity: a scandalous little book about sex, an amusing if shallow attack on the absurdities of a society now safely past.

Diderot's *Supplément* did not, any more than the *Lettres persanes* or the *Second discours*, change the world. It was not itself the political act that its author, through this text, showed that critical writing could and should be. It was an experiment, a model of critical writing as political action, but as such it demands our attention and our respect. For there is still a great deal to be learned from it about how the writer can both act responsibly and generate responsible action through engaging and shaping an active reader, and so, perhaps, change the world.

The Parameters of Dialogue

Victor Goldschmidt has written that the Platonic dialogue "wishes to form rather than inform."[2] For all the difference between Plato's dialogues and Diderot's, the end remains the same: to form readers by engaging them in a particular type of critical activity. In Diderot's *Supplément*, that end becomes indistinguishable from political action, which the text itself defines as critical activity. To understand how critical and political activities become one requires an inquiry first into the nature of dialogue and then into the *Supplément* as a dialogic model of critical activity in which both writer and reader are engaged. Their interaction as participants in a dialogue forms the focus of this text, and their joint activity is what will, according to the text itself, change the world, because it is both critical and political.

The end of a dialogue, as Goldschmidt argues, is to form rather than to inform, to change the world by changing the reader. Three means to

---

[2]Victor Goldschmidt, *Les Dialogues de Platon: Structure et méthode dialectique*, 3d ed. (Paris, 1947), pp. 2–3.

this end, all of which Diderot exploits in the *Supplément*, can be identified as formal aspects of the dialogue: it is nonmimetic; it is both universal and particular; and it is pedagogic.

In distinguishing between the drama and the dialogue, John Pedersen
points out that the drama, through its psychological imitation of ordinary
conversation, draws the reader (or audience) into the fiction, while "the
text of a dialogue sends the reader back into his own real world and to
the problems he must face."[3] The nonmimetic character of dialogic
discourse, the obvious artificiality that comes of being a verbal surface
with no hidden psychological depths, forces the reader to maintain a
critical distance from the representation. This distance, when looked at
from another angle, defines the reader's position as firmly rooted in the
real world, where political action can be taken.

A second and even more fundamental aspect of dialogue is its instantiation of both universality and particularity. For the dialogue requires two distinct particular voices, but also a shared language in which
they can communicate. Were the voices not particular, the dialogue
would be false; were the language not shared, communication would not
be possible. One could see in this dual nature of dialogue an ambivalence,
as Maurice Roelens does, or a constant striving through universalizing to
overcome the "noise" or obstacles to communication found in particularity, as does Michel Serres.[4] Diderot, however, takes advantage of this
dual foundation of dialogue, first by harnessing the energy entailed in a
perpetual motion from particular to universal and back again. Substantively, the universality of human reason is brought to bear on the concrete particularity of life and, conversely, particular, concrete action
based on the conclusions of empirical reasoning is made possible. Within
the structure of dialogue there is room for both the universality of
thought and the particularity of action.

Finally, as Cyrus Hamlin argues, "dialogue as a literary text provides a
model for reading and an implied pedagogy through a hermeneutic
interaction between reader and text."[5] In the *Supplément* this implicit

---

[3]"Le Dialogue—du classicisme aux Lumières: Réflexions sur l'évolution d'un genre,"
Studia Neophilologica 51 (1979): 306. Bertolt Brecht argues that this process of engage-
ment through distancing can occur in the theater. Similarities between Brechtian theater
and Diderotian dialogue will be discussed below.

[4]Maurice Roelens, "Le Dialogue philosophique, genre impossible? L'opinion des siècles classiques," *Cahiers de l'Association Internationale des Études Françaises*, no. 24 (1972),
p. 46; Michel Serres, "Platonic Dialogue," trans. Marilyn Sides, in *Hermes: Literature,
Science, Philosophy*, ed. Josué Harari and David F. Bell (Baltimore, 1982), pp. 65–70.

[5]Cyrus Hamlin, "Platonic Dialogue and Romantic Irony: Prolegomenon to a Theory
of Literary Narrative," *Canadian Review of Comparative Literature* 3 (1976):25.

characteristic of the dialogue is made explicit, as the characters identified only as *A* and *B* are none other than reader and writer. Through the reader's functional (rather than psychological) identification with *A* he learns first how to read and then how this one activity, in which he participates as he learns how to do it, serves as a model for other types of critical activity, including political reform. As the relationship between reader and writer is seen to be a model of all human relationships, so the activity by which that relationship is defined is the model of all human action.

The Model of Reading in the "Jugement"

Diderot's *Supplément au Voyage de Bougainville* is a lesson in how to read a text. It opens with a dialogic discussion of one book, Louis-Antoine de Bougainville's recently published *Voyage autour du monde*, and then introduces two new, fictional texts to be read by *A* and *B*, and also by Diderot's readers, you and me. The two fictional texts comprise the supplement within the *Supplément* and give a double meaning to the title of the work. This activity of reading, moreover, is a part and a model of critical activity in general. For the dialogue between *A* and *B*, which shows the reader how to read, is an instance also of the criticism of the text being read: first of Bougainville's *Voyage* and later of the supplement to it.

The *Supplément* opens in the cozy, familiar setting of a French living room on a cold and foggy day. Here *A* asks *B* how he is going to pass the time until the fog lifts. "I'm reading," replies *B*. *B*'s book is Bougainville's *Voyage*. Immediately a discussion of the book and its author ensues. Attention soon focuses on Tahiti, Bougainville's savage paradise. When *A* asks *B* if he has actually fallen for the myth of Tahiti, *B* responds: "It isn't a myth at all; and you wouldn't have any doubts about Bougainville's sincerity if you knew the supplement to his *Voyage*." The dialogue continues:

> *A*. And where is this supplement?
> *B*. There, on that table.
> *A*. Will you lend it to me?
> *B*. No; but we can run through it together, if you wish.
> *A*. I certainly do.[6]

[6]Denis Diderot, *Supplément au Voyage de Bougainville*, in *Oeuvres philosophiques*, ed. Paul Vernière (Paris, 1964), p. 464. All further references to the *Supplément* (*Supp.*) appear in the text.

These exchanges, which introduce the two fictional supplementary documents, bring together the two levels of text and, through them, two levels of readers as well: *A* and *B* within the text, you and me outside it.

For those of us outside the text, *B*'s mention of a supplement comes as a surprise because we thought we were already reading it. When *A* asks where the supplement is, *B* points to it by using the pointing word, "là"; we, in following the word, as *A* presumably follows the gesture, find ourselves looking at the same book, the one we have been reading and the one we are about to read.[7] As the two texts merge, so do two of the readers: *A* and us. Because *B* does not simply give the text to *A* (as Diderot does not simply give the text to us), the group of people reading it together expands to include all of us.[8] This identification is confirmed if we choose to continue reading, for in that choice we say implicitly what *A* says explicitly: "I certainly do" wish to read it. On the basis, then, of the interest aroused by discussion of Bougainville's *Voyage*, we—including *A*—consent to read together the supplement to it.

If we are to identify as readers with the voice *A*, what of his qualities are to become ours? Certainly *A*'s most striking characteristic in this section of the text is his tendency to doubt. In fact, it is because he is skeptical of Bougainville's idyllic description of Tahiti that *B* suggests *A* read the supplement. The critical stance of the reader both precedes and motivates his reading on the one hand and informs it on the other; it is also, as the dialogue that follows the reading of the supplementary documents shows, a means of generating critical reflection. Thus the first words *B* addresses to *A* at the conclusion of "Les Adieux du Vieillard" are: "Well! What do you think of that?"; and *A*'s response is a reaffirmation of his critical stance. "This speech strikes me as forceful," he says, "but through whatever there is that is abrupt and savage I seem to detect a few European ideas and turns of phrase" (*Supp.*, p. 472). The doubting and questioning that led to the reading of the text continue through and after it, and thus show reading to be part of a larger critical project of which it is the center. This centrality is reproduced structurally in the placing of the supplement within the *Supplément*, the text within the criticism.

The critical stance of Diderot's reader is one aspect of his freedom, for

[7]See David Berry, "The Technique of Literary Digression in the Fiction of Diderot," *Studies on Voltaire and the Eighteenth Century* 118 (1974): 174–75; Christie V. McDonald, "Le Dialogue, l'utopie: *Le Supplément au Voyage de Bougainville* par Diderot," *Canadian Review of Comparative Literature* 3 (1976): 72–73; and Jack Undank, *Diderot: Inside, Outside, and In-Between* (Madison, Wis., 1979), p. 52.

[8]On the eighteenth-century practice of reading together see Roger Chartier, *Lectures et lecteurs dans la France d'Ancien Régime* (Paris, 1987).

it depends upon remaining free of the text and its author, on maintaining one's distance from them. This is the freedom from the captivating illusion of fiction that Diderot, the creator of that illusion, seeks to ensure.[9] A's failure to be taken in by the fiction B presents, his refusal to suspend entirely his disbelief, is evidence that he is subordinating his passions to his reason. As Jean-Paul Sartre writes: "If I appeal to my [reader] so that he may carry the enterprise which I have begun to a successful conclusion, it is self-evident that I consider him as a pure freedom, [as a pure creative power,] as an unconditioned activity; thus, in no case can I address myself to his passivity, that is, try to affect him, to communicate to him, from the very first, emotions of fear, desire, or anger. . . . Freedom is alienated in the state of passion."[10] This is to say, as Sartre stresses, not that emotions cannot enter into the reading of the text but that they cannot control it, just as they cannot control the writing of it. Once that priority is established, the reader must be alienated from the text, rather than from his liberty, in order to judge it. The *Verfrem-dungseffekt* that Bertolt Brecht sought to achieve in the theater through stage and technical devices gives a name to this other kind of alienation, that which the external reader of the *Supplément* experiences each time A breaks the illusion B presents. "I hope," writes Brecht, that

> I've avoided one common artistic bloomer, that of trying to carry people away. Instinctively, I've kept my distance and ensured that the realization of my (poetical and philosophical) effects remains within bounds. The spectator's "splendid isolation" is left intact; it is not *sua res quae agitur*, he is not fobbed off with an invitation to feel sympathetically. . . . A higher type of interest can be got from making comparisons, from whatever is different, amazing, impossible to take in as a whole.[11]

The liberty of the reader, established first in his free choice to read the book before him, is reinforced each time A maintains his critical distance from the text in breaking its fictional illusion.[12]

As Sartre remarks, to be carried away or taken in, to be led by one's passions, is to be passive; the freedom manifested in and guaranteed by

[9]Yves Bénot remarks the same phenomenon in the epilogue to Diderot's *Les Deux Amis de Bourbonne*. See *Diderot: De l'athéisme à l'anticolonialisme* (Paris, 1970), p. 110; also Robert Niklaus, "Diderot et le conte philosophique," *Cahiers de l'Association Internationale des Études Françaises*, no. 13 (1961), p. 303; and Henri Coulet, "La Distanciation dans le roman et le conte philosophique."

[10]Jean-Paul Sartre, *What Is Literature?* trans. Bernard Frechtman (New York, 1965), p. 43.

[11]Bertolt Brecht, *Brecht on Theatre: The Development of an Aesthetic*, ed. and trans. John Willet (New York, 1964), p. 9.

[12]"You are perfectly free to leave that book on the table. But if you open it, you assume responsibility for it": Sartre, *What Is Literature?* p. 42.

the reader's critical stance implies his activity. In this way the term "critical stance" gives way to the more accurate "critical activity." In the *Supplément*, the very inclusion of *A* establishes his activity. The significance of *A*'s activity becomes clear in a comparison of the "Jugement du Voyage de Bougainville" with the text out of which Diderot developed it: a simple *compte rendu* of Bougainville's book. When Diderot transformed his review into a dialogue between *A* and *B*, he made of the reader an active participant in the analysis of that text, making explicit the implicit exigencies of the reader which guide the writer. The "Jugement" demonstrates the process of writing a book review, where the reviewer (*B*) must imagine the questions that the reader (*A*) can be assumed to want answered. Unlike the Platonic dialogue, in which the master controls the discourse, guiding it through predefined stages,[13] the "Jugement" is directed by the implied reader in his desire to understand.

Thus the paragraph in the *compte rendu* that begins, "The benefits of his voyage can be brought under three main points," is in the *Supplément* attributed to *B* and preceded by *A*'s question: "What do you think of his Voyage?"[14] *A* continues to ask the questions that the reviewer, Diderot, implicitly answered in his review: "And his style?"; "Was his route long?"; "Did he suffer a lot?"; but also, "And you, how do you explain it?" (*Supp.*, pp. 458–59)

The reader, always present implicitly, becomes explicit in the dialogue form; and in this transformation, in displaying to the reader his role in the creation of the text, Diderot demonstrates the reader's activity. Because, writes Sartre, "the literary object is a peculiar top which exists only in movement. To make it come into view, a concrete act called reading is necessary, and it only lasts as long as this act can last. Beyond that, there are only black marks on paper."[15] And Diderot, in emphasizing the role of the reader, brings to the surface the essential mobility of the text as text, as the instantiation of the act of reading. "The text," writes Georges Benrekassa of the *Supplément*, "is not a stagnant pool in which one could regard oneself indefinitely, a fixed result of sources that will dry up. It is porous, it is the site of a passage, of a series of operations; it is not itself at any given moment but the sum of the series of operations that can be tried upon it."[16]

[13]Goldschmidt, *Les Dialogues de Platon*, p. 12.

[14]Diderot, *Oeuvres complètes*, ed. Roger Lewinter, 15 vols. (Paris, 1970), 9:966; *Supp.*, p. 457.

[15]Sartre, *What Is Literature?*, pp. 34–35.

[16]Georges Benrekassa, "Dit et non-dit idéologique: À propos du *Supplément au Voyage de Bougainville*," *Dix-huitième Siècle*, no. 5 (1973), p. 39. See also Leo Spitzer, "The Style of Diderot," in *Linguistics and Literary History: Essays in Stylistics* (New York, 1962), p. 166; Undank, *Diderot*, p. 50; and Herbert Dieckmann, *Cinq leçons sur Diderot* (Geneva, 1959), p. 37.

The dialogue between *A* and *B* demonstrates that the reader not only gives the text its essential movement by imparting to it his own activity but is implicated in the correlative act of writing as well. To understand exactly how this process works, how the dialogue between *A* and *B* is implied in the review of Bougainville's *Voyage*, consider an unfinished writing of Diderot's, "Sur la diversité de nos jugements." There, after two paragraphs of the writer talking to himself, he arrives at: "I'm not sure that if frère Jacques had treated gardening to its fullest extent he wouldn't have had his revenge on Pluche." And immediately another voice enters. "I don't understand you," it says, and the first voice then recounts the anecdote to which his remark referred: "Pluche wrote the *Spectacle de la nature*; frère Jacques, gardener of Chartreux, found the work admirable throughout, except on gardening. At that point he exclaimed: 'Ah, Pluche! My friend, you don't know what you're talking about.'"[17]

If one is writing for an audience, one must have some sense of it, of who the potential reader is and what he knows; it is this potential reader who controls, ultimately, the limits of explanation and reference. If, as this essay begins, "the more one reflects on a subject, the bigger it gets," the limits, which exist neither in the subject itself nor in the reflections on it, must be set by the potential reader. The problem of writing becomes the problem of determining the reader. As the story of Pluche and frère Jacques demonstrates, "the worst is that the limits that must be prescribed, be they in the world, be they in one's study, are difficult to fix. Too far in one direction and you are verbose; to far in the other and you are inconclusive. You suppose your reader to be either too knowledgeable or too ignorant."[18]

The importance of the reader in the writing of the text is thus presented in three ways: in the introduction of the second voice asking for an explanation; in the anecdote of frère Jacques and Pluche; and in the direct discussion of the problem which follows. And the role of the reader, as explained in "Sur la diversité de nos jugements," is in great part that of *A* in the opening dialogue of the *Supplément*.

Bringing the reader's attention to his complicity in the making of the text robs him of the complacency of the passive spectator and leads him gradually to a more active and independent role vis-à-vis the author, as *A*'s later contributions to the "Jugement" demonstrate.[19] In considering a

[17]Diderot, *Oeuvres complètes*, 13:874.
[18]Ibid.
[19]Part of the reader's complacency lies simply in his sense of anonymity or hiddenness. Making the reader a participant in the dialogue is one way of revealing him. Another

problem raised by Bougainville's account, *A* begins to make positive contributions to the dialogue and to the reading of Bougainville's text. The questioner is no longer the reader but the author: "For the moment," says *B*, pointing to the globe, "do you see this island called 'Lancers'? On inspection of the spot that it occupies on the globe, there is no one who would not wonder [*se demande*] who it is that put men there. What means of communication linked them in times past to the rest of their species? What will become of them if they reproduce in a space that is no bigger than a league in diameter?" (*Supp.*, p. 460).

But it is not really *B* who poses these questions; the questions, he claims, pose themselves to anyone who considers the island's geography. Diderot continues to deny *B* the role of Platonic questioner, for *B* does no more here than articulate questions that *A*, as an average person, would ask himself. Whereas in the beginning of the dialogue *A* seemed to have been created in order to make explicit an implied correlate of *B* (a product of *B* the writer's imagination), *B* now represents the articulation of an implied aspect of *A*, the personification of the text, of what "strikes the reader," from the reader's point of view.

At this point, then, the reversal of the roles of questioner and questioned reflects a reversal of point of view from writer to reader. But at this same point the two voices balance out, becoming indistinguishable from each other. Because the questions raised appeal neither to the writer as writer nor to the reader as reader, they enter a realm where there are no characters, no roles, but simply the manifestation of common sense, general reflections on the way inhabitants of a small island might deal with the problem of overpopulation. In fact, *A*'s last suggestion ends in ellipses, and *B*'s next remark is the completion of *A*'s thought. What makes *A* indistinguishable from *B* identifies them also with the outside reader, since he too participates in the universal reason of common sense. We are all unified as point of view disappears entirely and ideas become themselves motivation for subsequent ideas. The movement of the text here is still what the reader lends it, but it is the movement of the discussion itself, in which the reader participates. At the points in the dialogue where *A* and *B* are indistinguishable, the dialectic of reasoned discussion supersedes that of the relationship between reader and writer. At these points the particularity of their roles in opposition to each other gives way to the necessary identity of universal reason or common sense.

A and *B* cannot be said to be characters in any usual sense. Their lack

---

technique, which Diderot employs in his novel *Jacques le fataliste*, is direct address. Either way, the reader is implicated and unveiled.

even of proper names must be seen as a conscious attempt to eliminate character as an element in the dialogue.[20] In place of personal characteristics that would define an individual character, *A* is endowed with the common sense that defines him as a human being. The identification between the reader and *A* remains on the level of reason, as opposed to that of emotions. The reader does not empathize with *A*, but identifies himself literally with him, to the extent that common sense is truly common.[21] It would be wrong, however, to say that *A* is nothing more than common sense, pure abstraction. As a reader, *A* may not have a personality, but he does have a history, one that he shares with the implied reader of the *Supplément*. This shared history consists of their reading past as readers in and of two other texts by Diderot: *Ceci n'est pas un conte* and *Madame de la Carlière*. The *Supplément* completes a triptych of texts, all three of which appeared in the *Correspondance littéraire* in 1773.

A and *B* are the interlocutors in all three texts of the triptych. From the beginning, *A* has been defined as a reader. Diderot opens *Ceci n'est pas un conte* with the following explanation: "When one creates a story, it is for someone who listens to it; and for as long as the story lasts, the storyteller seldom fails to be interrupted occasionally by his listener. This is why I have introduced into the narrative you are about to read . . . a character whose role approximates that of the listener."[22] This voice that fulfills the function of reader is initially nameless, but we recognize him in *A* in the *Supplément*. When we encounter him there he is already familiar, and we share with him the history of having read together the three stories that make up *Ceci n'est pas un conte* and *Madame de la Carlière*.

Beyond his common sense, then, *A* has particular attributes that identify him as a reader, displayed in his relations both to the author, *B*, and to the two texts, Bougainville's *Voyage* and the supplement to it. He is further particularized by his literary history, his known history being limited to the texts we have read with him. The discussion of the

[20]See Jacques Schérer, *Le Cardinal et l'orang-outang: Essai sur les inversions et les distances dans la pensée de Diderot* (Paris, 1972), p. 206. For a useful definition of character see Ducrot and Todorov, *Encyclopedic Dictionary*, pp. 225–26.

[21]Brecht's ideas about theater are again parallel here: "Nowadays the play's meaning is usually blurred by the fact that the actor plays to the audience's hearts. The figures portrayed are foisted on the audience and are falsified in the process. Contrary to the present custom they ought to be presented quite coldly, classically and objectively. For they are not matter for empathy, they are here to be understood. Feelings are private and limited. Against that the reason is fairly comprehensive and to be relied upon": *Brecht on Theatre*, p. 15.

[22]Diderot, *Oeuvres complètes*, 10:151.

weather with which the story of Madame de la Carlière ends, and which begins and ends the *Supplément*, creates an obvious link between texts which reminds the outside reader of this shared history. Even more explicit are the references to the characters of the preceding stories at the close of the *Supplément*. The particularization of *A* goes yet one step further, but still he is not individualized as a character. Beyond his common sense, his role as reader, and his literary history, *A* is a male member of a particular social and political community: contemporary France.

A and *B* are defined as reader and writer, respectively, in opposition to each other, but also in relation to the various texts that figure here: Bougainville's *Voyage* (or more precisely, the review of it embodied in the "Jugement"), the *Supplément* as a whole, the two stories told in *Ceci n'est pas un conte*, and *Madame de la Carlière*. These texts define *A* and *B* culturally. In *Ceci n'est pas un conte*, the narrator begins to tell the story of Tanié and Mme Reymer only after having established the roles of reader and writer. The story, however, begins with the introduction of Mme Reymer as an Alsatian personally known to both the reader and the writer.[23] Further indications at the beginning of the second story told in *Ceci n'est pas un conte* and of *Madame de la Carlière* confirm that the two voices in these texts belong to the cultural and social milieu of the characters whose stories are told and are roughly contemporary with them.

While the beginning of the story of Mme Reymer and Tanié simply places the reader and writer as contemporary Frenchmen, that of the subsequent stories gives them more precision. They are shown to be familiar with a fairly high intellectual and political milieu and are located in historical time through a reference to the military campaign of 1745.[24] The result is a full cultural (i.e., social, political, intellectual, historical) identification of the writer and reader within the stories with the characters of these stories; it is a cultural identification of the writer and the reader with the text. The purpose of this cultural identification, like that of the internal and external readers, cannot be to generate empathy or compassion, but rather to permit and further to stimulate reasoned evaluation. The cultural identification establishes the point of view of the interlocutors as members of a particular society to which the implied reader belongs.

The discussion of the weather which opens the "Jugement" identifies *A* and *B* with the voices of reader and writer in the preceding texts and

[23]Ibid., p. 123.
[24]Ibid., p. 158, 176.

thus establishes them as mid-eighteenth-century Frenchmen of a relatively high social and intellectual milieu. Since Bougainville, too, as A
and B describe him, belongs to this milieu, the identification of reader
and writer with the characters in the text continues. But it ends here as
well, for Bougainville's *Voyage* is the account of his confrontation with
cultures other than his own. The identification of A and B with Bougainville precludes necessarily their identification with members of other
cultures as members of those cultures (although it certainly does not
preclude identification with them on the universal level of common
sense). Whereas in the two preceding texts Diderot took care to demonstrate the familiarity of the stories he was recounting, here he takes as the
"story" a text that by its very nature, as the account of a voyage of
discovery, will generate an opposition between the familiar and the
unfamiliar. (This is, of course, the same opposition that Montesquieu
exploits in the *Lettres persanes*.)

Underlying the voyage of discovery as an activity and the account of
that voyage as a text is the assumption that there is something unfamiliar
to be discovered and recounted. Furthermore, the cultural identification
of A and B with the characters of the preceding stories makes the
otherness of other cultures both possible and necessary. Were it not for
this identification that particularizes the subject and in consequence his
object, one could remain exclusively on the universal level of humanity,
of common sense. But just as the reader and writer can merge with each
other when their particular points of view give way to the general
perspective of common sense, so too can the opposition between the
Frenchman and the Tahitian be suspended. This is to say not that the
opposition between cultural groups is a false one but that it is possible to
be both a Frenchman and a human being, just as it is possible to be both
a reader and a human being. The relationship between reader and
writer—the true opposition of their roles and the equally true unity of
their humanity as common sense—serves as a model for other kinds of
human relationships.

To the oppositions of reader versus writer and Frenchman versus
Tahitian must be added a third opposition that figures in the reader's
identification with A: man versus woman. Along with the cultural identification of A and B as Frenchmen goes their gender identification as
men, asserted throughout the triptych. Already in the story of Tanié and
Mme Reymer, it is revealed that A has been one of Mme Reymer's
lovers.[25] Unlike B, who takes the part of confidant in the story he tells, A
is neither neuter nor neutral. The reader, who is asked to identify with A

[25]Ibid., p. 157.

as a reader, must also identify with him as a man. The result is that, whether the actual reader is a man or a woman, he (or she) is forced to recognize gender as a factor in the reading of the text and in the full extent of critical activity of which reading is both an element and a model. One must be fully conscious not only of what one is doing (reading, being a reader) but of who one is culturally and sexually. And it is the writer who has the first responsibility to display this consciousness to the reader, for, as Diderot writes in his criticism of Thomas's *Essai sur le caractère, les moeurs et l'esprit des femmes*, the weakness of the book lies in the fact that it "has no sex whatever, it is neither male nor female; it's a castrato who has neither the nerve of man nor the nobility of woman."[26]

But if we must be able to identify *A* as a man in order to understand his point of view, and if this consciousness serves to raise that of the reader through identification or nonidentification with *A*, a question necessarily arises at the end of *Ceci n'est pas un conte*: is it possible to suspend or transcend this point of view? Of all the oppositions raised in the reader's identification with *A*, that between men and women most clearly illustrates the necessary particularity of concrete human beings. While one's particularity as a reader is only a temporary identification that derives from the activity of reading, and the particularity of cultural identification can be argued to be a mere social acquisition and thus superficial and changeable, sexual particularity is physical and permanent. Although *A* and *B* are not individuals, since they have no characters, no personalities, they are concrete particulars and not simply "abstract quantities labelled as mathematical symbols."[27] The gender identity of *A* and *B* shows the necessity of such particularity in its physical basis. It shows as well, in *A*'s implication in the story of Tanié and Mme Reymer, that such particularity must inform both our actions and our judgments.

When we are considering the action of a woman, for example, it is in the context of the relationship between men and women, in which we— as necessarily one or the other—are implicated. In order to see both sides, to use common sense, it is necessary to know not only the identification of the two sides but one's own relation to them. By the same token, in evaluating the information about Tahiti presented by Bougainville, or in the supplement to Bougainville, we must first realize that Tahiti is non-France, and that we (implicitly) are Frenchmen. To recog-

---

[26]Ibid., p. 32.
[27]Pamela Jean Bevier, "Diderot's Utopian Visions" (Ph.D. diss., Columbia University, 1976), p. 177. See also Anthony Strugnell, *Diderot's Politics: A Study of the Evolution of Diderot's Political Thought after the "Encyclopédie"* (The Hague, 1973), p. 32.

nize the Tahitian as Tahitian, it is necessary to recognize ourselves in opposition to him. And, although we are able to reason as universal human beings, in the end we must act as either men or women, Tahitians or Frenchmen, readers or writers. Such particularity is not incidental to our reading or to critical activity in general, but is that from which our general reflections emerge and toward which they are, ultimately, directed. In contrast to the abstract, universal man who Sartre tells us "can think of nothing but universal values,"[28] Diderot creates the concrete particulars, A and B. These "characters," like the dialogue form itself, like real human beings, are both universal and particular.

The "Jugement du voyage de Bougainville" is a model of reading, and reading is in turn a model of other types of human relationships. The identification of the external reader with A tells us how we are to read the text in front of us: the ability of A and B to suspend their points of view as reader and writer, to work together as reasonable human beings in reflecting on problems raised by the text, is based on the commonality of their reason, which we share with them. The "Jugement" shows that while we begin the reading as readers, the reading itself generates the general reflections that arise out of universal reason. In the end, however, we return to our roles, to the social context in which our activity takes place. The reader must read as reader and the writer must write as writer if the act of reading is to be accomplished. We must read a text both as readers and as reasonable human beings; we must read critically, always aware that there is a writer behind the text who may not be reliable, but accepting also our own complicity in the writing of the text and our ultimate responsibility for what it discloses through us (or we through it). Finally, it must not be forgotten that critical reading is a free activity: free because it is based on our reason rather than on our emotions; active because in our freedom we cannot be drawn in passively by our passions.

The reader's first-level identification with A as a reader is followed by the cultural and gender identifications that call upon the reader's concrete particularity outside the controlled activity, the closed world of the text and its reading. The link that connects these two levels of experience, inside and outside the text, is the shared history of reading the two preceding texts in the triptych.

Just as any text can present itself as a model of the relationship between reader and writer, any voyage can present itself as the model of an encounter between two cultures, and any culture presents a model of a relationship between men and women. The reading of Bougainville's

---

[28]Sartre, *What Is Literature?* p. 72.

Voyage provides a model of all three types of relationship. The movement from particular to universal and back to the particularities of concrete social activity operates simultaneously in all three dimensions of the text. Universal reason (common sense) becomes the common denominator of writer and reader, Frenchman and Tahitian, man and woman. While the particularities of role, culture, and gender allow concrete social activities to take place, the commonality of human beings, here found in reason, is the basis of the social in general. And the fundamental interaction of universal and particular which is instantiated in the three models described here is found most strikingly in the dialogue form.

In the "Jugement du voyage de Bougainville," Diderot creates a dialogic model of reading which, in its definition as critical activity, invites the reader's participation both as a human being through the use of common sense and as a concrete member of a particular society who is further particularized by his (or her) gender. It is this particularity that will send the reader back into the real world to apply the models of critical reading and reasoning to the concrete social relationships in which he participates. More immediately, however, in allowing the opposition between reader and writer to be suspended through the use of common sense, Diderot indicates how communication between representatives of two distinct cultures can be possible. In so doing he prepares us for the supplement within the *Supplément*.

CHAPTER SEVEN

The Dialogue between
Two Cultures

Fictionality and Representation in the "Adieux"

Acrucial effect of "Les Adieux du Vieillard," which follows the "Jugement du Voyage" in the *Supplément*, is to establish the validity of Tahiti as an alternative to France, as a potential partner in dialogue. In so doing, it sets up the conditions for a dialogue between representatives of the two cultures, which follows as "L'Entretien de l'Aumônier et d'Orou." The possibility of such a dialogue is established further in the marginal comments of *A* and *B* concerning the language and style in which the speech is presented.

As M. L. Perkins points out, the most significant structural feature of the supplement within the *Supplément* is its reversed chronology: it begins with farewells upon Bougainville's departure from Tahiti and then takes up his arrival on the island.[1] This chronological reversal is completed by the old man whose farewell speech is recorded in this section of the text. "Weep, miserable Tahitians! Weep," he says; "but let it be at the arrival, and not at the departure of these ambitious and evil men" (*Supp.*, p. 466). But in reversing chronology here, the Vieillard is doing more: he is inverting the meaning of Bougainville's "discovery" by presenting it from the Tahitian point of view. The chronological reversal is thus shown to be a case not of simple substitution but of reciprocity. It serves as a model of how each partner in a cultural dialogue (that is, any

[1]M. L. Perkins, "Community Planning in Diderot's *Supplément au Voyage de Bougainville*," *Kentucky Romance Quarterly* 21 (1974): 405.

member of one culture in the face of another) must perceive and relate to the other.

"You are neither a god nor a demon," cries the Vieillard:

> Who are you, then, to take slaves? Orou! you who understands the language of these men, tell all of us, as you told me personally, what they have written on that metal plate: *This country belongs to us*. This country is yours! and why? Because you have put your foot on it? If a Tahitian landed one day on your shores, and if he carved on one of your rocks or on the bark of one of your trees: *This country belongs to the natives of Tahiti*, what would you think of that? [*Supp.*, p. 467]

The Vieillard's reasoning here takes the following form: (*a*) You are neither greater nor lesser and are therefore a man. (*b*) How can you then assert yourself above those to whom you are equal? (*c*) If we are all men and thus all equal, then your right to declare Tahiti as your property implies the Tahitian's right to claim France as his property. (*d*) You see the absurdity and the injustice of the latter and from there can see that the former must be equally absurd and equally unjust.

The Vieillard displays here his common sense. His reasoning is based on the commonality of Tahitian and Frenchman, which implies equality and reciprocity. Only in terms of common sense and its implications of equality and reciprocity is the Vieillard able both to address the other in Bougainville and to make the comparisons of which his speech is composed, not only between Frenchmen and Tahitians but between the claiming of a colony and the theft of personal property, and between the transmission of venereal disease and murder by poisoning (*Supp.*, p. 469). If the "Jugement du voyage de Bougainville" provides a model of reading which includes universal reason as its central moment, "Les Adieux du Vieillard" focuses on that reasoning process, displaying its mechanism and its fundamental importance as the basis of dialogue between defined particulars.

The "Adieux" as a whole presents a reversal as well of the "Jugement," for there two Frenchmen discussed Tahiti, and here a Tahitian speaks about France. The object becomes subject, the subject object. The result is again the equality of the Tahitians and the Frenchmen as human beings, each equally able to reason about the other. It is the Tahitian, after all, who says, "We have respected our image in you" (*Supp.*, p. 468). The Frenchmen—including *A*, *B*, and the reader—must be reminded that the Tahitians, unlike other objects of study, are themselves subjects, watching the watchers, judging the judges.

The reversals that demonstrate the equality and reciprocity between Tahitian and Frenchman are founded in the universal reason shared by all human beings. The Vieillard's speech thus implies formally the dialogue that follows. It both establishes the Tahitian as a thinking subject rather than a mute object and it establishes the dialogue as the interaction between two thinking subjects. This interaction takes place not on the purely abstract level of thought, however, but in its concrete realization in language. And language is not only particular but one of the fundamental definitional particularities of culture. To maintain the particularity of the Vieillard as a true representative of another culture, as an authentic other, he must speak the language of that culture.[2]

While Diderot does not present a real solution to the problem of maintaining the particularity of Tahitian and Frenchman and at the same time overcoming the necessary particularity of their languages, he does signal the problem himself. In so doing he makes clear that his "solution" is a fiction of which the reader should be aware. The first indication of the problem arises in A and B's discussion of Aotourou, the Tahitian brought to France by Bougainville.

"Oh, Aotourou!" exclaims A. "Won't you be happy to see your father, your mother, your brothers, your sisters, your compatriots again? What will you tell them about us?" (Supp., p. 464). A's remark would make a perfect introduction, a cue line, for an imaginary supplement to Bougainville's Voyage: Aotourou, home from his voyage of discovery, telling his compatriots all about France. Such indeed is the obvious reversal of Bougainville's text. But B, far from taking his cue, replies instead to A's rhetorical question. What would Aotourou tell the folks back home? "Not much, and they won't even believe that." In explaining why the Tahitian would have little to say, B continues: "Because he will have understood little, and because he won't find in his own language any words that correspond to those he has some idea of" (Supp., p. 464).

The particularity of Aotourou's language is rooted in his society, for it is the simplicity of that culture that makes its language and those who speak it incapable not only of expressing ideas about the more complex French society but even of conceptualizing it. The question is one not simply of difference but of relative complexity. Clearly, a real Tahitian, such as Aotourou, would not be able to meet the conditions of dialogue that are established in the Supplément, despite the fact that, being human, he is endowed with common sense. Aotourou, therefore, does not figure in the fictional supplement, but is replaced by fictional representatives of his society who, because they are not real Tahitians, can find the words to conceive and express ideas about France.

[2]The particularity of culture is also definitional of the concept of language, according to the Encyclopédie, which defines langue as "the totality of usages proper to a nation for the expression of thoughts by the voice": Encyclopédie, 9:249.

Unlike his contemporary Nicolas Bricaire de la Dixmerie, who puts words in the mouth of Aotourou in his *Le Sauvage de Taïti aux Français*, and thus falsifies him both as an individual and as the anthropological evidence he constitutes, Diderot clearly distinguishes between the real Tahitian and the fictional ones.[3] While creating a Brechtian *Verfremdungseffekt*, this distinction also allows for the introduction of fictional representatives (rather than members) of Tahitian society, and for the dialogue between one of them and an equally fictional representative of French society.[4] Diderot thus capitalizes on fiction as representation in the supplement within the *Supplément*. As representatives of Tahitian society rather than Tahitians, the Vieillard and Orou both enjoy the particularity they represent and transcend it in a way that Aotourou cannot because, as fictional creations of a French imagination, they are able to communicate with the French and their representative. In their representational status as well they become universal, as the products of the reasoning faculty that is able to abstract and represent. Because the writer is endowed with this faculty, he is able to move from the particular to the general, or from the thing to its representation. Indeed, the Vieillard can be said to represent in part this faculty of universal reason, for his speech is both formed (stylistically) and informed by common sense.

The bounds of the supplement within the *Supplément* are defined by explicit references to the language in which it is couched. "How was Bougainville able to understand this farewell couched in a language that he did not know?" asks *A*. "You will see," replies *B*, and the supplement begins (*Supp.*, p. 465). At the conclusion of the Vieillard's speech, *B* asks *A* his opinion of it. *A*'s response brings out the improbability of the speech as truly Tahitian because of its language: "This speech strikes me

---

[3]Nicolas Bricaire de la Dixmerie, *Le Sauvage de Taïti aux Français, avec un envoi au philosophe ami des sauvages* (London and Paris, 1770).

[4]In his notes to the *Supplément*, Vernière points out that Bougainville says nothing of the ship's chaplain beyond his name. Diderot, who fails to name his chaplain, does just the reverse, and so allows his Frenchman to be as fictional and representative as the "Tahitian" Orou (*Supp.*, p. 475, n. 1).

Diderot's Vieillard does seem to originate in the *Voyage*, as Chinard indicates in his introduction to the text (p. 117). I would argue, however, that the case is one of Diderot's completing Bougainville's own fictionalizing, for it is Bougainville who writes of the Tahitian he calls the "vieillard": "his pensive and anxious air seemed to announce that he feared that these happy days, flowing by for him in the bosom of relaxation, would be disturbed by the arrival of a new race": Antoine de Bougainville, *Voyage autour du monde* (Paris, 1771), pp. 192–93. Bougainville's "vieillard" is a character in the myth of the Nouvelle Cythère, whereas Aotourou is a real person who has been interviewed in Paris, whose impressions have been recorded, who has a history and is a part of history.

as forceful; but through whatever there is that is abrupt and savage, I seem to detect some European ideas and turns of phrase." *B* then replies with an explanation that is so farfetched that no one could be drawn in by it. Instead of simply stopping at "Consider then that this is a translation from Tahitian into Spanish, and from Spanish into French," he continues to unnecessary heights of absurdity: "[The Vieillard] had gone, during the night, to see Orou, whom he had questioned, and in whose hut the use of the Spanish language had been preserved since time immemorial. Orou had written out the Vieillard's speech; and Bougainville had a copy of it in his hand while the Tahitian declaimed it" (*Supp.*, pp. 472–73).[5]

The tone of the rest of this conversation maintains the improbability of the supplement. *A* has agreed to play along with *B*, to accept the authenticity of the Vieillard's speech in order to be allowed to read the rest of the supplement. The game, in fact, is a continuation of the one that *A* and *B* play at the beginning of *Ceci n'est pas un conte* when, for the space of about thirty lines of text, *B*, the writer, teases *A*, the reader, and finally describes the scene to the reader outside the text: "Here, a little out of malice, I coughed, I spat, I slowly unfolded my handkerchief, I blew my nose, I opened my snuffbox, I took a pinch of snuff, and I heard my man, who said between his teeth: 'If the story is short, the preliminaries are long.' I was seized with the desire to call a servant on the pretext of some commission, but I didn't ask for anything and I spoke."[6] In the *Supplément*, the "Adieux" piques the curiosity of the reader in spite of its dubious authenticity. After hearing *B*'s explanation of why the speech sounds suspect, *A* admits that he now understands why Bougainville did not publish it, but he notes that the supplement continues and that his "curiosity for the rest is not slight" (*Supp.*, p. 473). If the obvious inauthenticity of the document kept Bougainville from publishing it, it does not keep *A* from wanting to read more of it.

The question of the document's authenticity is here shown to be of less importance than the useful conclusions that might be drawn from it. Since authenticity is conscientiously undermined as it is affirmed, one

---

[5]Vernière remarks that "this care for verisimilitude would seem stronger if Diderot had not learned from Bougainville that the Portuguese Fernandez de Queiro had probably discovered the Tahiti and Pomatou groups toward the end of the sixteenth century. . . . But why, like some Jules Verne hero, confuse the Portuguese and the Spanish?" (*Supp.*, p. 473, n. 1). Although it is impossible to determine absolutely whether Diderot's attempt at verisimilitude here is serious or intentionally overdone, I would argue that the confusion between Spanish and Portuguese is yet another piece of evidence in favor of the latter interpretation.

[6]Diderot, *Oeuvres complètes*, 10:153.

cannot accuse Diderot of "deception," as one critic has done.[7] And because the question of factuality has been set aside, the rhetorical game played by writer and reader is once again emphasized:[8]

> B. What follows will perhaps interest you less.
> A. That doesn't matter.
> B. It's a conversation between the ship's chaplain and a native of the island.
> A. Orou?
> B. Himself. [*Supp.*, p. 473]

The fiction is so transparent that A is able to predict its details. At this point the fiction is shown to be no longer interesting in itself, as a narrative, but interesting in the ideas and the confrontation between cultures it makes possible. The reader's narrative curiosity, as exposed in *Ceci n'est pas un conte*, is displaced, as A's curiosity here is shown to drive him in spite of the transparency of the fictional narrative. It is intellectual curiosity that drives the *Supplément*.

Fiction provides Diderot with a solution to the problem of communication between members of different cultures. It allows the Vieillard and Orou to be both alien and familiar, as Georges Benrekassa points out, in contrast to the authentic alien, Aotourou.[9] It allows them to represent one society in the language of another, and so to transcend the absolute particularity of alien cultures which would make verbal communication impossible.

---

[7]Berry, "Technique of Literary Digression," p. 175.

[8]Rousseau, too, had raised the question of the relationship between truth and factuality in the *Second Discours*. One finds none of Diderot's self-conscious playfulness, however, in Rousseau's "let us therefore begin by setting all the facts aside, for they do not affect the question" (*SD*, p. 132; 103).

In his dialogic preface to *La Nouvelle Héloïse*, Rousseau returned to the problem, repeatedly raising and refusing to answer the question of whether or not his text was a novel or a real correspondence (Rousseau, *Oeuvres complètes*, 2:12–30). And, of course, the *Confessions*, in which Rousseau narrates the story of his life, creating autobiography as a literary genre and himself as its first hero, does nothing to lay the question to rest.

The ambiguous relationship between truth and factuality was, indeed, at the bottom of eighteenth-century literature, as the *Lettres persanes* and the proliferation of documentary forms in general testify. But the ambiguity that was merely acknowledged by Montesquieu (in, for example, the reference to additional letters and the possibility of publishing them later) and that becomes pathological in Rousseau's repeated wrestling with it is exploited by Diderot playfully and to good purpose.

[9]Benrekassa, "Dit et non-dit idéologique," p. 37. Diderot reaffirms the improbability of the supplement in closing it when A says that Orou's discourse is "a bit modeled on the European," and B, no longer bothering to defend his fiction as fact, replies, "I don't doubt it" (*Supp.*, p. 503).

The equality and reciprocity that are presented as both the ground rule of dialogue and the product of universal reason which unites and transcends particular cultures is made technically possible in the *Supplément* through the self-conscious fictionality of the supplement within it. The "Adieux" and the commentary of *A* and *B* which enclose it make the dialogue between Orou and the Aumônier possible by defining the relationship between them, just as the "Jugement" makes the supplement as a whole possible by defining the relationship between writer and reader. Finally, the problem of language as one of communication between members of different cultures is technically resolved in terms of the other, semiotic axis of language: representation.

The best model for Diderot's resolution of this problem can be located in language itself, as the representation of ideas more even than as the fictional representation of an action. In fact, the Lockean conception of language as the representation of ideas rather than things allows for the transformation of Tahiti and France into the ideas that define them, and for the introduction of Orou and the Aumônier to represent them.[10] This process is initiated and demonstrated by the Vieillard in his manner of addressing Bougainville as a representative of France rather than as an individual; it is instantiated in the very creation of the Vieillard by Diderot.

Whereas the dual axes of language provided Montesquieu with the basic tension of the *Lettres persanes*, Diderot profits from this duality by using one axis to resolve a problem presented by the other. "Les Adieux du Vieillard" establishes Tahiti as a valid alternative to France through the introduction of a fictional representative who instantiates, initiates, and demonstrates the process of verbal abstraction and generalization, which, as one axis of language, makes possible the reciprocity and equality of communication in dialogue which is its counterpart.[11]

The Subject Matter of the Dialogue Selected

The "Adieux du Vieillard" is not a dialogue, except in the sense that it replies to Bougainville's *Voyage* and to *A* and *B*'s commentary on it. The direct verbal confrontation between representatives of the two cultures, France and Tahiti, takes place under the equal conditions provided by a pure fiction, the "Entretien de l'Aumônier et d'Orou." Through the freedom of fiction Diderot is able to establish the specific equality of his

[10]Locke, *Essay*, p. 267.

[11]Christie V. McDonald also sees a linguistic model at work here. See "The Reading and Writing of Utopia in Denis Diderot's *Supplément au Voyage de Bougainville*," *Science-Fiction Studies* 3 (November 1976): 249.

two interlocutors: they are of the same sex, and age, and both are educated men: the Aumônier represents the learning of the Church, the traditional European scholarly class; Orou is the only Tahitian with a knowledge of languages. The differences between Orou and the Aumônier (especially since, like *A*, *B*, and the Vieillard, they cannot be said to have developed characters or personalities) can be attributed only to the cultures they represent.

Once the "Entretien" is established as a dialogue and its interlocutors are identified, it is then necessary to select and introduce the topic of the dialogue, its subject matter or focus of attention. For the dialogue between two cultures must be instantiated not only in particular interlocutors who provide the voices but in a specific problem or topic that they can talk about. *A* and *B*, in discussing Bougainville's *Voyage*, found such a focus in his description of Tahiti, which raised the subject of comparative social systems. The dialogue between Orou and the Aumônier, as a dialogue within that between *A* and *B*, further specifies or localizes the subject matter. As primarily reader and writer, *A* and *B* found their topic in a book; Orou and the Aumônier, on the other hand, are primarily representatives of their societies, and so their dialogue arises out of their actual contact, their lived experience, rather than through the mediation of a text.[12] Furthermore, the direct experience of Orou and the Aumônier forms the mediated example, the text of *A* and *B*. The dia-

---

[12]These can be called primary and secondary experiences, but there is no reason why direct experience should be considered better than that gained through the reading of books. In fact, reading is crucial to the critical project because it provides the examples that enrich experience. In either case, it is the reflection upon the experience, either lived or read, that leads to understanding, knowledge, and, as I shall argue below, action and change.

The idea of example as a substitute for experience is found throughout the eighteenth century as a justification of novel writing, notably in Prévost's *Manon Lescaut*. In the "Avis de l'auteur," Prévost argues that example is crucial to moral instruction because, "all moral precepts being nothing but vague and general principles, it is very difficult to make any specific application of them to the details of *moeurs* and actions." Specifically, it is when one must make a moral choice, must weigh the applicable general precepts against one another, that experience and example become useful. "In this uncertainty, nothing but experience or example can reasonably determine the heart's inclination. Now, experience is certainly not an advantage of which everybody is free to avail himself; it depends on the different situations in which one is cast by fortune. Thus for many people only example remains to serve as a rule in the exercise of virtue." (*Histoire du Chevalier des Grieux et de Manon Lescaut*, ed. Frédéric Deloffre and Raymond Picard [Paris, 1965], p. 6). Like Usbek in the *Lettres persanes*, Prévost assumes a direct relationship between example and decision making. A recent study of Rousseau's *Confessions* focuses on the same assumption. See Christopher Kelly, *Rousseau's Exemplary Life: The "Confessions" as Political Philosophy* (Ithaca, 1987). Although Diderot's conception of that relationship is more complex, my purpose here is to stress the common idea that example is necessary as a substitute for the poverty of experience.

logue within the dialogue takes the same place structurally within the *Supplément* as the three stories do in *Ceci n'est pas un conte* and *Madame de la Carlière*: the exemplary text to be discussed critically by Diderot and his reader. And the preoccupation of those stories, the relationship between men and women, becomes also that of the dialogue between the Aumônier and Orou.

In becoming the subject matter of a dialogue between two cultures, the question of the relationship between men and women undergoes a transformation. Specific relationships are now interesting (important) not in their individuality, as in the story of the two real people, Mme Reymer and Tanié, or Mlle de la Chaux and Gardeil, but as representative of the social relations of a particular society. Diderot's insistence on the authenticity of the stories in *Ceci n'est pas un conte* and *Madame de la Carlière* can be seen as an insistence on their individuality, as opposed to the representative function of the fiction in the *Supplément*. Only by refining the problem of the relationship between men and women does one move from the individuality of direct experience or factual examples, with the complexity of many factors as possible causes, to the abstraction of a representative fiction that isolates the determinant aspect of the problematic relationship.

The parallel stories of *Ceci n'est pas un conte* demonstrate that neither all women nor all men are either good or bad, and thus that neither are responsible as men or women for the problems of the relationship. The story of Madame de la Carlière shows that the question of good and bad, or right and wrong, cannot be accounted for simply in terms of the particular man and woman involved. This turn is accomplished through the introduction of a third term, public opinion.[13] The "Entretien de l'Aumônier et d'Orou" eliminates individuality altogether and goes beyond public opinion to the two codes—civil and religious—that define and direct it. Finally, it is not simply these two codes that are inherently culpable; it is their interaction with the code of nature that creates the tensions and contradictions at the heart of the difficulties between men and women. The failure of particular relationships cannot be blamed on the individuals involved either as men or women (e.g., "all women are fickle") or as individuals (e.g., "he was just no good"). Rather, the interaction of the two codes by which these people are governed as members of a particular society and the one code to which they must submit as human beings regulates their actions as individuals: as men and women and as members of their society.

---

[13]On public opinion in *Madame de la Carlière* see Herbert Dieckmann's introduction to his edition of the *Supplément* (Geneva, 1955), pp. xciv–cxii.

Is the *Supplément* then simply a study of comparative sexual relations? When one views it in the context of the triptych and as its culmination, that is the obvious conclusion. In the context of the triptych, as Roger Lewinter demonstrates, the *Supplément* provides an abstract resolution of the problem posed concretely in the stories by identifying the determinant social and physical causes of the failure of relationships between French men and women.[14] But if the *Supplément* explains why French marriages fail, or why French men and women never seem to be happy together for long, that is only one side of its value. The other side must be sought in a reversal of the relative positions of the three codes and in the relationship between the sexes. We must look again at the "Entretien," not as an abstraction of the concrete situation presented in *Ceci n'est pas un conte* and *Madame de la Carlière* but as a dialogue between two cultures.

Because it is particular but not individual, the "Entretien" is at the same time an abstraction of individual stories and an instantiation of the formal requirements of the cultural dialogue. Like Rousseau's hypothetical history, Diderot's representational dialogue is both abstract and particular. The abstractions that serve to explain the stories of the triptych are generated from its particularity as an instantiation of the dialogue between two cultures. But in this same particularity the larger question of social relations in general is instantiated. That is, as the Aumônier and Orou's discussion of sexual relations abstracts from the concrete examples of the triptych, its subject matter (as well as the Aumônier's dilemma and subsequent acts) represents all social relations within societies, just as marriage represents all social institutions. In bringing together the two contexts in which it is placed, the "Entretien" responds equally to the questions raised in both. And in the end *A* and *B* have the last words; their dialogue gives meaning to the "Entretien."

"If all seems to turn here around sexuality, around its regulation," writes Benrekassa, "what is undertaken is in fact much greater. Orou underlines it: it is the magistrates, the priests, and the 'grand ouvrier' himself who are in question."[15] It is French society, represented by the religious and civil codes that regulate, structure, and thus define it, that is placed in question through the "Entretien de l'Aumônier et d'Orou," as a representation of the confrontation in dialogue between two cultures. The implications of the *Supplément* go far beyond the problem of sexual relations; while that problem responds to the problem raised in the triptych, here it is simply a subject matter borrowed from it to represent

---

[14]Roger Lewinter, "Introduction aux trois codes," in Diderot, *Oeuvres complètes*, 10:140.

[15]Benrekassa, "Le Dit et le non-dit idéologique," p. 37.

society as social relations. It is not because the dialogue between two cultures is an appropriate methodology with which to approach the problem of gender relations but because gender relations are representative of all social relations that the *Supplément* is necessarily an inquiry into French society and an attack on it. To understand the *Supplément* in this larger sense, then, it is necessary to read the "Entretien" not merely as the abstract solution to the problem raised in the triptych but as the instantiation and representation of the dialogue between two cultures.

The Dialogue Read

The Tahitian hospitality rite of offering the male guest a sleeping companion creates a dilemma for the Aumônier and sparks the dialogue with Orou. The customs of French society, represented by priestly celibacy, the French institution of marriage, and prohibitions against fornication and adultery, are immediately placed in conflict with those of Tahiti, represented by the hospitality rite. The first issue of this conflict, of the dialogue between two cultures, is a third term: nature. "I don't know what this thing is that you call religion," says Orou in response to the Aumônier's first refusal; "but I can only think ill of it, since it prevents you from enjoying an innocent pleasure to which nature, the sovereign mistress, invites us all" (*Supp.*, p. 476).

The "Entretien," which springs from the concrete predicament of the Aumônier, is initially and fundamentally an investigation of the bases of human action: on what basis does one act or choose between possible courses of action? What are the bases of human decision making that leads to action? The Aumônier is faced with the problem of sleeping or not sleeping with the daughter of his host. The dialogue that ensues between Orou and the Aumônier brings out the possible reasons for choosing one course of action over the other. When the Aumônier invokes "his religion, his *état*, good morals, and *honnêteté*," Orou counters with innocent pleasure, procreation, and the human qualities of generosity and what can be called common courtesy. Against the particular moral constraints of French society, Orou asserts that the Aumônier's "first duty is to be human and to be grateful" (*Supp.*, pp. 475–76).

In the guise of a dialogue between two cultures, then, the two initial positions represented by the Aumônier and Orou are really the particularity of French society and the universality of man.[16] It is thus not surprising that the Aumônier's dilemma is resolved not as a result of

---

[16]See Dieckmann, Introduction to *Supplément* (1955), p. xxxvii.

Orou's powers of persuasion but through the Aumônier's own "weakness" as a man before the temptation of Orou's daughter, Thia. He is weak in relation not to Orou, but to himself, as his general humanity proves stronger than his particular Frenchness. It is an inner debate that is sparked by the Frenchman's confrontation with Tahitian society, and one that ends but is not satisfactorily resolved. For in the end, we learn, "he stayed alone with [Thia], and . . . on saying: But my religion, but my *état*, he found himself the next morning lying beside this girl" (*Supp.*, p. 477).

The introductory scene of the dialogue poses the problem of decision making in terms of the internal debate between the individual as human being and the individual as a member of a particular society, assigning to the Tahitian the role of humanity in general. This is the internal struggle that *B* later calls the "constant war that lasts all one's life," between natural man and artificial man: "Sometimes the natural man is the stronger; sometimes he is knocked down by the moral and artificial man; and, in both cases, the sad monster is pulled about, tortured, tormented, laid out on the wheel" (*Supp.*, p. 511). In the case of the Aumônier, the natural man proves the stronger, but this momentary victory of one side does not resolve the conflict that makes each decision, each temptation, a trial. By sleeping with Thia the Aumônier has taken a course of action, but he has not made an informed, responsible choice; the question of which course of action is correct and why (if such a determination can be made) is still unanswered. The Aumônier's dilemma and the course of action he eventually takes dramatize the internal struggle articulated in the dialogue that presents it. The rest of the dialogue between the Aumônier and Orou then uses the internal conflict suffered by the Aumônier to launch a comparison of the two cultures, French and Tahitian. It begins when Orou questions the Frenchman about the beliefs and customs of France; the Aumônier, who has heard his own society severely criticized, then questions the Tahitian critic about Tahitian society.

The subtitle of the *Supplément* reads: "On the disadvantage of attaching moral ideas to certain physical actions that do not include them" (*Supp.*, p. 455). Its meaning becomes clear here in the center of the text when the Aumônier, in explaining the concept of God to Orou, says, "he spoke to our ancestors: he gave them laws; he prescribed for them the way in which he wished to be honored; he commanded them to perform certain actions as good; he prohibited them from doing others as evil" (*Supp.*, p. 479). Here religious dogma is presented as the origin of moral ideas that determine the correct (good) course of action in French society and generates one pole of the internal conflict suffered by the Aumônier.

Even without Orou's subsequent criticism of the content of the religious code, the reader must be critical of it in form, for it is clear that the relationship between man and man and between man and woman, defined by dialogue as equal and reciprocal, is in sharp contrast to that between man and God: God orders, man obeys. Already on the level of form, the dogmatic command is in conflict with dialogic common sense. As the product of revelation, it is also in conflict in its particularity, since it is not universally accessible, as reason is.

If the dogmatic form of the religious code strikes the reader as an unreasonable anomaly in the midst of a dialogue, it is the content of the code that Orou exposes as contrary to reason and nature. The definition of marriage which it prescribes, he argues, is contrary to nature because it is based on the assumption that "a feeling, thinking, and free being can be the property of a being like herself" and contrary to reason (*insensé*) because it "proscribes the changes that are within us; [because it] demands a constancy that cannot be and that violates the nature and the liberty of the male and the female" (*Supp.*, p. 480). Orou's critique goes one step further and articulates the implicit formal critique when, leaving the religious code behind, the Tahitian focuses on the authorities necessary to enforce it.

The conflict experienced by the Aumônier is finally completely externalized as the forces within him are identified with external authorities, each maintaining one code. Since conduct is guided not by reason but by concrete authorities, Orou asks, do the authorities not have the power to make what is just unjust, and what is unjust just? Once again the particularity of the three authorities—God, the Church, and the state—prevents them from being absolute and denies the possibility of their representing any absolutes—epistemological, moral, or aesthetic. If human reason, which is the only universal standard available to men, does not stand behind these authorities, then legality itself becomes the only basis for action: "There is nothing good that cannot be prohibited you; nothing evil that you cannot be ordered to do" (*Supp.*, p. 481).

At this point the multiplicity of authorities becomes a problem, because if convention is the only rule, there is no reason that two conventions should not conflict with each other. "Thus, in order to please the priest, you will have to quarrel with the magistrate; in order to satisfy the magistrate, you will have to disappoint the *grand ouvrier*; and in order to please the grand ouvrier, you will have to renounce nature. And do you know what will happen? you will scorn all three of them, and you will be neither a man nor a citizen nor a believer (*Supp.*, p. 481).

Orou, through his externalization and objectification of the

Aumônier's internal conflicts, has arrived at the same point that Usbek did in the *Lettres persanes*.[17] Usbek, too, found the religious code independent of its pretensions toward universality, and so began his inquiry into justice. For both Usbek and Orou, unless a knowable and universally applicable standard supports, not just the religious code but the civil code as well, it is impossible to be a good anything—neither man nor citizen nor believer. The problem with the religious code is not simply its content but its arbitrary particularity. The same criticism can be extended to all codes that are independent of a universally knowable universal standard. To say that the religious code is not a sure guide because it is contrary to reason and to nature leads necessarily (according to reason) to an equal condemnation of all particular codes whose justification is either discriminate revelation or conventional legality. And so Orou suggests as an alternative to these unsure and contradictory guides of judgment his own conception of a universal standard: "Do you want to know what, in all times and all places, is good and evil? Stick to the nature of things and actions: to your relationship with those like yourself; to the effects of your behavior on your individual utility and on the common good" (*Supp.*, p. 482).

The Aumônier's dilemma is presented initially as an internal struggle. Orou's analysis externalizes the struggle to reveal the collective forces of church and state as the opponents of universal human nature. Though the problem is posed as one of individual decision making or a personal moral choice, Orou's analysis demonstrates that in fact the individual cannot be separated from the collectivity, that although it is the individual who must make the choice, he makes it not as an individual but as a member of a collectivity and/or as a human being. Thus in analyzing the Aumônier, Orou ends by analyzing the society to which he belongs. Moral choice is a question not of conscience but of the social, religious, and political system in which it is made. Choices, in effect, are moral because there are collective authorities that attach moral values to otherwise neutral actions. And because individual moral choice is a matter of social organization rather than of private conscience, the discussion of the Aumônier's inner struggle evolves into a critique of his society. In this way, too, the dialogue between Orou and the Aumônier evolves into

---

[17]On exteriorization in various works of Diderot, see Otis Fellows, "Diderot's *Supplément* as Pendant for *La Religieuse*," in *Literature and History in the Age of Ideas: Essays in the French Enlightenment presented to George R. Havens*, ed. Charles G. S. Williams (Columbus, O., 1975), p. 239, and Jean Starobinski, "Diderot et la parole des autres," *Critique* 28 (1972): 15.

a dialogue between two cultures. Since Orou reveals the Aumônier to be an instantiation of the collective forces that are internalized as individual conscience, to analyze the Aumônier's conscience is to analyze the social forces that shape it.

The "Entretien" does not end with the critique of the Aumônier's society. Through the principles of equality and reciprocity, which define the dialogue formally, the analysis of the Aumônier gives way to that of Orou as the reciprocal instantiation of Tahitian society; or, more precisely, to an analysis of the social organization he instantiates and represents. And, the society itself being defined, it is in turn an instantiation of the principles that Orou has suggested to the Aumônier as the best guides for individual decision making and action: particular utility and the general good. The Tahiti described by Orou has its basis in principles that are universal and universally accessible through reason, as opposed to the conflicting particular and dogmatic authorities of French society. If Tahiti is to be viewed as a model, it is not for the specific organization that defines it but for the universality of the principles it instantiates. It is not the particularity of Tahiti that ought to be imitated but its foundation in universal principles.[18]

If the details of Tahitian society are not intended as models to be copied by the French, what is their function? They serve primarily to demonstrate that a society based on the principles named by Orou is possible, that the universal can be instantiated in a particular society as the basis of its organization. Only through the details of its social organization does Tahiti as an instantiation of universal principles—Orou's Tahiti, as opposed to Bougainville's—take on substance, the appearance of reality which makes it comparable to France.

Consider the process by which this second Tahiti has been generated. From the France that is shared in experience by Diderot and his reader (and, of course, A and B) are first abstracted its ruling principles, discovered to be civil and religious codes that have been internalized by France's representative (the Aumônier) and so guide his action. But because the Aumônier is a man as well as a Frenchman, the analysis that yields these codes also yields their opposites: universal and universally knowable principles, accessible through reason, based on nature. This second set of principles is then instantiated in the concrete but fictional society of Tahiti. The process is thus one of abstracting from the individual's dilemma the two opposing forces that define it; then of identifying one with the particular principles of French society and the other with the universal principles of nature, reason, and humanity; and finally of

[18]Perkins makes a similar argument in "Community Planning," pp. 414–17.

instantiating the universal principles in a fiction. There is thus an apparent symmetry between France and Tahiti as particular societies, a symmetry that is supported by the dialogue structure. The symmetry is only apparent, however, or at least incomplete, because France is assumed to be the instantiation simply of particular codes, while Tahiti instantiates only universals. In other words, for the purpose of comparison, Diderot is assuming that French civil and religious codes are completely arbitrary, completely independent of and opposed to any conception of universal human values. On the other side, as several critics have pointed out, Diderot omits any reference to the Tahitian religious rituals (including human sacrifice) described by Bougainville, choosing instead to invent customs that instantiate only the universal principles from which French society has become disengaged.[19]

The fictional dialogue compares not two existent cultures but opposing types of principles, one arbitrary, the other universal. The France of the Aumônier, however, is derived from the reality in which Diderot and his reader (and thus A and B) live. By the same token, Orou's Tahiti is derived from the myth of the Nouvelle Cythère presented in Bougainville's *Voyage*. As instantiations of opposing principles, Tahiti and France are defined in opposition to each other, but their origins in independent sources allow them to retain their separate identities. The details of Tahitian social life serve not only to oppose the island society to the Aumônier's France but also to continue and give depth to Bougainville's Tahiti.[20] In the details of Orou's Tahiti, two things come alive: Bougainville's narrative and Orou's own theory of the universal bases of action and society. The procedure used by Diderot to give viable comparative status to his Tahitian fiction, the apparent symmetry with France as a real country, derives from his use of Bougainville's text as a starting and reference point. This procedure is comparable to that used by Rousseau in the *Discours* to give factual status to what I have called the "second beginning" by identifying it with actual primitive societies. It must be stressed, however, that Diderot's fiction is conscientiously exposed as such, while Rousseau's is subtly masked.

Finally, the generation of Orou's Tahiti gives A and B something to talk about. That is, ultimately the dialogue between two cultures be-

---

[19]See, e.g., John Dunmore, "The Explorer and the Philosopher: Diderot's *Supplément au Voyage de Bougainville* and Girardoux's *Supplément au Voyage de Cook*," in *Captain James Cook: Image and Impact. South Seas Discoveries and the World of Letters*, ed. Walter Veit (Melbourne, 1972), p. 62; Fellows, "Diderot's *Supplément* as Pendant for *La Religieuse*," p. 237; and Pierre Hermand, *Les Idées morales de Diderot* (Paris, 1923), pp. 90–91.

[20]See Undank, *Diderot*, p. 50.

comes valuable as the subject of the continuing dialogue between *A* and
B. Diderot's purpose is not simply to give an account of an alien or
primitive culture nor is it merely to criticize what exists by means of
alien voices. The structure of the work points to an investigation of the
alien from the perspective and toward the reformation of Diderot's own
culture. The investigation, enclosed within this framework, gains significance only in terms of the culture through and for which it is conducted.
If, as Diderot writes in the article "Encyclopédie," "it is the presence of
man which makes the existence of all beings interesting,"[21] then it is only
the presence of one's own culture that makes the existence of other
cultures significant. If the passage from "Encyclopédie" is the precept
that guides the analysis of data about the physical world, then its implied
corollary directs the analysis of anthropological data. Knowledge is
viewed as equivalent to meaningful knowledge, and thus truth is bound
up with significance: in order that Bougainville's discoveries and the
supplement to them can be incorporated into knowledge, they must be
viewed in terms of the culture that examines them. If France and Tahiti
are defined in relation to each other through the dialogue between Orou
and the Aumônier, these definitions are not ends in themselves.

Just as the reading of Bougainville's *Voyage* was seen to stimulate
reflection to engage the reader's participation, so too does the reading of
the supplement to it. The parallel to the discussion of the Île des Lanciers
in the first dialogue, as a demonstration of reader participation, is here
found in *A*'s interruption of the dialogue between Orou and the
Aumônier to ask *B* to relate the story of Miss Polly Baker. When *A*
interrupts Orou to say: "What do I see here in the margin?" (*Supp.*, p.
488), the reader is immediately jarred into remembering that he too is
reading a book. He is reminded further that to read is not to be carried
along by the flow of the narrative, not to efface oneself before the text,
but to question it, examine it, act upon it. In bringing up the Polly Baker
story *A* demonstrates how one brings oneself to bear upon the text. The
reader is not a *tabula rasa* but a historical being with a reading past. This
shared reading past already includes at least *Ceci n'est pas un conte* and
Madame de la Carlière. To these texts are now added the story of Miss
Polly Baker, which eighteenth-century readers had learned originally
from Benjamin Franklin. The mental process expressed by "Hey, that
reminds me of . . ." introduces the Polly Baker story into the reading of
the dialogue between Orou and the Aumônier.[22] The awareness

---

[21]*Encyclopédie*, 5:641.

[22]It is most likely that Diderot was himself struck by the relevance of the two works to
each other in reading the Polly Baker story after he had written the dialogue. The story
that was originally published by Benjamin Franklin in 1747 was accepted as authentic by

of reading brings with it the self-awareness of the reader. In this moment of self-recognition the center of activity is displaced: whereas the objective definition of reading places the book as mediator between writer and reader (the object as center), in his self-awareness the reader becomes the center, the mediator between what he is reading and what he has read. The subject becomes the center of activity, and reading, as that activity, extends beyond the immediacy of *this* book to the process of learning as a whole. Just as the analysis of the *Supplément* displays its textual duality as both a whole made up of distinguishable parts and a distinguishable part of the whole triptych, the activity that corresponds to the textual object displays the duality of being both a definite activity in reference to a reader, a writer, and a text and the activity of which this particular act of reading is a part.

The moment at which the reader recognizes himself in the activity of reading depends on a reading past, but it extends forward as well into the future. All three moments of subjective time are realized here, as the integration of the past and the present through the mediation of the reading subject creates a possible future. In the "Suite du dialogue entre *A* et *B*," the final section of the *Supplément*, the reader will be asked to bring all the Polly Baker stories, all the stories of Taniés and Mme Reymers to bear on the text he has just read in order to elicit from that reading useful consequences. By inserting the story of Miss Polly in the middle of the "Entretien," Diderot not only breaks the mimetic spell of the narrative but shows the reader how he ought to be reading it, how to bring himself to bear upon the text as a person with a reading past, in order to generate a future. The Polly Baker story comes in the middle of the dialogue between Orou and the Aumônier, and also in the middle of the text as a whole; it is the pivot point of the reader's self-recognition. In displacing the center of activity, it makes necessary the continuation of the dialogue between *A* and *B* to give the supplement within the *Supplément* both a future and a meaning.

The future just described is, moreover, endless. Although the continuation of the dialogue between *A* and *B* will provide the symmetry necessary to enclose the fictional supplement, the *Supplément* itself is not

---

Abbé Raynal and appeared in his *Histoire des deux Indes* in 1770. In the *Supplément* it was certainly a late addition, as it does not appear in the manuscript of 1772 or 1773 or in the printed editions based on them. Diderot probably rediscovered the Polly Baker story in 1778 as he went over the *Histoire* to prepare an expanded edition, which was to appear in 1780. As Diderot reread the Polly Baker story, he was reminded of his own *Supplément*. He then simply reversed this mental process by having *A* be reminded of Miss Polly's story when he read the dialogue between the Aumônier and Orou. (See Vernière, *Supp.*, p. 491, n. 1.)

in that way completed. Every text must be seen as a center of its literary/intellectual context, able to give way to the reading subject as the new center of the greater intellectual project of which it is a part. When the *Supplément* is considered as a center of reading activity (as it is for me when I read it, as the supplement within it is for *A*), it becomes clear that the triptych provides only one side of its temporal context: as the third term in the triptych, the *Supplément* calls forth a future beyond itself and the reading past it seemingly completes. The future will provide the necessary symmetry, and that future is the responsibility of the reader. By taking over the central position, by displacing the text he is reading, the reader, in his activity, completes the text by acting upon it. By examining closely the critical activity of *A* and *B* as they complete in this way the supplement to Bougainville's *Voyage*, it will be possible to see that Diderot asks the reader to complete similarly the *Supplément au Voyage de Bougainville* by reflecting and acting upon it.

CHAPTER EIGHT

Critical Activity
as Political Action

T he final section of Diderot's text returns the reader to that cozy living room in which *A* and *B* had decided to read together the supplement to Bougainville's *Voyage*. Having finished that reading, they (and we with them) are now ready to reflect upon the text just read. In so doing, we, like *A* and *B*, begin to make comparisons between this new text and others that we have read. While *A* and *B* recalled the story of Polly Baker when they read the supplement to Bougainville, twentieth-century readers tend to think of Rousseau's *Second Discours* when they read the *Supplément*.

Indeed, it is almost impossible to read the *Supplément* without at some point thinking of Rousseau. Though he is nowhere named, Rousseau is as surely inscribed in Diderot's text as Bougainville himself. Herbert Dieckmann dedicates a section of his introduction to the *Supplément* to a comparison between it and the *Second Discours*, arguing that such a discussion should help to define the particular character of Diderot's text.[1] Other commentators, too, display their need to understand the *Supplément* in terms of the *Discours*.[2] What exactly the relationship is between the two texts is not obvious, however, and each commentator has defined it differently. The lack of agreement is not surprising, considering that interpretations of the two texts themselves vary widely: how does one determine definitively a relationship between two undetermined quantities?

[1]Dieckmann, Introduction to *Supplément* (1955), pp. lxxiii–xci.
[2]See especially Chinard's Introduction to the *Supplément* (1935); Jean Fabre, "Deux frères ennemis: Diderot et Jean-Jacques," *Diderot Studies* 3 (1961): 155–213; and Lester G. Crocker, *Diderot's Chaotic Order: Approach to Synthesis* (Princeton, 1974).

The relationship between the *Supplément* and the *Second Discours* has generally been based on a simple comparison of the states of nature portrayed in them. This approach, however, tends to create more problems than it solves, for as in Rousseau criticism in general, there is confusion as to what constitutes the state of nature in the *Second Discours*: either the completely savage state of part 1 or the "golden mean" of part 2 or the entire development of man up to the introduction of private property. On the other side, moreover, Diderot's Tahiti is uncritically accepted as a state of nature, to be compared with any of the possible states of nature in the *Discours*. Chinard, for example, writes that "Diderot's Tahitians are quite close to this 'homme sauvage' of whom Rousseau could say, 'his desires do not exceed his physical needs, the only needs that he knows in the universe are food, a female, and sleep; the only evils that he fears are pain and hunger.' "³

But while Chinard thus implies that Diderot's Tahiti is equivalent to the state described in the first part of the *Discours*, Dieckmann seems to assume that the state of nature in Rousseau extends up to the point where property is introduced, and that the Tahiti represented in the "Adieux du Vieillard" is that state. "The principal idea of the ['Adieux']," he writes, "is that the state of nature in Tahiti is threatened by the will to dominate of the members of the expedition, who not only declare that the island belongs to them but teach the natives the very concept of private property. Now, it is the concept of property that, according to Rousseau, distinguishes the state of society or civilization from the state of nature."⁴

In a third approach, Steven David Werner equates Tahiti with the "golden mean" when he concludes that "neither Diderot nor Rousseau had advocated a precipitous return to the forest. Like Jean-Jacques, Diderot had spoken warmly of the advantages of compromise: a golden mean between primitive society and the highly developed state. The *Supplément* speaks of a middle point of progress when man could be both happy and wise. It is also an idea which is implicit in Rousseau's *Discours*."⁵

Finally, Lester Crocker presents an ingenious interpretation by first assuming that Diderot means Tahiti to be a state of nature, and then accusing him of "cheating" because it really is not a Rousseauian state of nature. "Of course Diderot is cheating, *pour la cause*, since the Tahitians, as Rousseau had cogently urged, were not in the state of nature, but had

³Chinard, Introduction to *Supplément* (1935), pp. 52–53.
⁴Dieckmann, Introduction to *Supplément* (1955), p. lxxvii.
⁵Steven David Werner, "The *Encyclopédie* and the *Supplément au Voyage de Bougainville*: Diderot and the Range of Man" (Ph.D. diss., Columbia University, 1967), p. 94.

an advanced tribal organization with very many 'hindrances.' Diderot, however, had convinced himself that the Tahitians had stopped at the right point: 'a people wise enough to have by themselves halted at a middle stage.'"[6]

Considering the lack of agreement as to what constitutes the state of nature in Rousseau and the fact that Diderot never uses the term at all in the *Supplément*, a comparison of the two texts based on the states of nature portrayed in them tends to confuse rather than clarify the relationship.

A more subtle problem in determining the relationship between the *Discours* and the *Supplément* lies in the implicit use of Rousseau as the standard by which Diderot is measured. Not simply Tahiti, but the text as a whole and in its parts is analyzed and judged by a supposed Rousseauian standard. Thus Crocker writes that "Diderot does not really believe his ideal goals to be realizable. He is willing to settle for something less, and he surely would not have purchased order at the price that Rousseau realistically said had to be paid."[7] Even Dieckmann falls into this pattern, and the problem is most visible here because the analysis is more detailed, more profound. "If one places the *Supplément* in the perspective chosen by Rousseau," he writes,

> Diderot commits the same confusion in his way of conceiving the state of nature as the other philosophers refuted by Rousseau in his *Discours*. It is easy to imagine a "Réfutation suivie de l'ouvrage intitulé *Supplément*" by Rousseau. He would have criticized Diderot for suppressing the basic facts of Bougainville's report and inventing others; he would have shown that the conception of the state of nature in the *Supplément* was neither historical nor empirical, that it was not even logical according to the logic of natural reason which Diderot invoked.[8]

By hypothesizing an elaborate Rousseauian critique of the *Supplément*, Dieckmann introduces him as the standard by which Diderot is to be judged. What Dieckmann is doing, in fact, is transforming the chronological priority of Rousseau's *Discours* into a priority of value; the first thus becomes the judge of the second; the dead (in a manner of speaking) judges the living. Since the method is thoroughly counterhistorical, the relationship between texts determined by it can exist only in the mind of the critic or in the realm of transcendent ideas—ideas that float free of the human beings who create them and the world in which they live.

[6]Crocker, *Diderot's Chaotic Order*, pp. 123–24.
[7]Ibid., p. 122.
[8]Dieckmann, Introduction to *Supplément* (1955), p. lxxxv.

Such a method can expose a relationship between ideas but not between texts as the intellectual actions of the people who write them.

Instead of hypothesizing a probable Rousseauian response to Diderot, we can understand the relationship between the two texts by determining Diderot's actual response to Rousseau. Instead of placing the *Supplément* in the perspective chosen by Rousseau, one must place the *Second Discours* in that chosen by Diderot. Instead of starting from Rousseau's concept of the state of nature, one must look to the implicit references to the *Second Discours* in the *Supplément*, for it is in these references that Rousseau is inscribed in Diderot's text, and it is in this inscription that the connection between the two texts must be sought. To understand Diderot's stance toward Rousseau—whether he is completing the picture merely sketched out in the *Discours*, as Chinard argues, or renewing an old debate, as Jean Fabre claims[9]—one must look to the questions and the comments that invoke Rousseau in Diderot's text. In respect to the form of the *Supplément*, it is especially important to keep track of who is saying what.

The first clear reference to the *Second Discours* appears at the beginning of the "Suite du dialogue entre *A* et *B*," but neither *A* nor *B* makes it. The dialogue between Orou and the Aumônier completed, the Aumônier now closes his supplement to Bougainville's account of the voyage with his own reflections on the Tahiti he has just presented to us, here paraphrased by *B*:

> Here the good chaplain complained of the shortness of his stay in Tahiti, and of the difficulty of getting to know better the customs of a people wise enough to have stopped themselves half-way, or lucky enough to inhabit a climate whose fertility assures them a long torpidity; active enough to protect themselves from the basic wants of life, and indolent enough that their innocence, their repose, and their happiness had nothing to fear from a too rapid progress of enlightenment. [*Supp.*, p. 503]

There can be no question that, for the Aumônier, the Tahitians live in the spatial equivalent of that period of universal history described by Rousseau as "this period of the development of human faculties, maintaining a golden mean between the indolence of the primitive state and the petulant activity of our vanity"; the epoch that "must have been the happiest and most durable." It is the same epoch that Rousseau claims

[9]Chinard, Introduction to *Supplément* (1935), p. 51; Fabre, "Deux Frères ennemis," p. 203.

best describes "the point reached by most of the savage peoples known to us" (*SD*, pp. 170–71; 150–51).[10]

Is Diderot's purpose in identifying Tahiti with what he considers a Rousseauian golden age "to complete the picture that Jean-Jacques Rousseau had simply sketched in the *Discours*," as Chinard argues?[11] I suggest that his aim is rather to distinguish his own work from that of Rousseau by attributing the "éloge" to the good but simple Aumônier, who lacks the critical distance to make proper use of his experience. Just as much a participant as Bougainville, the Aumônier is unable to analyze his own data. Because his experience is direct rather than removed by critical distance, he is tempted only to the personal response of remaining in that other culture, instead of seeking general conclusions that would transcend both his own particularity and that of Tahiti. This personal response leaves the social whole unchanged, and as such it does not attack the problem at its source; it is a form of escape rather than a solution.

The Aumônier, who through his dialogue with Orou has become aware of both the conflict within himself and its origin in the conflicting "masters" he must serve in France, finds a simple solution in the fantasy of staying in the land where these conflicts do not exist. "He finished by protesting that these Tahitians would always be with him in memory, that he had been tempted to throw his clothes in the ship and spend the rest of his life among them." (*Supp.*, p. 504). While Diderot identifies this response with Rousseau by using a vocabulary that mimics the *Second Discours*, he does not endorse it. The futile dream of remaining in a fictional world, a personal solution to a socially imposed problem through escape from society, is first located in the *Second Disours* and then shown to be at best inadequate, at worst simply a fantasy.

"Despite this *éloge*," asks *A*, "what useful consequences can be drawn from the *moeurs* and strange customs of an uncivilized people?" (*Supp.*, p. 504). The distinction is drawn between the futility of seeking to live in the fictional world of Tahiti and the utility of analyzing that world. The purpose of creating such a fiction is not to escape from one's own society either physically or in dreams but to learn from an analysis of it. And Rousseau is implicated again in the wording of this rejection of his presumed solution to the conflicts of modern society, though the words here mimicked are not from the *Discours* but from the "Profession de foi du Vicaire Savoyard." "What good does it do," the Vicaire asks Montaigne, "to give to the most suspect travelers the authority denied the most celebrated writers? Will a few dubious and strange customs based

[10]See Chinard, note to *Supplément* (1935), p. 177, n. 1.
[11]Chinard, Introduction to *Supplément* (1935), p. 51.

on local causes that are unknown to us destroy the general induction drawn from the agreement of all peoples, opposed in everything else and agreeing only on this single point?"[12]

Whereas the Vicaire's question is rhetorical, A's is not, and the answer to it is to be found in the dialogue that follows. Yes, asserts Diderot, there is value in reflecting upon something that does not fit into our normal way of thinking, something that contradicts even the inductive reasoning of civilized man. The otherness of both anthropological evidence and fictions serves to change familiar ways of thinking. Sea stories, whether reliable or not, provide a contrast to the familiar and serve as the basis of a critical approach to it. They provide the distance that the direct experience of the Aumônier and the reasonings of the Vicaire lack.[13]

[12]Rousseau, *Oeuvres complètes*, 4:598. On the importance of Montaigne in the shaping of Diderot's thought, see Jerome Schwartz, *Diderot and Montaigne: The "Essais" and the Shaping of Diderot's Humanism* (Geneva, 1966). I would also suggest that the same essay, "Des cannibales"—which, Schwartz and others argue, was at least in the back of Diderot's mind when he wrote the *Supplément*, and to which Rousseau refers above in the *Émile*—was in the back of Rousseau's mind when he wrote the *Second Discours*. Consider Montaigne's description of the man from whom he learned the details of life in the New World:

> This man I had was a simple, crude fellow—a character fit to bear true witness; for clever people observe more things and more curiously, but they interpret them; and to lend weight and conviction to their interpretation, they cannot help altering history a little. . . . We need a man either very honest, or so simple that he has not the stuff to build up false inventions and give them plausibility; and wedded to no theory. Such was my man. . . . [Michel de Montaigne, "Of Cannibals," in *The Complete Essays of Montaigne*, trans. Donald M. Frame (Stanford, 1958), pp. 151–52]

It is against such simple travelers and tellers of tales that Rousseau lashed out in his note x of the *Discours*. Bougainville responded in his "Discours préliminaire" to the *Voyage*:

> I am a traveler and a sailor; that is to say, a liar and an imbecile in the eyes of that class of lazy and superb writers who, in the shadows of their studies, philosophize to the skies on the world and its inhabitants, and imperiously submit nature to their imaginations. A very singular procedure, quite inconceivable on the part of people who, having observed nothing themselves, do not write, do not dogmatize, except according to observations borrowed from these same travelers to whom they deny the faculty of thought. [*Voyage*, p. 17]

Diderot, choosing to supplement Bougainville rather than to supplant him, accepts the traveler's tale regardless of its questionable reliability and depends on the critical method to derive value from the evidence. Like Montaigne, Diderot distinguishes between observation and reflection by assigning these tasks to different people or groups of people. A and B are to Bougainville and the Aumônier as Montaigne is to his "man who had lived for ten or twelve years in that other world which has been discovered in our century" ("Of Cannibals," p. 150). Rousseau would have these tasks combined in sending the philosopher to make the observations (*SD*, pp. 213–14, n. x; 212–13, n. j).

[13]The reciprocity of spatial and temporal distance, already remarked in Montesquieu and Rousseau, can thus be converted further, as in this case between reality and imagina-

The next appearance of Rousseau in the *Supplément* is a further critique of the Vicaire Savoyard. *A* and *B* have just begun their analysis of the "Entretien," starting from *B*'s definition of *moeurs* as "a general submission to and a conduct consequent with the laws, good or bad," and *B* has named the three codes whose conflicting orders prevent observation of them and thus produce the worst condition possible in a society, the lack of *moeurs* altogether. *A* then suggests that either civil law should be based on nature and religious law thrown out as superfluous or all three codes should be maintained on condition that civil and religious laws "be nothing more than precise tracings of the first [nature], which we all carry engraved in our hearts, and which will always be the strongest" (*Supp.*, pp. 504–5). *A* has, in fact, stated the principle of moral judgment upheld by Rousseau's Vicaire Savoyard.

"It remains to me," says the Vicaire, "to seek what maxims I must draw upon for my conduct, and what rules I must prescribe for myself in order to fulfill my destiny on earth according to the intention of him who has placed me here. Following my usual method, I do not draw these rules from the principles of some high philosophy, but find them at the bottom of my heart, written by nature in indelible characters." And in looking into himself, the Vicaire comes to the following conclusion: "There is thus at the bottom of all souls an innate principle of justice and of virtue, by which, despite our own maxims, we judge our actions and those of others as good or evil, and this is the principle to which I give the name of conscience."[14]

With the introduction of the notion of individual conscience, the explanation of the Aumônier's dilemma threatens once again to be internalized, to be reduced from the social to the personal level. In fact, as the Vicaire had apostrophized earlier: "Man, seek not the author of evil, that author is yourself."[15] Such an individual explanation of moral judgment and the personal solutions (such as the Aumônier's) which it engenders and justifies, however, leaves the social whole unchanged. The conflict itself becomes externalized, as the individual, acting according to his conscience, acts against the civil and religious codes. "The society whose beautiful order your leader so praises," Orou had already explained, "will be nothing but a pack of hypocrites who secretly trample the laws underfoot; or of unfortunates who are the instruments of their own

tion, to produce the conditions of criticism. See Bevier, "Diderot's Utopian Visions," p. 174.

[14]Rousseau, *Oeuvres complètes*, 4:594, 598.

[15]Ibid., p. 588.

torture by submitting to it; or imbeciles, in whom prejudice has stifled completely the voice of nature; or defective creatures, to which nature disclaims all rights" (*Supp.*, p. 484).

By reinternalizing the origin of the Aumônier's conflict, the notion of individual conscience displaces the conflict itself to the external, social level. The Vicaire's method of reasoning, which begins with the individual, ends with him too, and in so doing generates a new source of conflict in the external relations of the individual to the social whole. And so when *A*, mimicking Rousseau's Vicaire, refers to the law of nature as "engraved in the bottom of our hearts," *B* immediately replies: "That's not quite right. We bring nothing with us at birth but an organization similar to that of other beings, the same needs, an attraction to the same pleasures, a common aversion to the same pains: that's what constitutes man such as he is, and ought to be the basis of a morality that suits him" (*Supp.*, p. 505).[16]

If we cannot simply consult our individual hearts or souls to discover the law of nature upon which civil and religious laws must be based, what means are available for knowing it? How can we determine what constitutes man as he is? Or, to borrow Rousseau's wording of the problem: "What experiments would be necessary to achieve knowledge of natural man? And what are the means for making these experiments in the midst of society?" (*SD*, pp. 123–24; 93). The first part of Rousseau's *Discours* is concerned with answering this question for, as he says, "it is this ignorance of the nature of man that throws so much uncertainty and obscurity on the true definition of natural right," and natural right must be at the basis of any definition of law and of the science of law (*SD*, p. 124; 93).

In the *Supplément*, *A* seems to follow the same reasoning as Rousseau in the *Discours* (just as earlier he followed Rousseau's reasoning in *Emile*). Admitting the difficulty of separating the natural from the artificial as Rousseau does, he still suggests that they try to do so. More precisely, he takes up the topic already raised in the "Entretien," the union of men and women, and submits it as a case by means of which to determine what is and is not natural. "Let's begin at the beginning," says *A*. "Let's really interrogate nature, and we'll see impartially how it will answer on this point" (*Supp.*, p. 506). *B*, without commenting on the validity of this procedure, consents to give it a try. They begin with marriage and agree that, narrowly defined as a mutual preference of one person for the other and of indeterminate duration, marriage can be said to be found in nature.

---

[16]Jacques Oudeis remarks the contrast with Rousseau's Vicaire on this point in "L'Idée de nature dans le *Supplément au Voyage de Bougainville*," *Revue de l'Enseignement Philosophique* 23 (1972–73): 3.

Similarly, they conclude that gallantry, too, can be said to be found in nature. But when it comes to determining what is not found in nature, the method breaks down.

A. Thus jealousy, according to you, is not [found] in nature?
B. That's not what I'm saying. Vices and virtues, all are equally [found] in nature. [*Supp.*, pp. 506–7]

"This remark brings to a close the inquiry into the foundation of natural morality," concludes Dieckmann; "the attempt to clarify the principles of this morality has quickly led to a disintegration of the concept of nature."[17]

Jealousy, although unjust, is not necessarily unnatural; coquetry, though deceitful, is not necessarily unnatural either for that reason alone. No simple equation of nature with virtue or artifice with vice is possible. Vice and virtue being social rather than natural categories, they cannot correspond directly to the idea of nature or its opposite. Rather, the actions and sentiments found in nature are contrasted to the vices and virtues that are the products of particular social organizations.

"As soon as the woman became the property of the man, and furtive pleasure was regarded as theft," says *B*, "one saw emerge the terms *pudeur, retenue, bienséance*; imaginary vices and virtues" (*Supp.*, p. 507). Everything is found in nature to some degree; it is the concept of virtue and vice that places positive or negative value on actions, proscribes or extends their original limits, and has as its end support of arbitrary laws that run counter to natural desires. *Pudeur*, for example, has its natural foundation in the physical weakness that follows lovemaking and that must be hidden from enemies for reasons of self-defense. It becomes artificial only when it is set free from the natural reason that gives rise to it and is called a virtue in itself. *Pudeur*, in other words, becomes dogmatic rather than reasonable when its aim is to support arbitrary laws rather than to follow natural desire. *Natural* and *artificial* correspond, respectively, to *reasonable* and *dogmatic*. The question to ask is not whether certain actions are natural but rather to what extent and under what conditions they are reasonable. And as Orou had argued earlier, the only reasonable standard you can use for judging human action is "the effect

---

[17]Dieckmann, Introduction to *Supplément* (1955), p. lii. *B*'s remark here, as well as an earlier one in response to the suggestion that coquetry is found in nature—"I'm not saying that"—appears first in the margins of the Naigeon manuscript now in the Bibliothèque Nationale (N.a. fr. 13783, p. 23). It would thus seem that Diderot definitively rejected this form of argument only after having tried it here in good faith. If he began by building on Rousseau, he ultimately was forced to reject Rousseau's method entirely.

of your conduct on your individual utility and the common good" (*Supp.*, p. 482).

The procedure of investigating nature directly, suggested by A in imitation of Rousseau and other theorists who seek to define a state of nature, fails to yield a basis of good legislation. If Diderot "has arrived at an impasse," if he "has blocked the inquiry that ought to have established the principle of reform," as Dieckmann argues, it is Rousseau's impasse and not his own. If Dieckmann is not surprised that Diderot "comes back to a critique of society," I am even less so, for not only does the opposite procedure fail to produce a basis of legislation, but it is in opposition to the methodological premises of the *Supplément* as a whole.[18]

The *Supplément*, it must be remembered, is an exercise in cultural comparison. Unlike Rousseau's historical method, which "begins at the beginning," Diderot's comparative approach begins at the "end," with contemporary France. Thus what Diderot retains of Rousseau's argument is not the narration of part 2, which describes the development of man from his origin in the wild, but that timeless state of nature described in part 1. "Nature," says *B*, "indecent if you wish, pushes one sex toward the other indiscriminately: and in a sad and savage state of man that one can perhaps conceive and that nowhere exists . . . " Here *A* interrupts to ask: "Not even in Tahiti?" and *B*, without further explanation, simply says, "no" (*Supp.*, p. 508). The reference to Rousseau's "state which no longer exists, which perhaps never existed, which probably never will exist" (*SD*, p. 123; 93), is obvious. Equally clear is the fact that Tahiti is not to be considered such a state. Rather, as the examination of the "Adieux du Vieillard" showed, Tahiti must be viewed as a civilized alternative to France for the purpose of comparison. The state of nature (the expression is still not used by Diderot) is not comparable in the same terms. Being theoretical rather than either factual or fictional, it is a pure product of reason. Its function is to serve as a control by explaining human action that is not based on arbitrary laws. Whereas Tahiti and France are discussed by Orou and the Aumônier in the comparative terms of good and bad, just and unjust, the state of nature is not susceptible to such human judgment. By introducing the third term, Tahiti, as the point of comparison with modern France, Diderot is able to isolate nature from the realm of comparison.[19]

In nature, everything is reasonable. To that extent, nature and reason

---

[18]Dieckmann, Introduction to *Supplément* (1955), p. liii.

[19]This procedure should have helped Diderot avoid the misinterpretation that plagues Rousseau and of which he himself was guilty. For Diderot, with the rest of his contempo-

are synonymous. Actions that are natural, however, become unreasonable when they are undertaken in other than their original context. For this reason, when one seeks to determine if an action is good or bad, just or unjust, one must ask not if it is found in nature but if it is reasonable in the particular social context and in the real circumstances in which it appears. A direct investigation of nature can explain the psychological or historical origin of a certain action or sentiment, but it cannot validate it. *A* and *B*'s discussion of the Île des Lanciers in their first dialogue is instructive on this point. In considering the inhabitants of the island, *B* raises the question: "What will become of them if they reproduce in a space that is no bigger than a league in diameter?" From this question certain hypotheses, such as cannibalism, infanticide, castration, and abortion, emerged (*Supp.*, pp. 460–61). Instead of asking whether the various practices they describe are natural, whether they exist in the state of nature, *A* and *B* examine the particular situation of a small island. Instead of interrogating abstract nature, they interrogate the nature of the Île des Lanciers. The size of the island can explain the need for actions that in the abstract would certainly be called unnatural. These unnatural acts, however, are not unnatural at all in the context of this island, where both self-interest and the general good of the society demand a limitation of the population. Like *pudeur* in French society, all these cruel and necessary practices have a reasonable origin. Like *pudeur* as well, however, they become unreasonable when they are transformed by religion into moral precepts and civil laws. As such they become objectified, valorized in themselves, and reason gives way to dogma.

The world, as both *B* and Orou assert, is forever changing (*Supp.*, pp. 480 and 507). In such a world, practices that are initially reasonable become unreasonable if the circumstances that give rise to them change. Institutions, laws, and precepts, in their rigidity and their objectivity, are necessarily in conflict with the world in flux from which they originate. Thus *A* calls the transformation from a practice that is based on particular circumstances into laws and precepts that by definition must be independent of particular circumstances "one of the most fatal of palingeneses" (*Supp.*, p. 461).

It is not nature but institutions, laws, and precepts that must be interrogated to determine if they continue to respond to the needs of the

---

raries, accused Rousseau of valorizing the savage state: "If Rousseau, instead of preaching to us to return to the forest, had taken the trouble to imagine a type of society half civilized and half savage, it would have been hard, I think, to dispute him" (*Oeuvres complètes*, 11:627). Unfortunately, Diderot's misinterpretation of Rousseau is simply displaced, as he is accused of nostalgia for Tahiti as a state of nature.

individuals and collectivities they were established to serve. Nature alone can only tell us what, in the absence of extenuating circumstances (such as the size of the Île des Lanciers or the lack of fertility of a particular region) would be reasonable. An investigation of the particular society is necessary to determine what is reasonable in its civil laws and moral precepts. As Montesquieu showed in the *Lettres persanes*, comparison of alternative social systems "denaturalizes" laws and precepts, revealing them as the products of human invention. This process is repeated in the *Supplément* by means of the dialogue between Orou and the Aumônier.[20] This cultural comparison, however, is only a first step toward the evaluation of established laws and precepts. One must then determine whether contemporary laws and precepts continue to reflect nature in general (defined as the commonality of all human beings) or reasonable modifications of it based on particular circumstances. The origin of most laws in nature, as *B* said earlier, "is lost in the night of time and tortures philosophers" (*Supp.*, p. 460). The recovery of such origins, however, must be viewed as of only antiquarian interest, for they are no longer reasons. That is, although the origin of a practice in nature was once its reason for existence, the fact that that origin is no longer accessible to reason shows it to be no longer reasonable—even though it must have been so at one time.[21]

Society's problems lie not in the nature—general or particular—that gave rise to social practices but in the laws, precepts, and institutions that extend these practices beyond their initial and proper function (*Supp.*, pp. 509–10). This unreasonable extension occurs both temporally, through the endurance of outmoded laws in a changing world, and "spatially": that is, by application of an absolute value to an act or sentiment whose reason is specific and local, such as *pudeur*. Thus a certain act or sentiment is first deemed necessary for the common good in specific circumstances or in response to specific local and temporal circumstances; then it is valorized, called a "virtue"; finally, it is institutionalized in law. Whereas the first valorization universalizes what was a local act, giving it positive value in all circumstances, the institutionalizing of that virtue gives it durability over time. The necessity that gave reason to the action is itself no longer necessary to motivate it; the moral and legal structures take on a life of their own, in themselves validating the actions and sentiments that are chronologically prior to them.

[20]There is, of course, a major difference between the cultural comparison made in the *Lettres persanes* and that of the *Supplément*. Whereas in the first case the two systems are revealed to be equally arbitrary, in the second Tahiti's social system, although as artificial as that of France, is not arbitrary.

[21]See Oudeis, "L'Idée de nature," p. 4.

What, then, is the value of laws, of the structure of society as a whole? Is the solution to the eternal conflict between natural and artificial man simply the elimination of the latter? If, as *B* argues, natural man is never destroyed, never even wholly dominated by artificial man, why not just let him destroy the rival who is powerless to destroy him? At this point it is apparent that there is no value in imposing the already arbitrary civil, religious, and moral system of France on primitive peoples whose systems are likely to be much more closely based on the exigencies of their natural situations.[22] To organize others is always to impose an order upon them, and that order will thus always be arbitrary and despotic, as *B* explains. "Beware the man who wants to put things in order," he warns. "To organize is always to make oneself the master of others by cramping them" (*Supp.*, p. 512).[23] But the question still remains: Even if we leave the rest of the world in peace, what are we to do in our own country, with our own complex system of arbitrary laws, institutions, and moral precepts? "What shall we do then? Should we return to nature? Should we submit to the laws?" (*Supp.*, p. 515). *A*'s initial question about what useful consequences can be drawn from the study of Tahiti ends ultimately in this question, which again is Rousseau's. "What!" he wrote in the *Second Discours*: "must we destroy societies, annihilate thine and mine, and go back to live in forests with bears?" (*SD*, p. 207, n. ix; 201, n. i).

Certainly Rousseau saw the futility of trying to go backward in time. But he also saw futility in trying to reform France, which he saw as headed down a path toward inevitable self-destruction. Though he could build in theory a society in which private conscience and public action would be reconciled, the *cité* of the *Contrat social* was not a guide for living in his own time. For Rousseau, the only immediate solution to the inner conflict experienced by Diderot's Aumônier was a personal one. In a world in which institutions and laws are based on the corrupt foundation of inequality, the only sure guide is that espoused by the Vicaire Savoyard, individual conscience. Diderot, however, denies the existence of individual conscience, and with it the self-sufficiency of the individual. For Diderot, the solution to the inner conflict experienced by the Aumônier and his fellow Frenchmen must be external, collective, social. Ultimately, moreover, it must be political.

Despite the fact that laws are too rigid, too durable to reflect con-

---

[22]On Diderot's anticolonialism see Bénot, *De l'athéisme à l'anticolonialisme*.

[23]*B*'s warning may also be a response to Rousseau's Vicaire Savoyard, who says: "The general evil can lie only in disorder, and I see in the system of the world an order that does not contradict this at all. . . . Take away our fatal progress, take away our errors and our vices, take away the work of man, and all is well": *Oeuvres complètes*, 4:588.

tinually a changing world; despite the fact that by their nature they generalize and thus tend to extend beyond the limitations and particularity of the circumstances out of which they emerge; despite the fact that, as the codification of moral precepts that ascribe an absolute value to acts and sentiments, they attach "moral ideas to certain physical actions with which they do not agree"; despite all these inherent faults, laws not only are necessary but are the very basis of *moeurs*, the measure, in turn, of a society's health. *Moeurs*, it must be remembered, have been defined by *B* as "a general submission to and a conduct consequent with laws, good or bad. If the laws are good, *moeurs* are good; if the laws are bad, *moeurs* are bad; if the laws, good or bad, are not obeyed, it is the worst condition of a society, there are no *moeurs* at all" (*Supp.*, p. 504).

The code of nature on which positive law must be based if the Aumônier's inner conflict is to be resolved is not engraved in our hearts but is simply the sum total of the commonality of all human beings. It is knowable through the faculty of reason, which, as common sense, is one aspect of this commonality. Opposed to this commonality, however, is the individuality of each human being and the particularity of circumstances that differentiate communities or nations. Were human beings simply their commonality, there would be no need for positive law. One must look to these two levels of distinction among people, the individual and the social, in order to understand the necessity and the importance of positive law.

The particularity of circumstances explains why the laws of Tahiti cannot be those of France. Thus M. L. Perkins writes that "appropriateness [for Diderot] means not what is applicable to all human nature, but to a group of men living under the environmental conditions of a given time and place. Not [Tahiti's] morals or its plans, but its ability and skill in planning are subject to successful adoption by all peoples."[24] Thus positive law must first adapt the general laws of nature to the particular conditions of the social group. This adaptation is possible through the use of reason, which is able to calculate positive laws as products of universal relations and circumstances. Although particular circumstances change over time as well as space, a constant critique of existent laws and their subsequent modification can correct laws that have either of themselves extended beyond their initial jurisdiction or become obsolete with changes in external circumstances. The same "calculating intelligence" that determines laws can evaluate them by asking if they (continue to) serve the general good of society and the human race as a whole, as well

[24]Perkins, "Community Planning," p. 411.

as the particular interests of the individuals subject to them.[25] Although positive law is always inadequate to the extent that it generalizes particular circumstances, it is necessary because it individualizes the universal law of nature. In respect to the circumstances that define a particular nation or community, the individuality of positive law is its virtue; its generality in respect to these same particulars, however, is its drawback.

Positive law must be understood in relation to the individual as well as the society. The fact that positive laws are always inadequate, or at least susceptible to becoming so over time, produces a situation in which one must choose whether or not to obey a law that one knows to be unjust. What does the critic (the reasonable person) do after analyzing current laws and finding them to be in need of change? Does one obey bad laws in the knowledge that they are bad, or obey instead a law of one's own calculation that is just?

It is at this point precisely that the *Supplément* as a text extends outward into the society it criticizes, for the responsibility of deciding what to do in the face of unjust laws is that of the reader as a person who has read the text. *A* and the reader merge once again as *A* asks: "What shall we do then?" They come together here outside the text in the reader's own world, rather than in *A*'s enclosed textual world. In *B*'s response, the text itself is seen to provide a model of responsible action, of the action of a person who is responsible for the awareness of unjust laws which the reading of the text has awakened in him.

We shall speak out against senseless laws until they are reformed; and, while we are waiting, we will submit ourselves to them. He who, on his own private authority, breaks a bad law authorizes everyone else to break the good ones. There are fewer problems with being a fool among fools than in being wise all by oneself. Let's tell ourselves, let's cry out incessantly, that shame, punishment, and ignominy have been attached to actions innocent in themselves; but let's not commit them, because shame, punishment, and ignominy are the worst of all evils. Let us imitate the good chaplain, be a monk in France, a savage in Tahiti. [*Supp.*, p. 515]

The *Supplément* is itself that cry, it is itself the means toward the reform of unjust laws. In exposing the "craziness" of these laws by setting forth the method of social criticism in which the reader participates, Diderot initiates the process of reform. Just as the first dialogue between *A* and *B* negates itself at the end as subject matter ("skip this preamble, which doesn't mean anything": *Supp.*, p. 465) to leave only the form—the relationship between reader, writer, and text and the meth-

[25]See Oudeis, "L'Idée de nature," pp. 4–5.

odology of reading that it describes—the *Supplément* as a whole negates itself as a text in revealing itself as responsible action, in identifying criticism as a moment of the reform it makes necessary.

Rousseau, too, argues that one must obey laws, even in the knowledge that they are unjust. The difference between his position and Diderot's, however, is substantial. For Rousseau the bonds of society are sacred, whereas for Diderot they are not. If it is better to obey bad laws than to disobey them, the reason lies in ourselves and our relation to society and its members, according to Diderot, not in some higher valorization of the social whole. For Rousseau, moreover, it is the constitution of society that is corrupt and that is the basis of unjust laws. Were Rousseau to advocate the uprooting of French society, the changing of its constitution, he would be the revolutionary he is often said to be. In not advocating revolutionary change he is left with no social or political change to advocate at all, since reforming any particular laws would not affect the fundamental inequality on which they rest.

For Rousseau, then, the reader can depend only on the goodwill of men who, obeying the higher law of divine virtue, work to counteract the inequality inherent in the constitution of society and the abuses to which it gives rise. Rousseau advocates neither the impossible return to the forest nor revolutionary action, but obedience to a divine morality that enjoins men to respect "the sacred bonds of the societies of which they are members" by, among other things, obeying scrupulously their laws and those who make and administer them (*SD*, p. 207, n. IX; 202, n. i).

Political reform is in no way a solution to the problem of the conflict between man and society, which Rousseau raises in much the same terms as Diderot does. "What is to be thought of intercourse in which the reason of each individual dictates to him maxims directly contrary to those that public reason preaches to the body of society, and in which each man finds his profit in the misfortune of others?" (*SD*, p. 202, n. IX; 193–94, n. i). For Rousseau, the cause of this contradiction is identifiable, but it is not subject to human action. For Rousseau, one can avoid the inner conflict that is the personal manifestation of this contradiction if one simply ignores the voice of society and listens only to one's own reason, one's own heart. To Diderot such a solution is both unacceptable, because it places the individual above the law on the basis of a nonexistent "higher law," and inadequate, because it denies the efficacy of legal reform to provide a real solution to the Aumônier's inner conflict.

For Diderot, positive law, with all its faults, is necessary because there is no higher law. Nature and nature's reason reveal a law that is fundamental to human beings but that is not for that reason higher than the positive laws that they themselves create. In itself, natural law cannot serve as a basis for individual human action because it is outside the particular structure of the society in which the individual lives, and it is that structure which forms the immediate context of his actions. If it is futile to interrogate nature directly, as the dialogue between A and B has shown, it is mad to act directly upon it. Madness, like morality, is a social term, meaningless in abstract nature, where all actions are amoral, where, all actions being instinctive, there are neither wise men nor fools. Knowledge, too, as the opening dialogue between A and B showed, is a product of human mediation, like morality, like the concept of madness, since it is only through the activity of A and B (of you and me) that the data provided by Bougainville can be converted into meaningful knowledge. Meaning is itself a human construct, that which makes words signify ideas or makes actions, otherwise devoid of value, either good or bad. Both knowledge and morality are the results of human meaning, of the placing of human value on something otherwise neutral. We have then the choice of applying what meaning we will, of interpreting what we observe and what we do according to standards of our own choosing. But we have the responsibility, living together as we do, to choose a standard that is both universally accessible and universally applicable. This applicability is found, according to Diderot, in the commonality of our physical beings; the accessibility is found in common sense; the two can be called nature and nature's reason. Any other standard must be deemed arbitrary. But if the universality of nature and of nature's reason justifies their use as a standard of judgment, a basis of positive law, the general acceptance of created laws as law is at least as important. Like language itself, positive law is conventional.

The analysis of the *Lettres persanes* demonstrated that the two axes of language—rhetorical and semiotic—are interdependent, that significance can be recognized only within the rhetorical community, and that the rhetorical (political) relationship can be stabilized only through a universal standard of meaning that lies outside that relationship. The *Supplément*, and especially B's final conclusion, reinstantiates that interdependence. For Diderot, not transcendent justice but nature and nature's reason provide the standard of morality, a standard that can be recognized only in the convention of positive law. Conversely, only when positive law is based upon natural law is it reasonable and not arbitrary, and in universal reason stabilized. To "speak another language," as Usbek did in the Persian court and as Rousseau advocates in the *Discours* but above all in the *Émile*, is futile. It is better to be "a fool among fools" while constantly crying out against this common idiocy.

Diderot, perhaps like those who pressured Usbek out of Persia, argues

further that the raising of private authority against positive law is an
invitation to others to do the same, and thus society as a whole is
threatened by anyone who invokes a "higher law."[26] Rhetoric and semiotics, community (communication) and meaning, convention and reason
are interdependent, and neither side of any pair can be sacrificed to the
other. In the end, when a choice must be made between the two, when
law is not based in reason or nature, one must obey because one lives in
society. It is because the particular society of France already exists, because it is the concrete reality in which one lives, that convention must
take precedence over reason. The lack of *moeurs*—that is, of obedience
to conventional law—as *B* has said, is the worst condition of *society*, for it
is as a member of one's society rather than as an abstract human being
that one must act, because it is as a member of that society that one lives.
Just as it is as a member of that society that one reads Bougainville. Or
Diderot.

   B's conclusion that one should imitate the Aumônier by being "a
monk in France, a savage in Tahiti" affirms the importance of cultural
particularity introduced in the initial dialogue between *A* and *B*. His
subsequent conclusion that one must above all be "scrupulously honest
and sincere with the fragile beings who cannot make us happy without
renouncing the most precious benefits of our societies" (*Supp.*, p. 515)
reiterates the necessary particularity of men and women which is at the
heart both of the conflict of universal and particular laws and of the
relational definition of human beings and their societies. That is,
the fundamental difference between men and women renders impossible
the complete similarity of all human beings and thus impossible too the

---

[26]Leland Thielemann is worth quoting at length on this point:
    Certain of Diderot's modern critics, who would have preferred a more absolutist
    Diderot, have argued that the philosopher refused the revolutionary implications of
    his analysis of eighteenth-century political institutions. They have made much of the
    passage in the *Supplément au voyage de Bougainville* in which he declared that he
    would not disobey bad laws for fear of encouraging disobedience to good laws. . . .
    In this declaration, however, Diderot expressed without equivocation one of the
    basic articles of the liberal critique both of Hobbes and of the advocates of "higher
    law" theories. The laws of convention were indeed the rule and guide of actions, but
    they do not create justice nor did they necessarily embody its eternal principle.
    Where thought was free, nothing prevented society from exchanging bad laws for
    good. . . . While recognizing as a necessity of social life the pragmatic justice of the
    positive law, he had read too much Cicero to regard the positive law as an infallible
    rule of justice and equity. ["Diderot and Hobbes," *Diderot Studies* 2 (1952): 253–54.]
The list of modern critics who express their disappointment with Diderot's "conformist"
final position, which they see as conflicting with the "revolutionary" or "anarchist"
criticism that precedes it, includes just about everyone who has written on the political
dimension of the text. Herbert Dieckmann stands out as a notable exception to the rule.

ability of universal laws to cover all aspects of human action. The fundamental need of men and women for each other—the insufficiency of one
without the other—also explains why the isolated individual cannot in
himself be the model of moral judgment and action. If modern society
has become too complex and contradictory in its legal and institutional
structure, it is because the differences between people have been un-
necessarily encumbered, not because the differences are themselves fab-
ricated. At the heart of all societies—and this is a universal—is the
relationship between its two irreducible members, man and woman.
Both the individual and the society must be understood in terms of this
relationship rather than in terms of man alone.

The relationship between men and women and their fundamental
difference within the universal category of human beings in turn serves
as the model of cultural differences within the same universal of humanity, as displayed in the opening dialogue of the *Supplément*. The reader
was led to realize there that he (or she) must necessarily read the text
both as man or woman and as Frenchman or Tahitian. And reading, in
turn, must be seen to be a model of all social activity, for the book defines
a community of reader and writer in which the reader's role is to read.
When *A* asks what we are supposed to do, to return to nature or to
submit to admittedly bad laws, *B*'s response is not that of abstract "man,"
or of a man without a country. It is the response of someone who realizes
that one's existence is bound up with that of one's own society.

B's answer reflects the inherent duality of the individual as a particular instantiation of the universal category "man" which is at the origin of
the need for positive law and must be at the basis of any reform of
society. This "natural" duality must replace (or be revealed beneath) the
factitious multiplication of contradictory laws and institutions that con-
found moral decision making and action rather than facilitate them. The
understanding that existing laws are nonsensical depends on the universal faculty of reason, common sense; the decision to obey these laws, to be
a fool among fools, depends on the need to live in the particular society
of which one is a member; to reconcile the conflict it is necessary to apply
continually the universal faculty of reason to the particular circumstances
of the society in which one lives. The cultural comparison is thus possible
only in terms of the calculation based on universal nature which makes
two cultures comparable through its mediation, while affirming their
difference in particularity. In the end, however, this comparison cannot
itself tell us what to do; it must be understood as a stage in the process of
coming to recognize and distinguish the universal and particular aspects
of one's own society.

The overall structure of the *Supplément*, in which the actual supplement to Bougainville's *Voyage* is enclosed within a dialogue between two Frenchmen, ensures that the reader is placed in the interior of his moral (and political) system. The structure of reading displayed in the first dialogue between *A* and *B* serves first as a model of how to read the text that is both the supplement and the *Supplément* and second as a model of responsible human action defined specifically as social criticism. *B*'s conclusion, that one must obey existing laws while crying out against them, is instantiated in the *Supplément* itself. Thus, far from being in opposition to the radical critique of the text, *B*'s conclusion completes that critique by converting it into responsible action toward changing what it criticizes. The gap between critical activity and political action is bridged in the identification of the process of criticism with the process of reform, which, through the identification of the internal and external readers of the text, moves from the text out into the world.[27]

[27]If there is an unresolved paradox in this text, as many critics argue, it is not within the text but outside it. (See, e.g., Hermand, *Les Idées morales de Diderot*, p. 97; H. Brugmans, "Les Paradoxes du philosophe," *Neophilologus* 41 [1957]: 177; and Vernière, Introduction to *Supplément*, p. 453.) The text in fact is a whisper rather than a cry, for to cry out against bad laws in the eighteenth century was tantamount to disobeying those laws. The paradox of the text, seen as the Aumônier's dilemma, is externalized just as it is for the Aumônier, as it is displaced from the text itself to the text's relationship to the society in which it exists and cannot act.

Conclusion

With Diderot, social and political criticism invaded the political arena, turning politics into one more form of critical activity. In his formulation, politics is a continual process of reform, and reform is simply criticism in action. Most important, the critic is now seen to be the agent of political change through reform. And the critic is not simply Diderot, the author of the *Supplément*, but the reader of that book as well. As such, the critic must be identified with an enlightened public. As the reading public expands, so grows the list of those qualified to evaluate and legislate, to engage in the criticism and reform that constitute Diderot's brand of politics.

Diderot's great innovation in the practice of criticism was to take the critical reader developed by Montesquieu and make of him an agent responsible for political change. Montesquieu's reader, who was forced to use his common sense in order to understand the *Lettres persanes*, became a practitioner of the comparative critical method. At the same time, the reader of the *Lettres persanes* became aware of himself as a Frenchman and of his society as specifically French. The comparative critical method in which Montesquieu instructed his reader depended upon both the universality of common sense and the particularity of concrete social reality. But in instructing the reader in this method, in forcing him out of the inertia of absolutist subjection and into the activity of criticism, Montesquieu left the reader frustrated. Although he could now oppose absolutism actively through criticism wherever absolutism was found— as politics, as religion, and as a way of thinking—he could not intervene. Society was simply too complex, the parts too tightly woven together for any single person—as king or subject, reader or critic—to be able to have an effect on it. Criticism was neither a rhetoric nor a politics; it was a dead end.

Rousseau extended Montesquieu's critique of society to much greater depth, but in so doing he neglected altogether the reader's potential for activity. No longer a participant in the criticism of society, Rousseau's reader was simply carried along by the narrated flow of events. Rather than experiencing the frustration of Montesquieu's reader, the passive spectator of Rousseau's *Second Discours* gained narrative satisfaction at the closing of the gap between original and modern man, intellectual satisfaction in the solution of Rousseau's conundrum. And so Rousseau's reader, in his passivity, should not have been surprised to learn that in fact there was nothing he could do anyway, since the society in which he lived was on a course that he was powerless to change.

In the *Supplément* Diderot reintroduced the reader into the text, and he did so with a vengeance. He dislodged the representation of society from its central position and placed there instead the dialogue between the reader and the writer, the activity of criticism itself. By emphasizing the activity of criticism over its subject matter, he broke down the barrier that Montesquieu had raised between the critic and the agent of political change when he had turned his critical attention away from the prince: he travestied the travesty of Anaïs and Ibrahim, returning the politically active critic to the real world of reader and writer. And the effect of this shift was to make of criticism a rhetoric, based as it now was on the rhetorical bond between reader and writer and the community it defined.

In this rhetoric can be seen a new form of politics, a politics not based on the authority of the absolute but one whose means—and perhaps even whose end—is reasoned discourse and whose authority is common sense. Because the monarchy is no longer the subject matter of criticism and the king no longer the reader to whom it is directed, the laws and institutions of France stand on their own as the subject matter of a criticism that has become a politics. That is, as itself a politics, Diderot's criticism bypasses courtier and king entirely, focusing directly on that which needs to be reformed. And the agents of this reform, the critical politicians, are the critical readers themselves, the enlightened public that had been created by fifty years of philosophic and critical activity.

To talk about criticism and political action in eighteenth-century France is, of course, to invite speculation on the relationship between the Enlightenment and the French Revolution. One must, however, overcome the temptation to make facile connections between complex phenomena. For if nothing else, this study should demonstrate that the Enlightenment, as embodied in three of its most important texts, was an extremely thoughtful and complex enterprise. Viewed through these works, the Enlightenment was much more than an age of popularization, slogans, and candy coating on old philosophic pills. It was rather that large-scale project whose aim, as Diderot wrote of the *Encyclopédie*, was to change the common way of thinking. I have tried to show the mechanics of this project in terms of the movement of Enlightenment political criticism from a rejection of the king as its subject and object and toward both a more profound social critique and the creation of an enlightened, critically active readership that might take responsibility for changing a social and political order that could no longer be identified with the monarchy. Whether that readership was in fact created, whether it did indeed take seriously the responsibility that was thrust upon it, and whether the taking of such responsibility was manifested in the Revolution—these questions lie beyond the bounds of the textual analysis in which I have here engaged.

My aim is simply to contribute to a better understanding of the Enlightenment itself by focusing attention on questions involving reading and readership as the implied correlate of authorial activity.[1] Before we can even begin to define a relationship between the Enlightenment and the Revolution, we must understand the Enlightenment not as a collection of ideas or common themes but as an intellectual and critical movement that gained definition as its leaders developed a self-consciousness and a consciousness of their common project over the course of the century. In Diderot's work of the 1770s we find the articulation of a mechanics of critical reading and writing which makes of them two aspects of this common project. The *Supplément* is simply the text that expresses and demonstrates most centrally and directly the mechanics of changing the common way of thinking through the development of a critical readership. It also draws most explicitly the political implications of why one ought to go about creating such an enlightened public, something that the article "Encyclopédie" in its discussion of cross-references had not done. Like the *Lettres persanes*, the *Encyclopédie* demanded a comparative critical method; unlike Montesquieu, however, by the

---

[1] Recent work on the problem of readership in early modern France, especially that of Roger Chartier, suggests that such a shift of focus has already begun. See Chartier, *Lectures et lecteurs*, as well as two volumes edited by Chartier that bring together the work of a number of scholars: *Pratiques de la lecture* (Marseille, 1985) and *Les Usages de l'imprimé* (Paris, 1987).

1770s Diderot took the bold step of suggesting that the mastering of such a critical method not only would qualify one to frame necessary reforms but would give the critic responsibility to do so.

The *Supplément au Voyage de Bougainville* is a crucial text for our understanding of the project of changing the common way of thinking, the most conscious and self-conscious articulation of a project that is now visible in its light. It can become our guide to the Enlightenment as a critical project that aimed to shape not simply ideas but readers. In one sense we can see Rousseau as such a critical reader who learned the lesson so well that nobody created a more profound critique of the Old Regime than he. If Montesquieu and his generation created the possibility of Rousseau, however, they also created the further possibility of Diderot, who could see himself as both reader and writer, as *A* and *B*, and tried to transform his own reader in his own image.

The Enlightenment, conceived in this way, is a world of texts, but it is also a world of readers and writers. My focus on literary form and structure has brought out the complex interaction between implied writers and readers which the Enlightenment, as a project directed toward changing the common way of thinking, entailed. But it also makes clear the importance of understanding better than we now do the implicit contexts in which these complex interactions took place and were meant to take place. Between texts and their historical contexts lie the rhetorical contexts in which these texts, as centers of communication, operate. To get at the rhetorical context of Enlightenment texts is, I think, to get at the Enlightenment as something greater than the sum of its texts. And to do so, one might begin by asking the following four questions: (1) What did it mean to read or to write in the eighteenth century? (2) Why did one read or write? (3) For whom did one write? (4) What was the situation of the reader and the writer in the eighteenth century? These four questions should be familiar, because they are simply modified versions of the four chapter headings in Sartre's *What Is Literature?* If we could answer them, we would be well on our way to understanding not only what literature is but what the Enlightenment was.

The close analysis of texts that I have engaged in here is a crucial step toward arriving at a definition of the Enlightenment as a community of discourse, a rhetorical context in which texts are written and read. And while I believe that it is also the best way of defining the problem, since it demonstrates how complex that problem really is, I am not suggesting that it is sufficient to an understanding of the Enlightenment as a historical phenomenon. But empirical work will not progress far without an appreciation and understanding of the complex mechanics of the project to change the common way of thinking. As Robert Darnton recently admitted, "to pass from the *what* to the *how* of reading is an extremely difficult step."[2] A combined effort of empirical and theoretical research will make the connection between the what and the how of reading and writing more accessible, and the definition of the Enlightenment as both a how and a what attainable.

[2]Robert Darnton, *The Great Cat Massacre and Other Episodes in French Cultural History* (New York, 1984), p. 222.

Works Cited

Allers, Ullrich S. "Rousseau's Second *Discourse.*" *Review of Politics* 20 (January 1958): 91–120.

Altman, Janet Gurkin. *Epistolarity: Approaches to a Form.* Columbus: Ohio State University Press, 1982.

Amelot de la Houssaie, [Abraham-Nicole]. *La Morale de Tacite: De la flaterie.* Paris, 1686.

Ansart-Dourlen, Michèle. *Dénaturation et violence dans la pensée de Jean-Jacques Rousseau.* Paris: Klincksieck, 1975.

Aristotle. *The "Art" of Rhetoric.* Trans. John Henry Freese. London: Heinemann, 1967.

———. *Poetics.* Trans. W. Hamilton Fyfe. Rev. ed. London: Heinemann, 1932.

Arnauld, Antoine. *The Art of Thinking: Port-Royal Logic.* Trans. James Dickoff and Patricia James. Indianapolis: Bobbs-Merrill, 1964.

Atkinson, Geoffrey. *The Extraordinary Voyage in French Literature before 1700.* New York: Columbia University Press, 1920.

Auerbach, Erich. *Mimesis: The Representation of Reality in Western Literature.* Trans. Willard Trask. New York: Doubleday, 1957.

Austin, J. L. *How to Do Things with Words.* 2d ed. Cambridge: Harvard University Press, 1975.

Baczko, Bronislaw. *Rousseau: Solitude et Communauté.* Paris: Mouton, 1974.

Baker, Keith Michael. *Condorcet: From Natural Philosophy to Social Mathematics.* Chicago: University of Chicago Press, 1975.

———. "Politics and Public Opinion under the Old Regime: Some Reflections." In *Press and Politics in Pre-Revolutionary France,* ed. Jack R. Censer and Jeremy D. Popkin, pp. 204–46. Berkeley: University of California Press, 1987.

Barrière, P. "Les Éléments personnels et les éléments Bordelais dans les *Lettres persanes.*" *Revue d'Histoire Littéraire de la France* 51 (1951): 17–36.

Bénot, Yves. *Diderot: De l'athéisme à l'anticolonialisme.* Paris: Maspero, 1970.

231

Benrekassa, Georges. "Dit et non-dit idéologique: À propos du *Supplément au Voyage de Bougainville.*" *Dix-huitième Siècle*, no. 5 (1973), pp. 29–40.

Berry, David. "The Technique of Literary Digression in the Fiction of Diderot." *Studies on Voltaire and the Eighteenth Century* 118 (1974): 115–272.

Bevier, Pamela Jean. "Diderot's Utopian Visions." Ph.D. dissertation, Columbia University, 1976.

Booth, Wayne C. "Metaphor as Rhetoric: The Problem of Evaluation." *Critical Inquiry* 5 (Autumn 1978): 49–72.

———. *The Rhetoric of Fiction*. Chicago: University of Chicago Press, 1961.

———. *A Rhetoric of Irony*. Chicago: University of Chicago Press, 1974.

Born, Lester K., ed. *The Education of a Christian Prince*, by Desiderius Erasmus. New York: Columbia University Press, 1936.

Bougainville, Antoine de. *Voyage autour du monde*. Paris, 1771.

Brady, Patrick. "The *Lettres persanes*: Rococo or Neoclassical?" *Studies on Voltaire and the Eighteenth Century* 53 (1967): 47–77.

Brecht, Bertolt. *Brecht on Theatre: The Development of an Aesthetic*. Ed. and trans. John Willet. New York: Hill & Wang, 1964.

Bricaire de la Dixmerie, Nicolas. *Le Sauvage de Taïti aux Français, avec un envoi au philosophe ami des sauvages*. London and Paris, 1770.

Broome, J. H. *Rousseau: A Study of His Thought*. New York: Barnes & Noble, 1963.

Brugmans, H. "Les Paradoxes du philosophe." *Neophilologus* 41 (1957): 173–80.

Burgelin, Pierre. *La Philosophie de l'existence de J.-J. Rousseau*. Paris: Presses Universitaires de France, 1952.

———. "Rousseau et l'histoire." In *De Ronsard à Breton: Recueil d'essais, hommages à Marcel Raymond*, pp. 110–15. Paris: Corti, 1967.

Cabeen, David. *Montesquieu: A Bibliography*. New York: New York Public Library, 1947.

———. "A Supplementary Montesquieu Bibliography." *Revue Internationale de Philosophie* 9 (1955): 409–34.

Caillois, Roger. Preface to *Oeuvres complètes*, by Montesquieu. 2 vols. Paris: Gallimard, 1949–51.

Canary, Robert H., and Henry Kozicki, eds. *The Writing of History: Literary Form and Historical Understanding*. Madison: University of Wisconsin Press, 1978.

Carr, J. L. "The Secret Chain of the *Lettres persanes.*" *Studies on Voltaire and the Eighteenth Century* 55 (1967): 333–44.

Cassirer, Ernst. *The Philosophy of the Enlightenment*. Trans. Fritz C. A. Koelln and James P. Pettegrove. Boston: Beacon Press, 1955.

———. *The Question of Jean-Jacques Rousseau*. Trans. Peter Gay. Bloomington: Indiana University Press, 1963.

Chartier, Roger. *Lectures et lecteurs dans la France d'Ancien Régime*. Paris: Seuil, 1987.

———, ed. *Pratiques de la lecture*. Marseille: Rivages, 1985.

———, ed. *Les Usages de l'imprimé*. Paris: Fayard, 1987.

Chinard, Gilbert. Introduction to *Supplément au Voyage de Bougainville*, by Denis Diderot. Paris: Droz, 1935.

Cohen, Ted. "Metaphor and the Cultivation of Intimacy." *Critical Inquiry* 5 (Autumn 1978): 3–12.

Cotta, Sergio. "Philosophie et politique dans l'oeuvre de Rousseau." *Archiv für Rechts- und Sozialphilosophie* 49 (1963): 171–89.

Coulet, Henri. "La Distanciation dans le roman et le conte philosophique." In *Roman et lumières au XVIIIe siècle*, colloque sous la présidence de W. Kraus et al., pp. 438–47. Paris: Éditions Sociales, 1970.

Crisafulli, Alessandro. "Montesquieu's Story of the Troglodytes: Its Background, Meaning, and Significance." *PMLA* 58 (June 1943): 372–92.

———. "Parallels to Ideas in *Lettres persanes*." *PMLA* 52 (June 1937): 773–77.

Crocker, Lester G. *Diderot's Chaotic Order: Approach to Synthesis*. Princeton: Princeton University Press, 1974.

———. "The Relation of Rousseau's Second *Discours* and the *Contrat social*." *Romanic Review* 51 (February 1960): 33–44.

Daguerressar, Pierre. *Morale et politique: Jean-Jacques Rousseau ou la fonction d'un refus*. Paris: Minard, 1977.

Darnton, Robert. *The Great Cat Massacre and Other Episodes in French Cultural History*. New York: Basic Books, 1984.

Dehaussy, Jacques. "La Dialectique de la souveraine liberté dans le *Contrat social*." In *Études sur le "Contrat social,"* pp. 119–41. Paris: Belles Lettres, 1964.

Delon, Michel. "Un Monde d'eunuques." *Europe*, no. 574 (1977), pp. 79–88.

Dictionnaire de l'Académie française, Le. 2 vols. Paris, 1694; rpt. Lille: L. Daniel, 1901.

Diderot, Denis. *Oeuvres complètes*. Ed. Roger Lewinter. 15 vols. Paris: Club Français du Livre, 1970.

———. *Oeuvres philosophiques*. Ed. Paul Vernière. Paris: Garnier, 1964.

Dieckmann, Herbert. *Cinq leçons sur Diderot*. Geneva: Droz, 1959.

———. Introduction to *Supplément au Voyage de Bougainville*, by Denis Diderot. Geneva: Droz, 1955.

Duchet, Michèle. *Anthropologie et histoire au siècle des lumières: Buffon, Voltaire, Rousseau, Helvétius, Diderot*. Paris: Maspero, 1971.

——— and Launay, Michel. "Synchrophonie et diachronie: *L'Essai sur l'origine des langues* et le second *Discours*." *Revue Internationale de Philosophie* 21 (1967): 421–42.

Ducrot, Oswald, and Todorov, Tzvetan. *Encyclopedic Dictionary of the Sciences of Language*. Trans. Catherine Porter. Baltimore: Johns Hopkins University Press, 1979.

Dumarsais, César. *Des tropes*. Nouvelle edition. Paris, 1757.

Dunmore, John. "The Explorer and the Philosopher: Diderot's *Supplément au Voyage de Bougainville* and Girardoux's *Supplément au Voyage de Cook*." In *Captain James Cook: Image and Impact. South Seas Discoveries and the World of Letters*, ed. Walter Veit, pp. 54–66. Melbourne: Hawthorne Press, 1972.

Ehrard, Jean. "Histoire des idées et histoire littéraire." In *Problèmes et méthodes de l'histoire littéraire*, pp. 68–80. Paris: Armand Colin, 1974.

———. "Tradition et innovation dans la littérature du XVIIIe siècle: Les Idées et les formes." In *La Littérature des Lumières en France et en Pologne: Ésthétique*.

Terminologie. Échanges, pp. 15–27. Acta Universitatis Wratislaviensis, no. 339. Warsaw: Panstwowe Wydawnictwo Naukowe, 1976.

Eigeldinger, Marc. *Jean-Jacques Rousseau: Univers mythique et cohérence*. Neuchâtel: Baconnière, 1978.

Elias, Norbert. *The Court Society*. Trans. Edmund Jephcott. New York: Random House, 1984.

Encyclopédie, ou Dictionnaire raisonné des sciences, des arts et des métiers. Ed. [Denis] Diderot and [Jean Le Rond] d'Alembert. 35 vols. Paris, 1751–80; rpt. Stuttgart–Bad Cannstatt: Frommann, 1966.

Engels, Friedrich. *Herr Eugen Dühring's Revolution in Science [Anti-Dühring]*. Trans. Emile Burns. New York: International Publishers, 1939.

Fabre, Jean. "Deux Frères ennemis: Diderot et Jean-Jacques." *Diderot Studies* 3 (1961): 155–213.

Fellows, Otis. "Diderot's *Supplément* as Pendant for *La Religieuse*." In *Literature and History in the Age of Ideas: Essays in the French Enlightenment presented to George R. Havens*, ed. Charles G. S. Williams, pp. 229–43. Columbus: Ohio State University Press, 1975.

Fénelon, François de Salignac de La Mothe-. *Les Aventures de Télémaque*. Paris: Garnier, 1968.

Fetscher, Iring. "Rousseau, auteur d'intention conservatrice et d'action révolutionnaire." In *Rousseau et la philosophie politique*, pp. 51–75. Paris: Presses Universitaires de France, 1965.

Foucault, Michel. *The Archaeology of Knowledge and the Discourse on Language*. Trans. A. M. Sheridan Smith. New York: Harper & Row, 1976.

France, Peter. *Rhetoric and Truth in France: Descartes to Diderot*. Oxford: Oxford University Press, 1972.

Frege, Gottlob. "Über Sinn und Bedeutung." *Zeitschrift für Philosophie und philosophische Kritik* 100 (1892): 25–50.

Gallie, W. B. *Philosophy and the Historical Understanding*. 2d ed. New York: Schocken, 1968.

[Gaultier, Abbé Jean-Baptiste]. *"Les Lettres persanes" convaincues d'impiété*. N.p., 1751.

Gay, Peter. *The Enlightenment: An Interpretation*. 2 vols. New York: Norton, 1977.

Genette, Gérard. "Boundaries of Narrative." Trans. Ann Levonas. *New Literary History* 8 (Autumn 1976): 1–13.

———. *Narrative Discourse: An Essay in Method*. Trans. J. E. Lewin. Ithaca: Cornell University Press, 1980.

———. "La Rhétorique restreinte." *Communications* 16 (1970): 158–71.

Goldschmidt, Victor. *Anthropologie et politique: Les Principes du système de Rousseau*. Paris: Vrin, 1974.

———. *Les Dialogues de Platon: Structure et méthode dialectique*. 3d ed. Paris: Presses Universitaires de France, 1947.

Goodman, Dena. "Story-Telling in the Republic of Letters: The Rhetorical Context of Diderot's *La Religieuse*." *Nouvelles de la République des Lettres*, no. 1 (1986), pp. 51–70.

———. "Towards a Critical Vocabulary for Interpretive Fictions of the Eighteenth Century." *Kentucky Romance Quarterly* 31 (Fall 1984): 259–68.

Gosselin, Gabriel. "L'Utopie de l'homme naturel dans le second discours de Rousseau ou la fonction de l'utopie dans la connaissance sociologique." In *Modèles et moyens de la réflexion politique au XVIIIe siècle*. Vol. 2: *Utopies et voyages imaginaires*, pp. 347–60. Lille: Université de Lille, 1978.

Gouhier, Henri. "Nature et histoire dans la pensée de Rousseau." *Annales de la Société Jean-Jacques Rousseau* 33 (1953–55): 7–48.

Grimsley, Ronald. "The Idea of Nature in *Lettres persanes*." *French Studies* 5 (October 1951): 293–306.

Grosrichard, Alain. *Structure du sérail: La Fiction du despotisme asiatique dans l'Occident classique*. Paris: Seuil, 1979.

Habermas, Jürgen. *L'Espace public: Archéologie de la publicité comme dimension constitutive de la société bourgeoise*. Trans. Marc B. de Launay. Paris: Payot, 1986.

Hamlin, Cyrus. "Platonic Dialogue and Romantic Irony: Prolegomenon to a Theory of Literary Narrative." *Canadian Review of Comparative Literature* 3 (1976): 5–26.

Hegel, G. W. F. *The Phenomenology of Mind*. Trans. J. B. Baillie. New York: Harper & Row, 1967.

Hermand, Pierre. *Les Idées morales de Diderot*. Paris: Presses Universitaires de France, 1923.

Hochart, Patrick. "Droit naturel et simulacre (l'évidence du signe)." *Les Cahiers pour l'Analyse*, no. 8 (1967), pp. 65–84.

Iser, Wolfgang. *The Implied Reader: Patterns of Communication in Prose Fiction from Bunyan to Beckett*. Baltimore: Johns Hopkins University Press, 1974.

Jost, François. "Le Roman épistolaire et la technique narrative au XVIIIe siècle." *Comparative Literature Studies* 3 (1966): 397–427.

Jouvenel, Bertrand de. "Essai sur la politique de Rousseau." In *Du Contrat social*, by Jean-Jacques Rousseau, pp. 15–160. Geneva: Cheval Ailé, 1947.

———. "Rousseau the Pessimistic Evolutionist." *Yale French Studies*, no. 28 (1961–62), pp. 83–96.

Kany, Charles E. *The Beginnings of the Epistolary Novel in France, Italy, and Spain*. Berkeley: University of California Press, 1937.

Kelly, Christopher. *Rousseau's Exemplary Life: The "Confessions" as Political Philosophy*. Ithaca: Cornell University Press, 1987.

Kelly, George Armstrong. *Idealism, Politics, and History: Sources of Hegelian Thought*. Cambridge: Cambridge University Press, 1969.

Kempf, Roger. "Les *Lettres Persanes*, ou Le Corps absent." *Tel Quel*, no. 22 (1965), pp. 81–86.

Keohane, Nannerl O. *Philosophy and the State in France: The Renaissance to the Enlightenment*. Princeton: Princeton University Press, 1980.

Koselleck, Reinhart. *Le Règne de la critique*. Trans. Hans Hildenbrand. Paris: Minuit, 1979.

Krieger, Leonard. *Kings and Philosophers, 1689–1789*. New York: Norton, 1970.

LaCapra, Dominick. "Rethinking Intellectual History and Reading Texts." In *Modern European Intellectual History: Reappraisals and New Perspectives*, ed. LaCapra and Steven L. Kaplan, pp. 47–85. Ithaca: Cornell University Press, 1982.

Locke, John. *An Essay Concerning Human Understanding*. Philadelphia, 1856.

Louch, A. R. "History as Narrative." *History and Theory* 8 (1969): 54–70.

Lovejoy, Arthur O. *Essays in the History of Ideas*. Baltimore: Johns Hopkins University Press, 1948.

McDonald, Christie V. "Le Dialogue, l'utopie: *Le Supplément au Voyage de Bougainville* par Diderot." *Canadian Review of Comparative Literature* 3 (1976): 63–74.

———. "The Reading and Writing of Utopia in Denis Diderot's *Supplément au Voyage de Bougainville*." *Science-Fiction Studies* 3 (November 1976): 248–54.

Manent, Pierre. *Naissances de la politique moderne*. Paris: Payot, 1977.

Marcil-Lacoste, Louise. "Le 'dogmatisme' des philosophes: L'Origine d'une distorsion." *Studies on Voltaire and the Eighteenth Century* 190 (1980): 209–14.

Mason, Sheila Mary. *Montesquieu's Idea of Justice*. The Hague: Nijhoff, 1975.

Masters, Roger D. *The Political Philosophy of Rousseau*. Princeton: Princeton University Press, 1968.

Melani, Nivea. "La Structure des *Lettres persanes*." *Annali dell'Istituto Universario Orientale, Sezione Romanza* (Naples) 10 (January 1968): 39–94.

Merry, Henry J. *Montesquieu's System of Natural Government*. West Lafayette, Ind.: Purdue University Press, 1970.

Mink, Louis O. "History and Fiction as Modes of Comprehension." *New Literary History* 1 (1970): 541–58.

Montaigne, Michel de. *The Complete Essays*. Trans. Donald M. Frame. Stanford: Stanford University Press, 1958.

Montesquieu, Charles-Louis de Secondat, baron de. *Lettres persanes*. Ed. Paul Vernière. Paris: Garnier, 1975.

———. *Oeuvres complètes*. Ed. Daniel Oster. Paris: Seuil, 1964.

———. *Persian Letters*. Trans. J. Robert Loy. New York: Meridian, 1961.

Mosconi, Jean. "Sur la théorie du devenir de l'entendement." *Les Cahiers pour l'Analyse*, no. 4 (1966), pp. 51–88.

Mousnier, Roland. "Les Concepts d'"ordres,' d'états,' de 'fidélité,' et de 'monarchie absolue' en France de la fin du xve siècle à la fin du xviiie." *Revue Historique* 247 (April–June 1972): 289–312.

———. *The Institutions of France under the Absolute Monarchy, 1598–1789: Society and the State*. Trans. Brian Pearce. Chicago: University of Chicago Press, 1974.

Niklaus, Robert. "Diderot et le conte philosophique." *Cahiers de l'Association Internationale des Études Françaises*, no. 13 (1961), pp. 299–315.

Oudeis, Jacques. "L'Idée de nature dans le *Supplément au Voyage de Bougainville*." *Revue de l'Enseignement Philosophique* 23 (1972–73): 1–10.

Ouellet, Réal. "Deux Théories romanesques au xviiie siècle: Le Roman 'bourgeois' et le roman épistolaire." *Études Littéraires* 1 (August 1968): 233–50.

Ouellet, Réal, and Vachon, Hélène. *"Lettres persanes" de Montesquieu*. Paris: Hachette, 1976.

Pedersen, John. "Le Dialogue—du classicisme aux Lumières: Réflexions sur l'évolution d'un genre." *Studia Neophilologica* 51 (1979): 305–13.

Perkins, M. L. "Community Planning in Diderot's *Supplément au Voyage de Bougainville*." *Kentucky Romance Quarterly* 21 (1974): 399–417.

Pickles, William. "The Notion of Time in Rousseau's Political Thought." In *Hobbes and Rousseau: A Collection of Critical Essays*, ed. Maurice Cranston and Richard S. Peters, pp. 366–400. Garden City, N.Y.: Doubleday, 1972.

Plattner, Marc F. *Rousseau's State of Nature: An Interpretation of the "Discourse on Inequality*." De Kalb: Northern Illinois University Press, 1979.

Polin, Raymond. *La Politique de la solitude: Essai sur la philosophie politique de Jean-Jacques Rousseau*. Paris: Sirey, 1971.

Porset, Charles. "Discours d'un anonyme sur l'inégalité, 1754." *Studies on Voltaire and the Eighteenth Century* 182 (1979): 7–27.

Prévost, Abbé [Antoine François]. *Histoire du Chevalier des Grieux et de Manon Lescaut*. Ed. Frédéric Deloffre and Raymond Picard. Paris: Garnier, 1965.

Richelieu, Armand-Jean du Plessis, cardinal de. *Testament politique*. Amsterdam, 1709.

Ricoeur, Paul. "The Model of the Text: Meaningful Action Considered as a Text." In *Interpretive Social Science: A Reader*, ed. Paul Rabinow and William M. Sullivan, pp. 73–101. Berkeley: University of California Press, 1979.

———. *The Rule of Metaphor: Interdisciplinary Studies in the Creation of Meaning in Language*. Trans. Robert Czerny. Toronto: University of Toronto Press, 1977.

Roelens, Maurice. "Le Dialogue philosophique, genre impossible? L'Opinion des siècles classiques." *Cahiers de l'Association Internationale des Études Françaises*, no. 24 (1972), pp. 43–58.

Romberg, Bertil. *Studies in the Narrative Technique of the First-Person Novel*. Stockholm: Almqvist & Wiksell, 1962.

Rosbottom, Ronald C. "Motifs in Epistolary Fiction: Analysis of a Narrative Sub-Genre." *L'Esprit Créateur* 17 (Winter 1977): 279–301.

Rousseau, Jean-Jacques. *The First and Second Discourses*. Ed. and trans. Roger D. Masters and Judith R. Masters. New York: St. Martin's Press, 1964.

———. *Oeuvres complètes*. Ed. Bernard Gagnebin and Marcel Raymond. 4 vols. Paris: Gallimard, 1957–69.

Roussel, Jean. "Rousseau, l'utopie et Thomas More." *Moreana* 15 (December 1978): 47–53.

Rousset, Jean. *Forme et signification: Essais sur les structures littéraires de Corneille à Claudel*. Paris: Corti, 1962.

Sacks, Sheldon. *Fiction and the Shape of Belief: A Study of Henry Fielding with Glances at Swift, Johnson, and Richardson*. Berkeley: University of California Press, 1964.

Sartre, Jean-Paul. *What Is Literature?* Trans. Bernard Frechtman. New York: Harper & Row, 1965.

Schérer, Jacques. *Le Cardinal et l'orang-outang: Essai sur les inversions et les distances dans la pensée de Diderot*. Paris: Société d'Édition d'Enseignement Supérieur, 1972.

Schwartz, Jerome. *Diderot and Montaigne: The "Essais" and the Shaping of Diderot's Humanism*. Geneva: Droz, 1966.

Serres, Michel. *Hermes: Literature, Science, Philosophy*. Ed. Josué V. Harari and David F. Bell. Baltimore: Johns Hopkins University Press, 1982.

Shackleton, Robert. *Montesquieu: A Critical Biography*. Oxford: Oxford University Press, 1961.

Shklar, Judith N. *Men and Citizens: A Study of Rousseau's Social Theory*. Cambridge: Cambridge University Press, 1969.

———. "Rousseau's Two Models: Sparta and the Age of Gold." *Political Science Quarterly* 81 (March 1966): 25–51.

Spear, Frederick A. *Bibliographie de Diderot: Répertoire analytique international*. Geneva: Droz, 1980.

Spink, John. "Rousseau and the Problems of Composition." In *Reappraisals of Rousseau: Studies in Honour of R. A. Leigh*, ed. Simon Harvey et al., pp. 163–80. Manchester: Manchester University Press, 1980.

Spitzer, Leo. *Linguistics and Literary History: Essays in Stylistics*. New York: Russell & Russell, 1962.

Starobinski, Jean. "Diderot et la parole des autres." *Critique* 28 (1972): 3–22.

———. Introduction to *Montesquieu par lui-même*, ed. Starobinski. Paris: Seuil, 1953.

———. *Jean-Jacques Rousseau: Transparency and Obstruction*. Trans. Arthur Goldhammer. Chicago: University of Chicago Press, 1988.

———. Preface to *Lettres persanes*, by Montesquieu. Paris: Gallimard, 1973.

Strauss, Leo. *Natural Right and History*. Chicago: University of Chicago Press, 1953.

Stricklen, Charles G., Jr. "The *Philosophes'* Political Mission: The Creation of an Idea, 1750–1789." *Studies on Voltaire and the Eighteenth Century* 86 (1971): 137–228.

Strugnell, Anthony. *Diderot's Politics: A Study of the Evolution of Diderot's Political Thought after the "Encyclopédie."* The Hague: Nijhoff, 1973.

Terrasse, Jean. *Jean-Jacques Rousseau et la quête de l'âge d'or*. Brussels: Palais des Académies, 1970.

Testud, Pierre. "Les *Lettres persanes*, roman épistolaire." *Revue d'Histoire Littéraire de la France* 66 (October–December 1966): 642–56.

Thelander, Dorothy R. *Laclos and the Epistolary Novel*. Geneva: Droz, 1963.

Thielemann, Leland. "Diderot and Hobbes." *Diderot Studies* 2 (1952): 221–78.

Tisserand, Roger. *Les Concurrents de J.-J. Rousseau à l'Académie de Dijon pour le prix de 1754*. Paris: Boivin, 1936.

Todorov, Tzvetan. "The Two Principles of Narrative." *Diacritics* 1 (Fall 1971): 37–44.

Undank, Jack. *Diderot: Inside, Outside, and In-Between*. Madison, Wis.: Coda Press, 1979.

Van Kley, Dale. *The Jansenists and the Expulsion of the Jesuits from France, 1757–1765*. New Haven: Yale University Press, 1975.

Vartanian, Aram. "Eroticism and Politics in the *Lettres persanes*." *Romanic Review* 60 (February 1969): 23–33.

Venturi, Franco. "Oriental Despotism." Trans. Lotte F. Jacoby and Ian M. Taylor. *Journal of the History of Ideas* 24 (January–March 1963): 133–42.

——. *Utopia and Reform in the Enlightenment*. Cambridge: Cambridge University Press, 1971.

Versini, Laurent. *Laclos et la tradition*. Paris: Klincksieck, 1968.

Werner, Steven David. "The *Encyclopédie* and the *Supplément au Voyage de Bougainville*: Diderot and the Range of Man." Ph.D. dissertation, Columbia University, 1967.

White, Hayden. *Metahistory: The Historical Imagination in Nineteenth-Century Europe*. Baltimore: Johns Hopkins University Press, 1973.

Wilson, Arthur M. *Diderot*. New York: Oxford University Press, 1972.

Index